The Mama Chronicles

The MAMA CHRONICLES

A Memoir

Teresa Nicholas

Teresa Nicholas

University Press of Mississippi / Jackson

Willie Morris Books in Memoir and Biography

The University Press of Mississippi is the scholarly publishing agency of
the Mississippi Institutions of Higher Learning: Alcorn State University,
Delta State University, Jackson State University, Mississippi State University,
Mississippi University for Women, Mississippi Valley State University,
University of Mississippi, and University of Southern Mississippi.

www.upress.state.ms.us

The University Press of Mississippi is a member
of the Association of University Presses.

Photographs are from the author's collection.

First printing 2021

∞

Library of Congress Cataloging-in-Publication Data

Names: Nicholas, Teresa, author.
Title: The mama chronicles : a memoir / Teresa Nicholas.
Description: Jackson : University Press of Mississippi, [2021] | Series:
Willie Morris books in memoir and biography
Identifiers: LCCN 2021006500 (print) | LCCN 2021006501 (ebook) | ISBN
9781496835253 (hardcover) | ISBN 9781496835277 (epub) | ISBN
9781496835260 (epub) | ISBN 9781496835284 (pdf) | ISBN 9781496835291
(pdf)
Subjects: LCSH: Nicholas, Teresa—Biography. | Mothers and
daughters—Mississippi. | Mississippi—Biography.
Classification: LCC CT275.N558 A3 2021 (print) | LCC CT275.N558 (ebook) |
DDC 976.2092 [B]—dc23
LC record available at https://lccn.loc.gov/2021006500
LC ebook record available at https://lccn.loc.gov/2021006501

British Library Cataloging-in-Publication Data available

For Debbie and Lisa

As always, for Gerry

And, of course, for Mama

Love bears all things, believes all things,
hopes all things, endures all things.
Love never fails.
—1 Corinthians 13:7–8

Love alters not with his brief hours and weeks,
But bears it out even to the edge of doom.
—William Shakespeare, Sonnet 116

PART ONE

One

My Mother's Green House

December 31, 2010. On a narrow street called Grand Avenue Extension, about two miles north of downtown Yazoo City, Mississippi, six sprawling, putty-colored buildings rise up from what not long ago was a cotton field. These are the Martha Coker Green Houses, a nursing home where my mother has lived for just over two years. Near the entrance to the spacious campus stands a mock traffic sign that reads "Slow: Elders at Play." My mother's room is in the second house on the right, Hilderbrand, named for its oldest elder, a wizened lady who died recently, well up in her nineties. In Green House parlance, *elder* equals *resident*. To enter the building, we ring the doorbell and wait. That's the protocol.

Behind the campus there lies a fallow field, where in grass chest high to a man hundreds of birds loop and dodge in their unwavering search for food. A chain hotel, newly constructed on the field's northern edge, advertises a nightly special. During the week its parking lot usually sits empty, but this weekend it's filled, likely with visitors to the nearby federal penitentiary.

Heavy skies skim the field. The weather is out of kilter today, Friday, New Year's Eve. It should be chilly, but it's warm, with a gusty, salty wind up from the Gulf. There's a chance of storms. Who doesn't fear a tornado? At the Fitness Center this morning, Fox News was detailing the damage already done by the storm system in Arkansas and Missouri. Yazoo City waits to see if it will have a third direct hit this year. In April a tornado slammed the town's outskirts, at the Four Points intersection, and in November another gave a glancing blow to the old Saxton Hardware building on Main Street. The spring tornado was the widest ever recorded in the state and stayed on the ground for 150 miles. Ten people were killed, buildings blown away, and wide swathes cut through the densely forested land.

An aide in blue scrubs opens the door, and my husband, Gerry, and I make our way along Hilderbrand's short entrance hall. Aides here are called "shahbaz," a Persian word meaning "royal falcon," meant to highlight their central role as all-around caregivers. The Green Houses are a new concept in eldercare, home-like in design, with private bedrooms (ten in all) and *en suite* baths clustered around an open kitchen, a living area known as the "hearth," and a large family-style dining table. The atmosphere of storm day hasn't yet penetrated the tight, new building.

The time is right after dinner, the noon meal, and most of the elders have already returned to their rooms for their naps. But my mother is still sitting in the hearth, her deluxe Tracer wheelchair braked to the left of the imitation fireplace; a soap opera plays overhead on the giant flat-screen TV. My mother exists in this highly internal world, the world of her wheelchair, the world of her small bedroom, and the blandly cheerful world of the hearth.

Our eyes meet across the large open space. I detect a straightening of her spine, the slightest improvement of her posture, when she notices us. Because it's Friday, her short, silky white hair is stiffly coiffed. There's nothing she would rather get out of bed for than her weekly appointment with Kathy, in the house's own beauty salon. The shahbaz have dressed her in bright pink socks, a light pink T-shirt, and a dark pink shawl edged with pompons. Pink in all its shades has become the color of her late eighties, inspired by a pair of powder-pink moccasins my sister Lisa gave her three Christmases ago. I'm not sure how she feels about this specialization of her wardrobe, but she appears to tolerate it, sometimes with amusement, as she does so many aspects of her constrained existence.

Another elder, the turbaned, porcelain-skinned Mrs. De León, glimpses Gerry and begins whispering nonstop from her blue leather Geri Chair. He drops on his knees beside her to say hello while I continue past the unlikely pair, threading through the field of end tables and padded recliners in the hearth, past built-ins with their staged vases and books.

When I stand before my mother, she extends her left hand, the fingertips purple, the back dappled with liver spots. I hold her hand briefly before dropping down beside her on the leather couch. When she offers her hand again, I realize what she's telling me.

"So they finally cut your nails," I say. "They look nice."

She nods, her lips turning up slightly.

Hattie, another aide in blue scrubs, comes over to say hello. Bosomy and big-boned, Hattie can seem comforting or imposing, depending on circumstances. She calls my mother "Mrs. Nicholas" rather than by her first name, Florence, and I'm "baby," though the fifty-something Hattie is several years younger than I am. Hattie is African American, as are most of the shahbaz. Most residents are white, although Green House policy is nondiscriminatory with regard to race, gender, religion, national origin, and income. It's not lost on me that in this racially complicated place the Black folks are still taking care of the white folks.

"Who cut her nails?" I ask, and Hattie whispers the name: Courtney, the nurse on duty. Nails are nursing staff purview. She goes on to tell me that the Catholics are holding a Mass in the private visiting room, located off the hearth, and they want my mother to attend. But Hattie isn't sure. After her hair appointment at eleven, my mother stayed up to eat the standard Friday dinner of fried catfish, so she's already been out of bed over two hours.

Hattie looks to me for a decision. Since my mother's watershed stroke, two years ago, I've become her interpreter. Diviner of her modest wants, reader of her impaired state. For clues I have my

mother's good left hand, though she can sometimes squeeze out
a short sentence or choose between two possibilities by repeating
a word. She can also nod or shake her head, though she often gets
these two confused. Sometimes she nods yes while saying no.

I press my lips close to her ear and take in her sweet, sharp
smell. "Do you want to go to Mass or back to bed?"

She stares straight ahead, eyes like points of coal behind oversize beige frames.

"Mass or bed?" I repeat. "You pick."

"Bed," she manages, her voice oddly wheezy.

The stalwart Hattie goes off to find another shahbaz. It takes
two aides to get my five-ten, nearly two-hundred-pound mother
out of her wheelchair and into her bed, even with all of Hattie's
strength and the automatic lift. Just then the nurse who cut
Mama's nails strides by, and I shout thanks to Courtney across
the hearth.

After they transfer my mother, the shahbaz open the door to her
room, my cue to enter. It's a tasteful room, cheerfully furnished.
There's a chifforobe, a matching chest of drawers where the TV
sits, and a night table piled with creams, wipes, and a machine
for breathing treatments. To this standard-issue furniture we've
added a slender mahogany bookcase and an occasional table from
home, along with the blue Med-Lift chair she once dubbed, when
she could still use it, her "favorite thing in the whole world." She
lies, as usual, on her back, at about a thirty-degree incline. Hattie
is fussing over her, arranging the oxygen cannulas on her face and
wriggling the extra pillows onto her stroked side, one under her
right elbow and another under her right leg. I position the stuffed
animals: Boo Boo, a sock monkey that Lisa commissioned from
the local yarn shop, whose practically life-size head goes on the
pillow next to my mother's; and Tempe, her plush bear, named for
her grandmother Temperance, who guards the foot of the bed.
Mama tolerates this behavior from me, like a bored mother dog
overlooking her puppy's silliness.

When she's finally set up to watch TV, I ask my mother if she prefers an old movie on TCM or a rerun of *Bonanza*. But she starts chopping at the air with her left hand. She inhales deeply, her wide belly moving like a bellows under the pink sheets.

Hattie feels inside her scrub-shirt pockets. "I don't have my panic button, but I think the nurse is still in the house. I'll go get her."

I kneel at my mother's paralyzed right side (not the best place to grab her attention). "What's the matter?" I ask.

Before she can try to tell me, Courtney steps into the room, pausing at the door to disinfect her hands at the hanging dispenser. She's in her thirties, athletic, friendly yet professional. Mama fans her left fingers at the nurse, in a gesture similar to hello but faster, with each finger moving independently.

From the bedside, Courtney looks down at my mother. "What's wrong?" she asks.

Mama keeps waving at her.

I glance past their bent-head tableau to the family photos that Lisa has framed for the wall above the bed. My mother, from fifty years ago, with both arms around Sol Boy, the mother–son pair posed on the sidewalk at Grandma Hood's house, during one of our weekly visits. My mother's face is wide at the temples but thin at the jawline, haloed by wavy, black-dark hair. My little brother is chubby-legged, about to squirm away. There are standard grammar school pictures of Lisa and our big sister, Debbie, with cowlick hair and toothy smiles, and a formal portrait of my father as a toddler in a blue knit dress and a tasseled cap—apparently, in the twenties, in Yazoo, you dressed a little boy in girl's clothing. In the pictures we are suspended in these moments of old time, before so many things started to go wrong: Sol and Daddy's early deaths; Lisa's and Debbie's chronic illnesses; and now this, with my mother.

Courtney is repeating her question. "What's wrong?"

"Police academy," Mama blurts out. Then she reaches to pick up the box of tissues from the over-the-bed table and frowns into it.

"Police academy?" Courtney and I ask in chorus.

"Police academy," my mother nods, annoyed. She jabs the tissue box at Courtney. I stifle a laugh and so, I think, does the young nurse. Part of me would like to tease Mama about the non sequitur, to play up the funny, but I know this isn't the time.

"It's frustrating," I say instead, and she frowns harder at the box, "but try to get out just one word that will help us understand what you want. Or better yet, point."

She puts the tissue box down with a thud and raises her left arm high in the air and points her index finger toward the ceiling.

"Say one word," I repeat. "Just one."

"Police," she says.

Courtney inspects the box and mumbles, "Well, there are tissues in there," as if that might be the source of my mother's anxiety. But nearly ten minutes have passed, and she has to leave. In the background I can hear several call buttons ringing at once, their tones sweetly intertwining. Anyway, it's clear my mother isn't having an emergency. If I can figure out what she needs, Courtney tells me wearily, I should come find her in the house.

With the nurse gone, Mama picks up the tissue box again. Again she looks inside as if she's never seen a tissue box before. But this time she says, "Bottle."

"Bottle?" I inspect the box too. "Bottle of what? Bottle of Tylenol?"

She shakes her head.

"Bottle of milk of magnesia?" But as soon as I ask, I realize that seems unlikely.

"Bottle," she sputters, "of rubbing alcohol." Only she pronounces it, "al-key-hol."

Finally I think I've got it. Mama used to apply this clear liquid whenever she had an itch. I ask, "Is that red patch on your hairline bothering you again?"

She drops the box and reaches around behind her right ear. She looks up at me, black eyes clouded with torture. With her fingernails newly cut, she can't get purchase there.

I run into the hallway, past the kitchen and toward the hearth. The place is deserted except for Gerry, who's now seated next to the whispering Mrs. De León. As I pass Miss Inez's room, I glimpse her in a wheelchair, undressed from the waist up except for her pointy white bra. Nurse Courtney is standing over her, trying to cajole her into putting her shirt back on. I arm-wave to her like a drowning woman and hurry to my mother's room. Gerry gestures a question, but I keep going. I'm eager to release that look from my mother's eyes.

I perch on her bed, stroking her right hand. "She's coming," I say. "The nurse is coming. She's helping someone else." My mother scans my face as if memorizing me.

"You enjoyed the catfish at lunch?" I ask, trying to distract her. She wheezes, "I am tired of catfish."

I'm thrilled she's spoken an entire sentence. "Well," I say, paraphrasing Samuel Johnson's pronouncement about London, "when you're tired of catfish, you're tired of life."

"I am tired of life," she counters. Which declaration falls dead as a hammer.

Gerry appears in the doorway. His middle-aged face is still handsome, with a soft, round chin and nose, blue eyes, and black, curly hair. He knits his dark brows and mouths, "What is it?" and I mouth back, "Itch." He approaches my mother on her left side and squeezes her good hand. She flashes him a broad smile. Anything for Gerry. He's a Yankee—upstate New York, Troy—though this is his thirty-second Christmas in Mississippi. For twenty-five years we lived in a commuter town outside Manhattan, before expatriating to Mexico eight years ago. When we're not here with my mother, we're in the small hill town of San Miguel de Allende, in the Central Highlands, about three hours north of Mexico City.

A few minutes later Courtney breezes back in and snaps on a pair of fresh latex gloves. She rubs a glob of ointment on my mother's itchy neck.

"Is that what you wanted?" I ask her. She beams at Courtney.

And so begins this Friday afternoon, those dragged-out hours after dinner that my mother used to call "evening," when she could still talk. I take a seat in the straight-backed chair, Gerry in the blue recliner. The TV is set to TCM. This week we've seen *National Velvet*, *In the Good Old Summertime*, and *Ben-Hur*; today the channel is broadcasting *Arsenic and Old Lace*. All during our visit my mother has been sleeping a lot, as many as eighteen hours a day, but she eyes Cary Grant closely. When the movie ends, I ask if she prefers to look at another flick with the debonair actor or *Bonanza*, and she surprises me by choosing the western.

I change the channel, and she leans forward an inch. When *Bonanza* premiered, in 1959, I was five. We watched the show *en famille* in the tiny living room of our dilapidated duplex: my father spread-eagled in the green wing chair and the rest of us sardined on the red Naugahyde couch. For years on Sunday nights, the Cartwrights riveted us—thrice-widowed Ben and his three sons, brainy Adam, goofy Hoss, and loveable Little Joe. Theirs was a perfect family, minus a mother. The series, broadcast in reruns every afternoon, recently marked its fiftieth anniversary; I rented the entire first season on tape so my mother and I could binge watch. Today we're lucky. The show is pivotal, about the day Hoss was born. We watch as Hoss's mother takes an arrow in the back. We've seen enough of *Bonanza* to know that no woman in love with any Cartwright can live for more than one episode.

At five o'clock Hattie drops by to ask my mother if she'll be getting up for supper. It's New Year's Eve, she reminds her. Mama flurry-waves at Hattie. She shakes her head. But I advise Hattie that this "no" shake could really have been a "yes" nod. How can I tell? The signs are subtle, having to do with the ease with which the "no" was given. And sure enough, just as I interpret the shake, my mother reverses herself with a nod.

Elders and guests alike, we take seats at the long wooden dining table. The storm is only just arriving in Mississippi, crossing over the great river to our west. The shahbaz have the TV weather on full-blast, and they've turned on the all-weather radio with its litany of warnings and watches. Adding to the din, they blow noisemakers. We don paper party hats, but on this tornado-heightened holiday eve the lightheartedness seems forced.

Mrs. De León looks pretty with her white hair pulled back in a bun and tied with a blue ribbon. She's whispering again to Gerry. The shahbaz believe he reminds her of her late husband, though Gerry looks nothing like the Latin Mr. De León, whose lone photo graces her chest of drawers. I chitchat with the petite, cheerful Mrs. Clark, the only Hilderbrand elder who's ambulatory. When she finishes her cake, she reaches for her walker and leaves the table under her own deliberate steam. Mr. Barnwell, with his few remaining teeth, holds out for ice cream, even though the evening's festive menu has included Hattie's homemade chicken salad, ground fine as paste for the dentally challenged. My patient mother feeds herself left-handed, with measured movements, trying not to drop crumbs on her shirtfront. Finally the shahbaz escort those who've finished their meals from the table to the hearth. Those who couldn't eat, or didn't, will continue at table, and the aides will move among them, encouraging them and if necessary taking up knife and fork for them.

I push my mother's wheelchair near the fireplace so we can join the weather watch. Tornado warnings out earlier for Vicksburg have been extended east to the capital, Jackson. Both cities are south of us, about an hour away. Then the weatherman announces that a tornado has been sighted near Byram, a small town south of the capital. With Doppler radar, stations can follow tornadoes on the ground street by street. I detect a trace of excitement in the meteorologist's voice, building to contained urgency.

One night, a few years back, I was visiting my mother in the duplex when the town's tornado siren went off. As the wind blew and rain drummed the decades-old roof, I announced to my mother (aping the weatherman) that we needed to get out of the living room, with its two big windows, and into our "safe place." We wouldn't all fit in the closet, I said inanely, and suggested we wait out the storm in the hall. Fifty years ago, when our family moved into this duplex, my father tore out the dividing wall, creating a center hallway. "You can go sit in that hall if you want to," my mother told me that night, "but I'm staying right here." She rode out the storm in her canary-colored recliner, while I cowered in the unlighted hall, in a child's wooden school chair, one of several my father had collected over the years. The tornado ripped off the roof of an apartment building a few blocks away.

This evening, New Year's Eve, my mother is again unperturbed, idly studying the red "watch boxes" on the TV screen that outline this tornado's path. I don't know if she can't make out what's happening or if she truly feels no concern. Who doesn't fear a tornado? She didn't fear that one a few years ago, and I would bet she's not afraid of tonight's either. Though I'm aware there's a greater chance of falling off a cliff or contracting leprosy, I'm expecting the worst. As my mother used to tell me, "You always was a worrier."

The Green Houses have a protocol for storms, and the shahbaz have drilled in it: move the elders near the hearth, as far as possible from the wall of windows in the dining area. My mother is already where she needs to be. So shortly after six, Gerry and I get ready to leave. I go into Mama's bedroom to perform my ritual checks: draw the blinds; adjust the air; lay the principal stuffed animals on the bed; place her princess phone on the table within reach, in case my sisters call; click on the night lamp for added coziness.

Back at the hearth, I bend over her. "I fixed your room. Do you need anything else?"

"Naw," she whispers, blinking rapidly. Of course, there is so much that she needs.

"'Night," I say. I plant a kiss on her high forehead. I dangle Horton, a small blue stuffed elephant, and let him mock-kiss her cheek. He's a purchase we made right after her big stroke, supposed to help with cognitive rehab.

"What's his name?" I prompt.

"Timothy," she answers. Other names she has for him: Sebastian and Humboldt.

Gerry kisses her cheek. "Goodnight, Mama," he says. We take a step back. With her left hand, she waves at us, me and Gerry and "Timothy." A true wave, a bye wave. Jaunty. Fingers flying. She unleashes a smile, forty-watt. She has remarkably unwrinkled skin for eighty-seven, even when smiling.

I lay the little elephant on her lap and walk backward toward the front door. She's looking at me all the way. One last wave. One last smile. I haven't said anything to her, but in less than a week we're leaving again for Mexico.

Gerry dashes off into the wild, wet night to get the car. But I stand outside Hilderbrand's door, trying to glimpse her through the fogged window. To get back in, I must ring the doorbell. That's the protocol. Would she still be there? Staring at the TV?

"You so crazy," she used to say, when she could still talk.

Two

Partway Back, Midway Between

Less than a mile—that's the distance from the nursing home to
Willie Belle's house, next door to our duplex. It may be New Year's
Eve, but there's no traffic in this small southern town on the edge
of the Mississippi Delta. This is a mixed neighborhood—some
fine old houses on Grand Avenue, a corner grocery store, a bank
branch, a Shell station. The night is pitch dark, and the rain lands
on our windshield in ridiculous, fat drops. In two minutes' time we
pull into my aunt's driveway, parking behind her house. Everybody
comes and goes from the back of Willie Belle's, directly into her
den. Only the mail carrier and Jehovah's Witnesses use the front
door. From my aunt's driveway I can see "our" block, the Nicholas
family block, our houses lined up on Thirteenth Street: the bungalow that once belonged to my paternal grandparents, my father's
sister's and brother's homes, and our duplex. Willie Belle—not a
Nicholas but a Hood, married to my mother's twin—bought the
house due north of ours about a dozen years ago.

When Willie Belle moved here our block was still vibrant, at
least still lived in, but now many of the houses are vacant, including
my grandparents' bungalow. Once as elegantly got up as a lady in
a fine feathered hat, the spacious, high-ceilinged bungalow, along
with its large, lush garden, has suffered mightily from neglect. For
the eight years my grandmother Vashti lived in the Martha Coker

Convalescent Home (precursor to the Green Houses) and for several years after she died, the bungalow sat empty. Finally one Mr. Rochester, a widower from Florida, made the family a decent offer, declaring he would renovate.

And so the sale was made, with the proceeds divided among my father's sister, Pauline; his brother, Moe; and my mother. And Mr. Rochester did prove to be handy. He Sheetrocked the breakfast room and painted the outside clapboards yellow. He hung a wooden swing on the front porch, where he could be seen entertaining his frequent visitors during the long southern twilights. Pauline, whenever she related the story about the sale of our homeplace, where we'd all lived at one time or another, concluded, "God sent us Mr. Rochester." But then Mr. Rochester moved on, for reasons unknown. For a while, a family with a lot of children lived there. Then they too left for reasons unknown.

Now, next door to the bungalow, in Pauline's own front yard, a red and white Mashburn Realty sign stands erect as a sentinel, its stark colors aberrant against the winter-brown grass. A few days ago, in Stub's Restaurant—the day's specials, barbecue chicken, chicken fried steak, and a fried pork chop, served with your choice of three sides—a round-waisted, graying woman turned to me at the steam table and said in a loud voice, "I didn't know Pauline had moved in with her daughter! She's not doing well at all!" Before turning back to select her sides, she finished, "But she don't give up!"

Next door to Pauline's ranch is our duplex, also usually vacant except for the four months a year, parceled out one per season, that Gerry and I stay there. Other nearby houses remain untenanted, month after month, year after year: Mrs. Carter's and Mr. and Mrs. Upton's and Mr. Gerrard's. Mr. Gerrard survived his house getting cleft in two by a tree but some months later died abruptly. Willie Belle's only year-round neighbors are a newcomer, Mr. Smith, a kindly, stooped Black man, a refugee from Katrina; and Moe, the only full-time Nicholas left. Moe, who has lived on this block for seventy years, remembers learning to roller-skate on a Grand Avenue devoid of traffic even in the daytime. When he fell, he said, his little face "kissed the hot asphalt."

Gerry and I arrive at Willie Belle's shortly before seven, when the first nighttime movie rolls on TCM. She's expecting us, and so, uncharacteristically, she's left the sliding glass door to her den unlocked. She remains seated in her recliner while we let ourselves inside. Formalities are unnecessary; Willie Belle's house is like our second home. Built in the early fifties, the neo-colonial, with its redbrick foundation and white vinyl siding, mock shutters, and fancy grillwork, shelters you from the harsh Mississippi climate. In our duplex, dampness swells the old, warped wood until the doors don't close.

"Come in this house," she says, as we shed our raingear.

Willie Belle sits in her padded brown recliner while maintaining perfect First Baptist Church posture, her blue-jeaned legs stretched out on the footrest. Because it's Friday, her ash-brown hair is freshly styled—also by Kathy, but in her salon on Fifteenth Street. My aunt still resembles that high-cheeked blond girl who was voted, of the three in her class, "Miss Louise High of 1948." The next year she married my mother's twin, Lawrence, in her hometown, about fifteen miles north of Yazoo City. I don't know what Louise was like when my aunt and uncle took their vows in the quaint Methodist Church on Ash Street, but now the tiny Delta town consists of a few run-down blocks, including a one-room jailhouse with the date 1909 scrawled over the doorway. My aunt's father used to be the jailer.

At eighty, Willie Belle is two years into retirement from her own job in law enforcement, as a secretary at the Yazoo County Sheriff's Department. Six or so years younger than my mother, she lives by a Great Depression philosophy not so different from my mother's, occasionally sloganizing from her recliner, "Ain't no need to worry," "Ain't nothing you can do about it," and "Just get on with it," often while munching miniature chocolates from her glass candy dishes.

"Get you something to eat," my aunt instructs. On the little round table between her den and kitchen she's put out a platter of nibbles, including dill pickles and locally made cheese straws that taste of cheddar and cayenne pepper. We pick at the cheese straws, chase them down with the pickles. Tonight it's just us. Willie Bell's two sons "live off" with their wives, though not far. It's not easy growing old by yourself, even in a small southern town where your church brings you a hot plate dinner on Thursdays and where, unasked, your neighbor, the kindly Katrina refugee, hauls your empty garbage can back up under your carport after the city truck passes.

Gerry slumps his lanky frame on the blue and white loveseat while I stretch out on the matching couch. "Y'all want to watch this?" my aunt asks about TCM's feature, a Marx Brothers film. I sense her polite lack of interest, so after a brief back and forth about the comedians she channel-surfs, landing on Times Square coverage of the singer Kei$ha. Memory rises before me like a vapor. It's from another rainy New Year's Eve in Yazoo City, over forty years ago, in the living room of the duplex. I'm alone with my father in front of the family's Zenith, also tuned to Times Square. My mother has retreated to her bed; my siblings, off somewhere. On that mild night, Daddy is dressed in a pair of stringy cutoffs, his thick white calves practically hairless. The poverty and paucity of life in the duplex hang about me. As he and I sit uncompanionably with the front door open, watching the frantic cars skid by on the grease-slick street, I vow to leave and one day to live in New York City.

But now I'm back, at least partway.

From Willie Belle's cocoon of a couch I can make out an occasional thunderclap, nothing alarming. At ten o'clock we switch channels to the local news. Maybe the storm's a bust, the disappointed weatherman admits. During the lull in the weather, we prepare to decamp. "Y'all coming over tomorrow for black-eyed peas?" Willie Belle asks. As we wish each other Happy New Year,

I tell my aunt we're planning to eat our good-luck peas at the nursing home. Gerry and I slog through the puddled yard between our two properties and up onto the duplex's front porch, which welcomes us with its flash-on safety light.

My family had lived with my grandparents for nine years when my father bought this duplex, with a two-thousand-dollar mortgage, and had it trucked to the corner lot opposite their bungalow. It was my grandparents who deeded them the lot—"for and in consideration of the natural love and affection for which we bear our son and daughter-in-law," the document says. Though my mother had longed for her own house, she didn't much take to the duplex. It was old construction, from the thirties, with nine-foot ceilings, but instead of an elegant flow, the rooms ran like boxcars on a freight train. With no foundation, the duplex stood propped on concrete blocks. Paint peeled off the clapboards, and the wallpaper hung in shreds. Termites tunneled the floorboards. But worse, the duplex smelled ugly, of grime and mildew. Of being rented too often and unloved too long.

My father talked about "fixing it up," and in a shed he built behind it, painted red and dubbed the Little House, he amassed faucets, screws, nails, lengths of pipe, squares of linoleum, and even lumber, but to no avail. My mother pitched everything she had at the duplex—brooms, mops, the anemic horsepower of an ancient Electrolux. But she couldn't Pine-Sol away what was wrong with it. The duplex embodied our poverty, shame, and despair, and the dominance wielded by my father, Solomon Thomas Nicholas Jr., called Sol Jr., pronounced "Soljune." After his death my mother finally "fixed up" the duplex, twice, but still it reflects paucity, especially with her absence.

As we step inside the living room, we're greeted by her canary-colored recliner. There's no use lighting the gas space heaters to try to dispel tonight's damp. We can't sleep with them on, an old-time Daddy rule we still obey for fear of asphyxiating. Gerry and I kiss New Year's in front of the Sony, and he heads off to huddle under the down comforter while I sit in the recliner to check the weather one last time. Since we're here only part of the year, we don't splurge on cable but instead use a portable antenna to try to capture the signal. We call the duplex, among other epithets, "the house of poor reception," where the four channels we do receive often break up into digital shards and disappear entirely. But tonight, even in all this weather, we're getting stations from deep in the Delta. And there's enough of a picture to see that Yazoo County remains under a tornado warning.

Then, for the first time that evening, the siren sounds.

I grab a raincoat and shoes—I want to be fully dressed when disaster happens—and rouse Gerry. There are two closets in the duplex, as there was once two of everything—kitchens, dining and living rooms, bathrooms, bedrooms. One closet is off the living room, but its door is blocked by a loveseat. The other is off my mother's bedroom. Her closet hasn't been cleaned out since she left for the nursing home. There are two rows of hanging clothes, a metal shoe rack, and suspended from the door, a cloth shoe bag. There's also a large foam wedge, a bag of Christmas-tree balls, and a box of fifty-year-old dress patterns. Unlike her bedroom, which was paneled about thirty years ago, my mother's closet retains the duplex's original wallpaper—floral, faded, crumbling. Gerry tosses the foam wedge out into the bedroom and stumbles in without complaining. He's still in pajamas, but he's conceded slippers. I take with us a flashlight, our flip phones, and the solar-powered weather radio, which has to be hand-cranked every few minutes. It's a tight fit for a safe place.

At the top of this closet is a trapdoor leading to the attic. There's nothing up there except the giant, rusted-out attic fan, with barely room under the eaves for that. As I sit on the floor, under that flimsy ceiling, the storm sounds huge, as if wind and rain and thunder and siren are funneling directly into the closet. Outside the door, the lights flicker.

I dial Willie Belle. She's in her closet too. "What are you doing?" I ask.

"Reading," she says.

"With what?"

"My flashlight."

The noise grows thicker with hail. I call the Green Houses. The nightshift shahbaz picks up. "Everything's fine," she says. I don't press: is my mother in her room, trapped in her too-wide hospital bed that won't fit through the door? Or did they use the automatic lift, put her in the wheelchair, and take her to the hearth, their safe place?

At 11:45, Gerry announces he's going back to bed. I creep into the living room. Miraculously, the TV is still broadcasting. A funnel cloud has passed over Yazoo City and possibly touched down in Midway, an unincorporated community about fifteen miles east, where my mother was born. A community so imprecise it's not on Google Maps.

At 1:43, I look at the clock for the last time that evening, then crawl into bed.

———

There is irony in my being here with my mother as her caregiver. Growing up, I didn't feel close to her. I didn't feel I knew her. And when it came time for college, I fulfilled my rainy New Year's Eve vow, left and lived far away from her and from this place.

My memory of my mother divides into two parts—B.D. and A.D. Before Duplex, I hardly recall her presence. When I was eight months old, she gave birth to twin boys who died—Fred lived two days and Ed lived three. For my first five years, I have only passing memories of her. A Sunday ride in our red Chevrolet coupe, along the high road to Vicksburg with my parents, my mother's touch soft as she shielded me from falling forward, in that dodgy era before seat belts. A day when I cried at the bathroom door in the bungalow for her to let me in, and my grandmother Vashti, smelling of hairspray and lanolin, took me on her lap instead.

Mainly I recall the absence of my mother, an absence filled with other memories, other sensations. Aside from Vashti's generous lap, they were of the contours of the bungalow's ample backyard, with its exciting dips and rises. They were of the dense leaves on the many trees and the way the sunlight pierced them in thrilling ways. They were of the bungalow's tall and rickety back steps, the pleasure I took in sitting on them by myself, eating white-bread-and-mayonnaise sandwiches. And they were of the climbing red rose on the bungalow's back wall and the stand of purple larkspur inside the gate, and of the prolific fig and pear trees, and the careful study we made of these fruits and flowers, Vashti and I. These memories were of me with my grandmother.

Then came the winter day, in February around my fifth birthday, when we moved down the block, away from the bungalow, away from my grandmother and into the duplex. After Duplex, I recall a string of less bright memories, and I remember my mother. How in the dark I would beg her to comfort me, but from her bedroom up the hall she would call out, "Go back to sleep, young'un." How one stifling hot day she closed me up in my room until I taught myself to tie my shoelaces. How she would mete out whippings with a branch from the backyard privet hedge, her hand no longer soft but expert, if unenthusiastic. How, adding to the indignity, I had to select the branch. How one time, while she was fashioning my ponytail, I whined that I didn't want to go on our weekly visit to see her mother, Grandma Hood, and she popped me on the top of my head with the hairbrush.

All this strife culminated in an incident I'll call "The Note." In third grade I wrote her a shakily penciled message on blue-lined paper that began, "Dear Mrs. Nicholas." What eight-year-old addresses her mother by her married name? It continued: "You are mean. Why?" The injustice: Sol Boy had stomped his feet at the dinner table and "you blambed it on me." I closed by imploring, "Please be nice to me MOTHER." She was supposed to sign and return the note, agreeing by her checkmark to be nicer. But days passed without any answer. When finally, feelings doubly hurt, I screwed up my child's courage to ask why, she said she didn't recall ever getting any note, though I'd left it squarely on her pillow slip.

But our problems went deeper than any child's grievances, to how she fit into our family. She was the outsider: hills to my father's flatland; country to his city; Scots–Irish to his Lebanese; dirt farmer to his small-town merchant. She was chicken feet and chitterlings to his kibbe and imjadra. Her family was poor as snakes, his well off enough to commission baby portraits of little boys in blue dresses. My father's family didn't honor the poor country girl she'd been, but then neither did my mother. She didn't talk much about her past, claiming she didn't remember it. Or that nobody wanted to hear about it.

What I knew, I mostly learned during those weekly trips to visit Grandma Hood. In her modest frame house on Dunn Avenue, on one of Yazoo City's hilliest streets, on that last ridge of hills before the Mississippi Delta began, my mother's family would sit together in the living room, with an oscillating fan and three-quarter-drawn shades. How fitting that the Hood home straddled the hills and the Delta, because that's what their lives had done. There they would remain for hours, hooting and hollering over their former hardships.

What I knew of my mother's history I could render in catch-phrases. Catchphrase Number One: "My daddy died when I was five." My mother was born in 1924 in the low hills around Midway, but her father, John Wesley Hood, a "dirt farmer," she said, left soon after with his family to try farming in the Delta. Then, at forty-three, he died. "Of the Hood heart," my mother said. Since no one ever went to a doctor, she didn't know what this might be, just that many relatives had died of it. Her father's death was her first memory.

Catchphrase Number Two: "My aunts low-rated me at his funeral." Grandma Hood managed to get her husband's body back to Midway to be buried in the Primitive Baptist churchyard.

When my mother fell asleep in the pew during the service, on a Mississippi-hot August day, her aunts dressed her down. This was her second memory.

Catchphrase Number Three: "My children will never eat last." My mother had twenty-eight aunts and uncles. When they visited, which was often, Grandma Hood would make the children eat after all of them. "All we got was the feet," my mother would wail years afterward, about what was left when the platter of fried chicken got around to them.

On the few occasions when I'd asked my mother to talk about her past, she would drop her head and snap, "You ask too many questions, young'un." Though I might have been curious, I also felt shame. It was a child's shame, in retrospect making only a child's sense. I was ashamed that her family sat around telling hardship stories in the Dunn Avenue living room rather than watching TV, the way the Nicholases did. I was ashamed of the way they talked, their voices gruff and guttural, their grammar rough and filled with "ain'ts" and double negatives. I was ashamed of their plain clothes and even of their last name, Hood, which I'd begun to associate with a certain class of student that was better off avoided in the social strata of Yazoo grammar school life. I was ashamed of the little I did know of the Hoods' history and their dirt farming, which sounded not only unproductive, but unclean.

I came up not knowing much about my mother and, I believed, not close to her. And there things stood, for fifty years. But since leaving New York, since living in Mexico, and especially since living part-time in Yazoo City, I've tried to know my mother. This is her story and that of her people—those hardscrabble, too-poor-to-paint, mean-acting, knee-slapping, dirt-farming, hill-country folk. And it's our story, mine and hers, the story of our late-to-get-going mother-daughter relationship. While I still remember what happened, I plan to set it down. What happened to my mother, but not only to her, to all of us.

PART TWO

Three

The Letters and How It All Began

Nine years before that New Year's Eve storm, on a fall day, I called my mother. Just routine. Probably it was cloudy in the New York suburbs, as it is so often there in the late fall, when the skies turn dull and the air turns damp and biting. When drabness settles over the northeast like a gray army blanket. I'm sure it was a Sunday. In the three decades since I'd left Mississippi, I'd kept in touch through regular Sunday-afternoon phone calls.

I saw my mother twice a year, at Christmas and for her birthday in March, but through our phone calls I got to know her routine. She lived a quiet life. She had to. Since my father died, in 1994, she lived on his Social Security, about eight hundred dollars a month. Every morning her bare feet hit the carpeted bedroom floor when the sun reached her east-facing windows. She padded to the kitchen in navy slippers. Drank a mug of Maxwell House from her recliner while watching the *Today* show. Spent her day in the chair watching old movies, with interruptions to bathe in the cast-iron tub and to steam her dinner (meat + 2) in the plastic contraption on her kitchen counter. For supper she might soak a hunk of cornbread in a glass of buttermilk. Once a week she bought groceries at the Winn-Dixie and had her hair done at Grand Creations on Grand Avenue; three times a week she lifted weights and rode a stationary bicycle at the Fitness Center. On

Saturdays she and Willie Belle ate dinner—the catfish plate, served with hush puppies, at River Bend Catfish House. On Sundays she'd stopped going to Mass, saying she didn't like to sit alone in the "family" pew. Maybe she ventured out to Kmart. I always found her home when I phoned.

To make that call, I climbed on our brass bed on top of the fraying quilt—little blue and yellow and red squares, Mississippi made—to use my fifties desk phone, with its rotary dial that made such satisfying clicks as you brought the finger wheel around to the stop. Daddy had mailed it to me right before he died, after another one of our arguments. He obsessed over collecting vintage telephones, rewiring them, storing them in his bureau drawers, so as a makeup gift the phone had meaning for him. When I was growing up, we'd fought about race and politics and religion and the length of my skirts. Our latest blowouts had been about the efficacy of microwave ovens and whether I loved my young niece enough.

When I thought of home, I thought of New York, not Mississippi, though Mississippi was home in another way: in the way of a home stored away in a bureau drawer, in the way of a place that had shaped me, a place that had nurtured me with much pain and yes, with some pleasure. Though Mississippi had changed in the three decades since I'd left, I'd stored it in my memory as the confounding place it always had been. New York was my adult home, the place where I felt I belonged. The place I fit.

"Mm-hello," my mother answered. I asked her my usual first question.

"Doing fine." Her usual reply.

I could envision how she looked. She kept a beige princess phone tucked under her recliner seat and fished it out to talk. With her left hand she cradled the receiver and with her right she palmed her jaw. She was seventy-seven years old, but she drew her long legs under her, pretzel-like. Usually she wore a mask of calmness on her broad, smooth face, but on this Sunday afternoon I could hear a smidgen of excitement in her breathless voice.

"Did you know about the magnolia tree being cut at the church? It was them birds."

I'd noticed these tiny black birds on one of my recent visits. They flew around the neighborhood at dusk, landing as a twittering mass in the tallest trees. During our last call, she'd complained the birds were making "doody" all over her back steps. "They stop in the hackberry," she'd said, "but they roost in the churchyard across the street. Fly out of that magnolia tree every morning, looking like a big dark cloud."

"Yes," I said, "you told me all about the tree being cut down."

She went silent, apparently disappointed that she'd scooped herself. Then she asked, "Well, did I tell you they dug up the stump?"

I laughed at the update. "We're planning another trip," I told her after a pause, "this time to Mexico." I went on about our upcoming post-Christmas jaunt to Mexico's Central Highlands, mostly to avoid talking about the publishing company where I worked. Once a fun, funky independent, the company had been swallowed up first by a magazine magnate and then by a global conglomerate. On weekends, I wanted to forget about my job as production director for a division of the world's largest book publisher. Lately we'd been traveling a lot, to far-flung places like Peru, Ecuador, Cuba, and Papua New Guinea.

My mother interjected a few "mm-hmms" to let me know she was listening.

Finally I asked, "Is anything else new there? Other than the stump?"

Maybe she'd intended to tell me all along, or maybe she only told me because she'd scooped her earlier news about the magnolia. But I was surprised when she replied, "This week I saw a cardiologist in Jackson."

—

That was all she wanted to say, except to add, "Naw, it ain't nothing." But then why go to a cardiologist? Had her family doctor, the burly Dr. Lamar, discovered something wrong with her during a routine visit? Was it the dreaded Hood heart? By this point the Hood heart had felled her father and four of her seven siblings. Maybe she had the defect too, whatever that might be. Was she ailing? She was always "doing fine." Wasn't she?

How did she even get to the appointment in Jackson? There were two types of drivers in Yazoo: those who ventured the hour-long trip to the lower Delta's go-to city, and those who didn't. My mother was strictly a local driver. Once this hadn't mattered, because back then people shopped for clothes and groceries on Yazoo's Main Street and ate out in its hometown restaurants. There were fancy places like the Tenderloin Grill, where Herbie Holmes and his Orchestra played and the lyrics of "Darkness on the Delta" might be heard wafting across the dance floor while patrons "lingered in the shelter of the night." People visited hometown doctors and, when they had to, King's Daughters Hospital, which had been a state-of-the art facility when it opened in the nineteen-fifties. Yazoo City had once been the richest town in the Mississippi Delta, or so reported the *New York Times* right after the big fire of 1904, which had leveled two hundred of its prime buildings.

By the time I left, in 1972, Main Street had long been rebuilt in solid red brick. And it was still lively, especially on Saturdays, when the country folk came to shop. But now much of the four-block downtown was empty, and some buildings had their storefronts haphazardly boarded up. There was talk of not-so-petty crime, and meth and crack use. My widowed aunts lived with steel bars on their windows and pickups parked out front so a potential burglar would expect to find a man at home. The economic life of Yazoo had all but moved to the city's outskirts, to Highway 49 and a strip of shopping centers, one even named "Yazooville." And the medical life of the town had all but moved to Jackson.

Before the weekend was up, I called my mother back to clarify some details. Charlene, her former lawn lady, had driven her to the cardiologist. On coming to Yazoo City for the first time, bubbly

Charlene (who was from "somewhere up north," my mother said) noticed the kudzu vines growing outside of town, covering the hills and gullies like a vast green carpet. Believing this worthless vine to be an enormous crop of wild cucumbers, Charlene dreamed about the steady money she would make canning pickles. When canning hadn't worked out, Charlene took in ironing and mowed lawns, but she'd had to stop when her legs got too "wobbly." These days she ran errands for Yazoo's widows and escorted them to their Jackson doctors. On Wednesday, my mother told me, she had an appointment with the same cardiologist. Charlene would again be driving.

Wednesday came and went. She and Charlene had thoroughly enjoyed themselves, my mother reported. They'd made a day of it, ordering a plate lunch at a southern-style cafeteria called Piccadilly and taking a turn around a big-box store. I imagined the unlikely pair: my big-boned mother riding her usual shotgun, the diminutive Charlene sunken and chatty behind the oversize wheel of my mother's white 1990 Ford Crown Victoria. For follow-up, Mama would visit Dr. Lamar. He would have the reports from the cardiologist, and they would explain everything. For good measure, she added, "It still ain't nothing."

My mother didn't know if it was "nothing," but she knew that I, the worrier, would need reassuring. Throughout my childhood, I may not have been close to my mother, but I was afraid of losing her. And so with this current medical news my mind went right to her past health crises and hospital stays, when she would disappear for spells into King's Daughters. "Women's problems," Vashti, my unsparing grandmother, explained during one admittance. I was ten at the time, and afraid my mother was going to die—a fear only made worse by my grandmother's lurid descriptions. My mother had been "bleeding to death" in her hospital room, Vashti told me, when my father found her and called for the doctor "in the nick of time." Grandma didn't tell me what was actually wrong with my mother, but later I learned she'd had an ectopic pregnancy. While she was in the hospital, things in the duplex went upside down, with beds unmade, dishes unwashed, food unprepared, and our emotions topsy-turvy as well. When she finally came home, my mother seemed hollow as a seashell.

A few years later, when I was in high school, she went into the hospital again. I had use of an old Rambler station wagon and could have visited her after school, but I let days pass. Finally she sent me a message through my father: where was I? I couldn't tell her of my old fear of losing her, and how I dreaded seeing her in the hospital. But one afternoon I went. When I walked into that antiseptic room and found her lying on her back I couldn't speak. I'd anticipated seeing her neck bandaged, believing she'd had a thyroid operation. But there was no bandage. That time I never did learn what was wrong.

In my life After Duplex, my mother had ignored me, closed me up in a hot room, switched my bare legs, bopped me on the head with a hairbrush, and dismissed me as overly inquisitive, but she and I had also shared some happier memories—of one high summer's noon when she encouraged me to master my twenty-four-inch Challenger bike in the street in front of our house, and of other summer days when, sensing my embarrassment about the condition of the duplex, she packed lunches for me to share with friends at Goose Egg Park.

She painstakingly sewed all my school dresses, and we looked forward to selecting the patterns and materials. Even as a teenager, I liked hunting for fabric with her, thumbing through the oversize pattern books, laying out the tissues on the dining table, pinning and cutting the shapes. She did all the sewing, at first on my great-grandmother Mugga's pedal-powered machine, and later on her electric Singer. When it came time for college, she wanted to make me a special skirt. She seemed sad that I was going so far away, to a school (Swarthmore) and a state (Pennsylvania) whose names she couldn't quite pronounce. She sewed me a floor-length, black-and-red-checked skirt that I was supposed to wear when I went to the opera. She looked proud when I tried it on for her to measure the hem, and then she pressed it and carefully folded it away in the blue footlocker I planned to carry up north.

Four years later, I still hadn't worn that skirt. On the few occasions I'd gone into Philadelphia for a concert, the even fewer times for an opera, I'd worn jeans. Life had lost its formality—had already lost it when she'd sewed the skirt, but we hadn't known. I ended up giving it away to a friend, a short girl from Chicago who cut it down to fit her. I'd never needed it, and the skirt and my mother's sewing it added up to a heavy sadness that seemed to embody all our miscues and misunderstandings. We hadn't fought during my teenage years; my father and I had fought, but she and I had passed each other like unfamiliar ships navigating the unsettled waters of the duplex's close quarters. No, I hadn't needed the skirt, and then I'd proceeded to live my adult life as if I hadn't needed my mother.

In the fall of 2001, which inaugurated such a season of uncertainty for those of us living in New York, I didn't know that I was also about to embark on a season of questioning my After Duplex memories, especially my certainties about my mother and our relationship.

—

After her next visit to Dr. Lamar, my mother still couldn't explain what was wrong with her. She seemed a little vexed that I wanted to know so badly, but she agreed to mail me copies of the letters the cardiologist had sent to Dr. Lamar. In November, they arrived. On the back of the first letter she'd written: "These explain all. Mama."

Case #105088 is a seventy-seven-year-old white female with
hypertension, diabetes mellitus, and hypothyroidism who has no
previous history of heart disease. She does exercise three to five
days per week for about forty-five to sixty minutes and does ride
a stationary bike. Unfortunately, she cannot walk on a treadmill
due to pain in her legs and feet so she has to use a stationary bike
to exercise. She really has not had any chest discomfort whatso-
ever but does not do any strenuous exercise. She has no orthop-
nea, PND, or dyspnea on exertion but does have some mild
lower extremity edema. She has had no palpitations or syncope.
She has no history of hyperlipidemia. Blood pressure 160/90 in
the right arm, 160/80 in the left arm. Pulse 74 and regular, respira-
tions 18 and unlabored. Neck supple without JVD or bruits. Good
carotid upstroke. No thyromegaly noted. Cardiovascular exam
was regular rate and rhythm without murmur, gallop, or rub. No
lift or thrill. PMI nondisplaced. Lungs clear. Abdomen unremark-
able. Extremities revealed no clubbing, cyanosis, or edema. Pulses
were 1+ and equal in all extremities. EKG sinus rate of 84 with
nonspecific ST abnormalities.

I'd seen my mother's lackadaisical *modus operandi* in Yazoo's
cavernous Fitness Center—how she lolled on the back-extension
machine; pedaled a halting rhythm on the stationary bike; dawdled
on the UBE, a kind of bicycle for the shoulders. As for the doctor's
lingo, I took comfort in the number of times he'd written "no" or
"good" next to something. I took comfort that my mother had no
"murmur, gallop, or rub," no "lift or thrill." But he'd noted that she'd
smoked for twenty years and had a strong family history of early
heart disease. Since she couldn't take a stress test on a treadmill, he
wanted her to have an IV adenosine Myoview scan, the chemical
equivalent. She was now a case with a work-up in progress.

In his second letter, written after the chemical stress test, the
cardiologist reported, "Case #105088 had resting non-specific ST
abnormalities that worsened during IV Adenosine administration

and had some mild chest discomfort. There was a very small inferior reperfusion defect that had normal inferior wall motion and had some mild septal hypokinesis ejection fraction 48%."

"These explain all," my mother had written in her spidery script. They explained nothing, at least to me.

I called my sister Debbie, a pediatric anesthesiologist in South Carolina. I sent her copies of the letters. What did they mean? "This is the bad part," she told me. "She had evidence of chemically induced angina. And there's evidence that could indicate an old heart attack."

The cardiologist's second letter had concluded: "I offered a cardiac catheterization but the patient elected empiric medical therapy. She is not having any symptoms at home and does not want to proceed with cardiac catheterization. She understands the risk of myocardial infarction and death. She is willing to take the risk." He prescribed my mother a new blood pressure pill, a daily aspirin, and as-needed nitroglycerin.

There would be no persuading her, a woman who at the age of five had watched her father die of a heart attack, to take care of her own heart problem before it became too late. Once again, I was afraid of losing her. The way I'd "lost" her after the twins died, the way I'd nearly lost her as a ten-year-old, as a teenager.

The vial of nitro went right into her black handbag. Like her princess telephone, she kept it handy, under the recliner. *She understands the risk of death.* And so, finally, did I.

Four

On the Way to Somewhere Else

That Christmas holiday we stopped in Mississippi to check on my mother before our trip to Mexico. I was pushing down the news of her test results from the fall. And she was helping: on the phone, nothing was ever new, and she was always "doing fine." Her daily routine was simple enough that it didn't seem to tax her faltering heart. Even the vexing black birds had flown off after the Methodists cut down their magnolia tree. The nitro went unused.

We got to Jackson after the weak winter sun had set, rented a car, and "pointed" it toward Yazoo City, as Aunt Willie Belle would say. If the weather had not been warm that night, but cold and rainy, she would have added, "And don't brake on them bridges." One holiday Gerry and I had been traveling this same stretch of interstate when it started sleeting, and we watched as the car directly in front of us slid sideways off an overpass. Mississippi might be a landscape of little change for my mother—nothing ever new—but to me it could be unpredictable and dangerous, even at the most mundane of times.

We got to Yazoo City early on the night before Christmas Eve. We found my mother slumped in her yellow recliner in the dark, except for the play of light and shadow from the TV. The house looked neat but was undecorated for the holiday. My mother seemed the same, gray-maned and sweatpant-clad. After she shoulder-hugged us hello, shyly, without getting up, Gerry and I sat down next to her on the twin loveseats. We were staying only three days and would spend our visit on these flowered couches, which she'd bought at Unclaimed Freight after the duplex was fixed up the first time. Hardly a year after my father died, she withdrew ten thousand dollars from the small nest egg he'd accumulated in two of the town's banks, even while fretting she should be saving it for "that day when I have to go into the nursing home." Her first bid for the renovation was from an ex-con Willie Belle had met in the sheriff's office. But in the end familiarity won out over frugality, and my mother hired her cousin Mike for the job.

Mike hung fresh Sheetrock and installed light blue carpet in the bedrooms, mounted butcher-block counters and put down linoleum in the kitchen, and painted everything in my mother's new favorite wall color, China Doll. After he finished, my sister Lisa dug a narrow trench around the front porch and planted "Red Ruffles," an azalea that flowered crimson in the spring, along with a camellia bush that produced milky white blossoms in the winter. My mother tore down the makeshift Little House my father had built out back, replacing it with a tan metal storage shed, and she installed a metal carport, likewise tan.

Without my father around, the new-old duplex was weirdly quiet. Where he used to clomp his leather clodhoppers over the wooden floors, my mother wore soft slippers and padded through the carpeted rooms. I wondered if she missed him and all the noise he used to make. I suspect that if I'd asked, she would have replied, "Well, of course," though that wouldn't have gone far in explaining their marriage. I wondered too if my mother wished that my father had lived to see the duplex fixed up. But if he'd been alive, the work wouldn't have gotten done. She maintained that he couldn't have withstood the disruption, but there were other reasons. Money was one. Another was his opinion of change. One Christmas I sent my parents a microwave, and the gift got him so mad he yelled into the phone, "We don't need no microwave," and vowed he wouldn't ever use the "new-fangled contraption." Something of this attitude—mistrust of the new, of almost anything that altered the present or threatened his precious memory of the past—must have factored into his refusal to fix up the duplex, despite amassing all those faucet handles and two-by-fours in the Little House.

After high school I'd left and never come back here to live, absorbed with my life in my Manhattan steel-and-concrete office building and our suburban clapboard farmhouse on the Harlem Line. While my father was alive, I'd come back to give my mother relief from him, and after he died I'd come back to help relieve her loneliness. I'd felt protective of my mother, even as I believed we weren't close, and I'd never wanted her to be alone, especially on her birthday and at Christmas. So I'd come back, out of obligation toward my mother but also out of sentiment (with all the word's meanings, even "homesickness"), seeking my past, circling around the unresolved feelings about my father and about leaving this place. Maybe I'd come back out of a combination of love, tamped-down hunger for a relationship with my mother I'd never had, and a big dose of survivor guilt.

Our stopover visit started off like all the others we'd spent with my mother in the seven years since Daddy's death. We lounged in the living room, in the warm beige tones of China Doll, my mother in her recliner, Gerry and I on the loveseats, with the TV tuned to TCM. I lay on the loveseat next to her, my feet sticking over the armrest, so close I could have reached out my big toe and touched her arm. Wrung out from work, I dozed during the endless play of old movies. Gerry slept a foot away on his own loveseat.

But late on the afternoon of Christmas Eve, my mother and I began to talk. We reminisced about Christmases past, about things we'd often reminisced about. The year she forgot to line the German chocolate cake pans with wax paper and had to bake the three layers twice. How she and my father had saved for our presents all year long using the Bank of Yazoo's Christmas club plan. How each fall they hid our presents in the car, and how from all over the neighborhood on Christmas Eve would come the sound of trunks slamming. How every year, on a cold December day, we would visit the Rusche farm to cut fresh holly and a giant cedar tree. The living room furniture would be carted out, some onto the front porch, so the tree could be hauled in, tied to a nail on the wall, and strung with old-timey balls and colored lights. This afternoon, when our talk turned to my father's over-the-top Christmas sentimentality, I suggested we get out his favorite decorations.

I piled the tattered cardboard boxes at my mother's feet. She stayed close to the heater, her legs bound in the yellow snuggle sack she wriggled into whenever it got cold. These boxes, many the original packaging from the fifties, held glass figurines, dimpled baubles, shiny balls, plastic holly, red velvet ribbons, strings of fat, multicolored lights, and a white plush tree skirt. One contained the "silver" angel that had floated on top of our tree and another the little lightbulbs painted like Frosty the Snowman and Santa Claus. After the family stopped reuniting for Christmas, my father dispensed with a live tree and just displayed his dollar-store decorations, including his prized foot-high Santa Claus doll. The Santa's white beard was now matted with age, his red tunic stained, but there was still a jingle in his handbell.

"Put him yonder on the cocktail table," my mother said quietly, from her chair. She was swigging a double cup of late-afternoon coffee, loaded up with the fatty milk she couldn't do without. I placed the tatty doll next to the pink glass candy dish.

"And we always put that silly little tree right on the Sony," she added, meaning the eight-inch plastic fir with its concealed eyes and mouth, complete with bright-red tongue. Whenever anybody walked too close, the tree's hidden face would come alive and sing a jolly "Ho, ho, ho!" This never failed to get a belly laugh from my father.

My mother felt little nostalgia for Daddy's Santa doll or for the jokey tree—she didn't share his cheap sentimentality—but she did have a sense of humor. And she was loyal. She'd treated Daddy with sweet consideration, even when he was on his worst behavior, throwing tantrums and storming out of the house to punish us with the fear of desertion. With his prized decorations displayed like little invocations of Christmases past, she made sure he was with us still. I didn't mind; in some ways I was like him. I also looked to the past and didn't much court change, which was why I'd stayed at the same publishing company for twenty-five years. As for my mother, as she sipped her coffee and provided color commentary about Daddy's hokey trimmings, I took note of her soft accented voice and how, without trying, she could always tug me back to this place I didn't call home.

But even as I felt enwombed by her presence and by the new-old duplex, a competing awareness clamored for my attention. I flashed to the times over the years when she'd participated in, not just directed, the decorating, when she'd been the one to cut down the cedar Christmas tree. She used to stand for hours cooking the turkey, casseroles, and desserts in our tiny kitchen; she pre-washed the crystal, china, and silver, and then washed them again when the meal was over. This year, on the morning after Christmas, as we were leaving for the Jackson airport, as I was about to close her front door, I glanced back. My mother sat hunched in the yellow recliner with her knees crossed man-style. She was wearing the fleece Debbie had sent her for Christmas, her short, snowy hair contrasting with the jacket's royal-blue fabric. She gripped her pencil and an oversize paperback of word-find puzzles. Was it because I was returning to my world that I suddenly saw her more clearly?

She'd taken on the shape of the recliner, with her chest caved in, her stomach poked out. When had her upper back started to curve? When had she started sitting down so hard, blowing out a puff of air? When had her pace become so slow, the steps so measured? Now when she walked she watched her feet, her head craned like a giant bird's. When had she gotten so old? As I slipped her front door closed, she didn't look up. I left feeling guilty for not staying longer and for not doing more for her. Guilty for leaving her alone again.

And it wasn't only my mother who'd changed. Since leaving Yazoo City I'd gone back regularly, if infrequently, seeking my past, but this visit I had trouble finding that past. Reminiscing with my mother, I couldn't summon up half of what I used to remember about the Yazoo City of my childhood; the time and place where I grew up seemed no longer to exist, even deep inside me. With the dimming of memory, I felt I'd crossed into middle age.

When we landed in Mexico City I discovered I'd filched my mother's keys. They lay heavy in my hand, a riotous mess of steel. They were spares, but I imagined her hunting everywhere for them. While Gerry filled out papers to rent a car, I called her. She answered with her lazy "Mm-hello," and I promised to mail them when we got back to New York.

This quick trip to the Central Highlands and the colonial cities of Zacatecas, Guanajuato, and San Miguel de Allende was to explore Mexico's "heartland." Four years earlier, on our first visit to the country, we'd picked up a rental car in Cancun and driven west on the deserted Yucatan Peninsula toward the ruins of Chichen Itza. But this would be different. Zacatecas, with its pink limestone buildings, and Guanajuato, with its colorful houses jumbled on the hillsides, were charming and sophisticated cities. Late one afternoon we arrived in the small, rustic town of San Miguel de Allende. We bumped along a lengthy construction detour on its southern edge, somehow ending up on the hill above the main square. After a slow descent on a narrow, cobblestoned street, we finally made it to the square just before sunset, coming to a stop in front of an old hotel.

Within minutes the staff parked the car and checked us into a second-floor room. Gerry and I stood on the balcony looking down on the neatly landscaped square, bordered on four sides by buzz-cut laurel trees. In the center was an old-fashioned wrought-iron bandstand. Across the way, a pink confection of a church rose before us. The buildings all around us were colonial in spirit, with nothing to break the venerable style. To the west, the town seemed to fall away, revealing a great, open plain trimmed by blue-tinged mountains.

We had been searching for something, especially after the events of the past fall. After September 11 we'd vowed to stay in New York, but we planned to sell our eighty-year-old farmhouse to get out from under its high taxes. Gerry was putting together a book proposal about the Prussian naturalist Alexander von Humboldt and his nineteenth-century exploration of Latin America, part of which we'd retraced on a recent hiking trip to the Ecuadorean Andes. He had only to figure out how to free himself from his own responsibilities at a publishing house to write the book. As for me, every day I arrived at my office at seven-thirty, as I always had, but I wrote short stories until the official starting hour. I felt guilty, but not guilty enough to stop. If our publisher happened by my office, I would hide whatever I was writing under the many stacks of papers on my desk.

Then on that warm winter afternoon in central Mexico, a few days after Christmas, while standing on a hotel balcony in San Miguel de Allende, looking west over the valley toward the mountains I didn't yet know by name, I turned to Gerry and said these unexpected words: "I think I could live here."

Also not one to court change, not lightly, he said, "I think I could too." We knew no one in the town, and almost nothing about it, but already we had a feeling of belonging. Except for New York City, I'd never felt so immediately attached to a place.

During the past fall, though I'd tried ignoring the news of my mother's medical tests, I'd been afraid that the quiet years since my father's death were about to end for her. That she might be entering a new, unstable phase of her life. I wasn't sure how, but in San Miguel I had an inkling that the quiet years were also about to end for Gerry and me—but that we would will them to end, and that this would entail a new country. Mexico.

Five

And Then They Really Ended

Seven months later, Debbie and I, dressed in shorts and shirtsleeves, stood side by side in my mother's kitchen. My big sister and I hadn't been together during the summer for probably thirty years. The galley-style kitchen looked out over the backyard: the picture window Mike had installed over the new stainless steel double sink just about framed the giant hackberry tree. Since sunlight couldn't filter through the tree's dense canopy, a shadow spread near the back door—a summer shadow, green-tinged, deep, and unmoving. There were no breezes; we'd gone beyond them. There was only oppressive heat and wild growth. My mother protested that her St. Augustine grass grew at the rate of an inch a day. Fruits dropped from Willie Belle's two huge fig trees, slicking the bare ground beneath. Nature seemed heavy with memory, deep in itself, evocative of other days, older days.

We were making Lebanese cabbage rolls for a throwback Sunday dinner. We'd already boiled the cabbage, and now Debbie and I worked at the butcherblock counter, separating the warm, pliable leaves to receive the spicy meat stuffing. Tomorrow my mother would have surgery, a CABG, or coronary artery bypass graft, which the doctors referred to as a "cabbage." Had we done this unconsciously? Cooked cabbage rolls before her CABG? My

father's Lebanese food had always been our special fare, but we
could have baked kibbe.

How had the surgery come about? Something had sent my
mother back to the doctor. Perhaps her breathlessness had worsened, or she'd started having chest pains and dipping into the nitro
vial in her bag. Or perhaps she'd simply accepted that she needed
fixing. Simply made the decision, in her practical way, to "go on
and get it over with." I don't recall, and I blame my preoccupation
with my job and our house in New York.

A month ago, in early June, I'd stood looking down on her
stretched out on a hospital gurney at a large medical complex in
Jackson. She'd been in a holding pen, waiting for a cardiac catheterization. I'd encouraged her to wave her arms and raise her legs,
as much to entertain us as to prove to myself she was still capable
of it. "You are so much fun," she'd said. And it had felt like fun,
joshing her. But after the procedure, back in her private room, any
movement was out of the question. Afterward she rested with a
sandbag on the cut in her groin where they'd inserted the tube that
they'd threaded to her heart. (The sandbag was her reminder to lie
still until the wound clotted.) I waited impatiently by the window,
watching her stare at the ceiling, hoping for the cardiologist's call.
Then the phone rang.

The "cath" showed blockages in the right coronary artery, the
left coronary artery, and the left anterior descending artery, the
specialist said. Bad news succinctly delivered. Was that what it
meant to have the "Hood heart"? My mother would need surgery,
and fast, he continued, but first she needed a carotid arteriogram,
a dye study of the arteries in her neck, because these were also
suspect. Within a day we found out that my mother's left carotid
artery was blocked; within a week she'd had the surgery to reopen
it. Debbie, who stayed with her in Jackson through the neck surgery, reported that she'd done well under the anesthesia. She hadn't
"stroked." She'd "emerged with her faculties intact."

But on this hot, slow Sunday in July, all that prep lay in my mother's past. I thought of this as a "what if" day, as in "what if she doesn't pull through?" and I'd arranged things in New York so I could be with her. At twelve o'clock, after the Baptists finished their services, Willie Belle came over, towing my first cousin and her young granddaughter from Atlanta along with her. Dottie liked to time her yearly trip to Mississippi during high summer so she could eat figs straight from Willie Belle's trees. The six of us crowded around my mother's dining table and passed the cabbage rolls. When a local grocery had started selling fried kibbe from its deli case, Lebanese food had become unexpectedly popular in town. My aunt was used to the strong spices, the cinnamon, allspice, and pepper, from sampling my mother's Lebanese cooking, and she'd already developed a taste for them. I wasn't sure about my cousins.

At the table, we chitchatted, mostly about the color of Debbie's hair. She explained that the purple streaks helped her relate to her young patients before their surgeries. Nobody was mentioning my mother's operation until, with fork in midair, she declared, apropos of the elephant in the room, "Well, I'll be almost back to normal in two weeks." Which made me wonder how she defined "almost." Not to mention "normal." She narrowed her eyes, stared out the window toward the deserted street, and chewed her cabbage roll.

After dinner she relaxed in her recliner with her feet propped up while Willie Belle told a favorite story about the time she'd met Alec Baldwin. He'd been deep in Yazoo County filming *Ghosts of Mississippi*, and because of her job at the sheriff's office, my aunt got to visit the set. She was as impressed by the eats as she was by the famously blue-eyed actor—especially by a dish of chicken and mushrooms that "came out of a truck." The drink selections proved similarly memorable. "Something called cappuccino," she recalled. "Coffee from Italy, they said. And the water was from France."

Late in the afternoon Lisa arrived, and we were all together. Though she had a four-hour drive from Picayune, in south Mississippi, Lisa visited Mama often, possible because as a freelance editor, she could somewhat make her own schedule. She was the youngest, the "baby of the family," as my father liked to call her. She'd lived like an only child in the duplex after the rest of us had moved out, and she and Mama had stayed close. Her arrival got my mother up to brew a fresh pot of Maxwell House. Dottie pulled me aside. "I don't know if Aunt Florence is really that calm or she's just pretending," she said. "But I didn't want to ask."

It wasn't pretense. Except for a loud sigh at four-thirty the next morning, as we were leaving for the hospital in the pitch black, I heard nothing from her to indicate worry. Even the sigh was more of a "let's-go-get-this-over-with" call to action.

—

After our long predawn drive from Yazoo City, my sisters and I strolled down the Jackson hospital's airy, plant-filled medical mall, taking turns pushing my mother in a saggy loaner wheelchair. Then we all bunched around her in the surgical holding pen, while the nursing staff peppered her with routine questions. After the nurse drew blood, as if on cue the anesthesiologist entered, pulling the thin white privacy curtain around us. He had a husky physique and seemed like a practical man. A deer and dove hunter, probably.

"My doctor daughter," my mother said, introducing Debbie. The two specialists shared shoptalk—medical schools attended, residencies completed, hospitals worked at—before he turned back to his patient. "Well, did you bring your own nurse too?"

I could see my mother hesitate. "Naw, I'll have to use one of y'all's," she replied. Comments like these had led Gerry to describe her as fey. Was she teasing the doctor or answering him earnestly? He didn't know either, but he laughed. Then he gave her a sedative, and she said, "I need to lie back," though she was already supine on the gurney.

My sisters and I staked out space in the designated waiting area on two worn-out couches, near a black wall phone where we would get news from my mother's medical team. Willie Belle; my cousin Danny, my aunt's older son; and Ada, my mother's only remaining sibling, soon joined us. I didn't have experience waiting in hospitals, but Willie Belle, who'd tended to my uncle Lawrence during his heart attacks and surgeries, elevated waiting to an art form. She and Aunt Ada settled in and started chatting. All around us were other extended families, on other worn-out couches, anticipating their own surgical updates.

My sisters and I took turns answering the wall phone. At eight o'clock they called to say they'd begun. I asked Debbie what it meant to begin. "It means they've divided her breastbone and exposed her heart. They've connected her to a heart-lung machine to take over the job of the heart and lungs." She added, "It means her heart is stilled."

We talked little after that, just remarks to pass the time and tamp down the nerves. But the phone calls kept coming and kept the stress level up. At nine they'd finished taking the leg vein they planned to use for the right and left coronary arteries. At ten they'd taken the chest artery they planned to use for the left anterior descending artery. By eleven she was "off bypass," the heart-lung machine, and they were "closing her." At twelve they called to warn us. "Keep your composure, because you'll be seeing your loved one soon."

They had wheeled her into a pod-like space, steps off a central nurses' station. She looked entirely unlike the person we'd said goodbye to only hours earlier. Her face appeared twice its normal size. She was on a breathing tube. Other tubes protruded from her, and she was hooked up to a battery of machines. Liquids spilled from her, filling pouches and bulbs. On her legs, plastic cuffs inflated and deflated to reduce the likelihood of blood clots. Strangest of all, she seemed bathed in ethereal whiteness, from her gray hair, her broad, bloodless face, the thin white sheet covering her, and the stark white wall behind her.

"Not bad," Debbie said, "for someone who was dead for two hours today."

"She's doing great," a nurse interjected. "And she looks much younger than her seventy-eight years."

"What makes you say she's doing great?" I asked. This must have been the moment when the medical team thought we would lose our composure. When we saw our "loved one" overtaken by tubes, drains, and machines, and looking otherworldly.

"Her blood pressure's stable, and she's breathing on her own with only an assist from the ventilator," the nurse replied. Though she was deeply unconscious, my mother's face twitched at that instant, and a grimace passed over her like a fleeting cloud.

By afternoon she was off the ventilator and breathing deep into her swollen belly. "Difficult to breathe higher," the nurse said. "But she's still doing great." Her eyes remained closed, but when Lisa shouted, "We love you, Mama!" they fluttered open. Maybe my mother had been right. Maybe she would be almost back to normal in two weeks. By the end of the day, the heart surgeon was touting her as his star patient.

—

But I had things to do, and so the morning after my mother's CABG I sat on a plane on the Jackson runway, headed back to New York. At about the same time, she was out of bed, sitting in a chair in the Cardiac Care Unit. A little while later, guided by her nurses and Debbie, she took a few steps outside the room. Debbie asked her if she'd "passed flatus" yet.

My mother shook her head, surprised probably by the Latin but surely by the personal nature of my sister's question.

"You've got to pass flatus," Debbie went on.

She demurred. "I don't want to do that."

"Mother, you need to fart," Debbie insisted. "If you don't, we'll have to lap the nurses' station again."

"I'll do it then."

Mama described her first post-op steps as "doing the Tim Conway shuffle," a reference to his Old Man character's foot-dragging on *The Carol Burnett Show*. She felt "dead tired," she said. During afternoon rounds the heart surgeon decided she was ready to move out of the CCU. Day two and she was still his star. After she settled into her private room, her "vitals" were still good. But, she told my sisters, she was starting to feel "poorly."

⁓

The next day at noon I was back at my desk, fighting to calm down. That morning I'd walked across Midtown Manhattan in the thick heat to tell my corporate boss I was leaving the publishing company. At the same hour Gerry was also giving notice. We'd found a buyer for our house, and our plan was to leave New York in September. We were headed to San Miguel de Allende, the Mexican hill town we'd fallen so hard for the previous December.

Afterward Gerry would quip to bewildered friends, "After selling our house and quitting our jobs, the next logical step was moving to a foreign country." But the move would only be temporary—we intended to put our things in storage and be back in New York within six months. Then we would buy a house in another commuter town with lower taxes and find jobs that taxed us less. During the sabbatical, Gerry would finish the Humboldt manuscript, and I would start a coming-to-grips memoir about growing up in Mississippi during the Civil Rights era. The coming-to-grips part had to do with my father.

That was the plan, which for months we'd kept secret. It hadn't been the snap decision that Gerry's joke implied. We'd been daydreaming about this course for years. Things had come to a head late one night after another long day at the office. I'd been loading the dishwasher. "How much longer do I have to wait to do what I've always wanted?" I'd asked, during an unusual acrimonious exchange. I'd even let fly the word *divorce*.

But both of us wanted to write, and that meant no regular income to pay the bills. After psychotherapy and antidepressants, we'd arrived at this compromise. Six months off to write. Plus, we would learn Spanish and immerse ourselves in another culture. Mexico, close on our border yet far away in spirit, seemed about perfect. In June we'd circled back to San Miguel for a few days to judge if its pull would hold up. And it had—the sculpted, blue-tinged mountains; the rustic, colorful buildings with thick walls and central patios; the narrow, cobbled streets; the perfumed blend of Catholic and indigenous cultures; and above all the inexplicable serenity of the very old.

But as I sat at my desk that July day, I was faced not with the excitement of what we'd planned but with the irretrievability of what we'd done. As I was mulling over how to break my resignation to my colleagues and staff, whose lives I was also disrupting, the phone rang at my desk. It was Debbie. There had been a setback with my mother's recovery. She was weak all over, but especially on her right side. She couldn't speak or follow simple commands, and she was refusing food and drink. Because she couldn't get out of bed the bladder catheter had been put back in. Her recovery had ground to a halt. My doctor-sister seemed uncharacteristically rattled. "Mama is languishing," she said. "Refusing to cooperate."

My mother had given out. Or had she given up? Debbie's description seemed to imply opposite states. "Languishing" suggested a physical setback, while "refusing to cooperate" indicated a willfulness to fail. But only two things seemed clear on that humid summer morning, as so many old fears about my mother came rushing back. As I sat at my desk, poised on the cusp of huge change, my mother, in her hospital bed, appeared hugely changed. And for both of us, the quiet years had ended, and with a holler.

Six

When You Peel a Banana

In a less medically specific moment, Debbie had also used the term "goofy" to describe my mother's condition. But why was she goofy? Was it the pain medications? Or had she suffered another stroke? She'd already had one stroke, in the early nineties, as she and my father were driving away from this same hospital after my uncle Lawrence's angioplasty. Daddy made a U-turn over the boulevard's landscaped median to drive her straight to the emergency room. After she came to, she could still talk, though for a while she used wacky metaphors. Her team of doctors, for example, she referred to as a "herd of elephants."

If she'd had another stroke, when had it happened? Was it happening yesterday morning when she lapped the nurses' station doing the "Tim Conway shuffle"? Or during the evening, in her private room, when she complained of feeling poorly? Or did it happen overnight, when she was by herself? Is that when she went goofy? And if she'd had a stroke, what type did she have? (There were types?) The heart surgeon pulled her off the pain pills and called in a neurologist. As I sat at my desk that Wednesday, mulling these questions, a new team was assembling in Jackson to solve the medical mystery she'd presented.

All that day, I got telephone updates from my sisters, sometimes every few minutes. In the morning my mother underwent a CT scan to rule out a brain hemorrhage. Later a kind and efficient speech pathologist came by the room to examine her. The therapist determined that she couldn't process complex sentences, but that she could understand simple ones. She couldn't write either. And she seemed frustrated and downhearted.

At noon my mother sat up in bed while waiting for her lunch tray. Debbie told her, "Mama, when that tray comes, I want you to eat, eat, eat!" She didn't, but after a nap she stared at the TV and spoke a garbled sentence. Although her vital signs were good, her heart was going in and out of atrial fibrillation, beating irregularly. In the late afternoon the surgeon visited and reminded my mother that before the operation he'd been worried about neurological complications. A Mr. Lumpkin, from Mended Heart, a patient support group, also stopped by. The last phone call of the day came from Lisa, saying that the earlier CT scan showed no "deep stroking." The neurologist theorized that my mother's atrial fibrillation had "thrown a clot to the brain." In that case there shouldn't be a "bad outcome," the specialist said, and her symptoms should improve with therapy.

That night my mother slept well, and the next morning her heart was no longer "fibbing," Debbie reported. Her voice sounded stronger. This would be a day of yet more tests, an MRI of the brain and a cranial Doppler study. But first, Mama sat out of bed and walked twenty feet with a physical therapist. The effort exhausted her, and she said, "I can't feel the floor." Back in her room, she ate the legs off a gingerbread man.

After all the studies, the neurologist concluded that a clot in the repaired carotid artery had broken off and embolized to the brain's left hemisphere. So the first operation that she'd had to prevent a stroke had triggered a stroke, though that was said to be good news, because the clot was "fresh" and would break up. Before, her left carotid had been partially open, but now it was closed. Instead the circle of Willis, a loop of vessels at the base of the skull, was supplying blood to my mother's brain. Only a

third of all people, the neurologist said, "enjoy" a complete circle
of Willis. My mother, apparently, enjoyed it.

The medical team planned on discharging her to a nearby
stroke rehabilitation center. They hoped that with blood thinners
her body would reabsorb the clot and the left carotid artery would
open up again. They hoped that with rehab her speech would
improve, and she might regain enough fine muscular control to
write again. "But she's different," Debbie explained. "You can't have
a fast conversation with her. That goes right by."

A week later my mother went by ambulance to a major rehab
center near the hospital, where she was given a big, bright room
all to herself. That made her happy, but she dreaded meals in the
dining hall because she didn't know anybody. Lisa volunteered
to sleep in the duplex and drive to Jackson every morning to
attend my mother's therapy sessions and then keep her company
at lunch. I stayed in New York to finish out my month's notice,
pack up our house, and move our belongings into storage. And
before my health insurance ran out, I also carved out a day to have
arthroscopic surgery on my left knee. Selling our house, packing
and moving our things, quitting our jobs, my mother's heart surgery and stroke, my own surgery and physical therapy, preparing
to move to a foreign country. The quiet years, over.

My mother had accepted a stopover in rehab so she could learn
to function again. But her schedule there was ten times busier than
in her real life, with multiple daily sessions of speech, physical, and
occupational therapy. Lisa and I talked often, mostly about the
little crises that kept popping up. One day I had my sister ask our
mother a question, if she knew what year it was, to which Mama
answered, "Don't she know?"

But my mother had been left with a kind of neurological damage that Lisa began calling "the banana problem." During an early

therapy session, a pleasant young woman named Heather posed this diagnostic question: "Do you eat a banana before you peel it?"

To which my mother wholeheartedly assured her, "Yes."

Heather patiently explained the correct sequence for eating a banana and asked my mother to think about it hard. Again the therapist posed her question, and again my mother gave her answer—that you eat a banana before you peel it.

As her first week in rehab drew to a close, my mother was scheduled for another session with Heather. Just before they were to meet, she asked Lisa if Heather was the one who'd asked her about the banana. Sensing that she was anticipating the question, even that she wanted to cram for it, Lisa asked, "Mama, do you eat a banana before you peel it?"

To which our mother replied, "Yes."

Lisa then explained again why the answer should be "no."

To which our mother exclaimed, "Well, I disagree!"

That was her mental status when she was discharged from rehab toward the end of August. She believed, or at least she said, that you ate a banana before you peeled it.

—

The Tuesday after Labor Day found me standing next to my mother in her living room. On our way to Mexico again, this time for six months, Gerry and I were spending three weeks in Yazoo City. Everything we owned in New York was crammed into a climate-controlled storage unit in Westchester County, next to Luther Vandross's spare wardrobe. As an added benefit, the facility played classical music twenty-four-seven to the units' contents.

Since my mother's living room faced due west, it didn't receive any direct sun until late afternoon, and even then the two giant sycamores in the front yard blocked much of the light. That was why she left the lamp next to her recliner permanently switched on. But that morning the lamp was off, and absent its artificial glow the dim space seemed to embody our off-kilter situation. Her silvery head was bowed, and I got a good look at the growth on her crown, which she called "that knob up top my head." She'd had this unsightly "knob" for so long that it seemed as much a part of her body as her arms and legs, but I figured we should see a specialist about it too, as long as we were seeing about everything else.

She'd woken up "wobbly-kneed," she'd reported, but had managed to dress herself in black pants and a white T-shirt. She'd put on and tied a pair of white tennis shoes. She was ready to venture out to her therapy appointment, but I didn't want to let her go.

"Do you have any money on you?" I asked.

She nodded. Since the stroke, she seldom spoke if she didn't have to.

"How about an I.D.?"

She removed a clip from her pants pocket, then shoved it back inside.

"Okay," I said. "I'll watch from the window."

I kissed her forehead, and she cracked open the front door and edged out. As I watched through the fanlight, I saw her stop before trying the porch steps. There were only three, but no railing. She two-footed them sideways, then made her way past the sycamores without tripping on the knotted roots that ran along the surface. She stopped at the curb, turning her head left and right before attempting to cross the street. Cars flew by, heading north, away from downtown. Should I have gone with her, held her hand on her first day out by herself?

She touched one foot down on the concrete, then the other, and made it to the sidewalk in front of St. John's Methodist Church. There the sun found her, illuminating her hair, skin, shirt, and those shoes—all shades of white, contrasting with her dark pants. Two blocks, not even, that was the distance she had to cover, but her size-ten feet appeared too small for the task, her near-six-foot frame towering above them.

We'd met this therapist a few days ago in her office, a converted house where the living/waiting room was outfitted with tiny chairs and cuddle toys and blocks in primary colors. She'd ushered us into her office and outlined how she might help. My mother needed practice speaking and writing and computing math. It had felt like a small miracle, finding this specialist nearby, and then she'd agreed to take my mother, a client so obviously outside her usual practice. Mama didn't register any doubt about the thin young woman and her black BMW with the license plate that read BLACK BARBIE. She liked her from the start.

These days felt off-kilter not because our stopover marked the beginning of our sabbatical, but because I didn't know what to do with myself. For the first time since kindergarten I had no routine. I had a book to write, but I didn't know how to start. Even the weather felt jarring. After Labor Day I'd expected the temperatures to cool, as they did in New York, and the trees to take on bright fall colors. But September in Mississippi wasn't so much a precursor to fall as an extension of summer, though with drier days, which were better for picking the cotton that grew right up to the town's edge. Gerry was working under a deadline on the Humboldt manuscript, but I told myself to let these weeks be for my mother. In the mornings I watched as she made her way up the street to therapy, and in the afternoons I drove her to the gym for cardio rehab. With nothing else to do, I languished.

One Saturday morning, desperate for a diversion, Gerry and I did what many do in the Delta during the fall. We went dove hunting. We got up early and dressed in borrowed camouflage clothing—pants, shirts, vests, and even hats. After meeting up with my cousin Zack at a rusted-out cotton gin in Holmes County, we piled into his pickup and drove to a field that he'd planted with sunflowers. We set up campstools. Insects almost as big as doves buzzed our ears; when the darkness thinned to gray, I recognized them as dragonflies. An hour later, Zack, who'd situated himself in a nearby field, pulled up on his four-wheeler. "I thought I would show y'all what flying doves look like," he said. Which was a polite way of saying that we didn't know what we were doing. Gerry did manage to shoot the tail feathers off two low flyers, but we bagged nothing and left feeling like Elmer Fudd.

During these weeks, my mother kept getting better. And except for the banana question, she took everything in stride. Her handwriting became more legible. As she hunched over the dining table, doggedly balancing her checkbook, her grasp of numbers improved. She became steadier on her feet and resumed her routines: in the mornings, pricking her finger to check her glucose level, and in the evenings, repeating the procedure. Around eight each night I would hear water running in the basin, the echoing sound of the brush against her teeth, and then she would pad down the hall to her bedroom in her purple bathrobe, stopping to say goodnight. After she fell asleep, I would look in on her. My tall, stocky mother liked starting the night curled on her right side. These rootless weeks, I felt myself becoming tied to her. She, who was so rooted, drew me to her without trying, and without making demands. She simply went ahead with her daily routines, one moment at a time. She so lived in the moment that I began to feel I lived in her moments.

She really was "almost back to normal." I suspected she might be humoring us, in particular Debbie, who'd proposed the extra therapy. I suspected she might even be waiting for us to leave, biding her time until she could get back in her recliner, where she could sit out the days uninterrupted by self-improvement. But I was also biding time, waiting for our flight to Mexico. Perhaps it was wrong to leave a seventy-eight-year-old who couldn't explain the sequence of peeling and eating a banana, but I couldn't admit this lapse was a reason to stay. It was hard to believe she wasn't all right. Off we went, south toward Mexico.

Seven

Magic and Misery in San Miguel de Allende

On September 21, a full, white moon eyed our small plane as it circled the airport in León, in the Mexican state of Guanajuato, a few hours before the autumnal equinox. By the spring equinox we would be back in New York, but landing in Mexico that first night of fall felt like the beginning of something permanent, not the beginning of something temporary. We quickly passed through immigration, receiving six-month tourist visas, and met up with our van driver outside of customs. Once past the city of Guanajuato we rarely saw another car as we made our way southeast over the mountains to San Miguel.

Around midnight, we rang the bell at our pension, located a few steps off the town's main square. The owner, Alma, her hair in curlers, opened the stately wooden door and helped us drag our bags over the entryway's stones to our suite: a living room with a sixties-vintage sofa, and up the spiral staircase, a cramped loft bedroom with a small writing desk. As we'd driven through town we'd seen scores of young men dressed in dark pants, white shirts, and red bandanas, and now a group of them was gathering in the hole-in-the-wall cantina across the street, whooping in high-pitched voices. We wouldn't realize until the next day that we'd arrived during the *Sanmiguelada*, the yearly running of the bulls.

The sun came up late and the air felt chilly, so unlike the humid Mississippi mornings we'd left behind. On our way to the dining room we paused outside the door to our suite, struck by the casual beauty of the classic colonial house and its central patio awash with geraniums, bougainvillea, and orange and lime trees. After breakfast, Alma presented us with a copy of the local English-language newspaper, and we began house hunting.

By two o'clock, when we returned to the pension for the main meal, or *comida*, we'd seen three places to rent and decided which one we wanted: a little pink house built into the ruins of a stable on the grounds of an old hacienda. There was one hitch—the efficient Swiss landlady was insisting we sign a year's lease for the furnished rental. We figured we could still leave Mexico after six months and pay the penalty the lease stipulated, but we made ourselves wait a day to tell her we would take it. It seemed easy, relocating to Mexico.

But the next evening Gerry spiked a fever of 104 degrees, and Alma had to find a doctor to make a house call. He felt better after a few days of antibiotics, but then his computer crashed, and he lost the files for his manuscript. We'd thought it romantic to lie under the bedroom's exposed beams while raindrops dampened our pillows, but we'd left the laptop plugged in during the storm, and a power surge had damaged its circuitry. Once again Alma recommended a specialist, one who could restore computers. After two weeks at the pension, we didn't have reason to believe we would want to stay in Mexico for longer than six months.

We began to learn about the town. San Miguel el Grande had been founded in 1542 along the Camino Real de Tierra Adentro, which for three hundred years was the main route for transporting silver from the mines in Zacatecas and Guanajuato to Mexico City and Santa Fe, New Mexico. In 1826 the town adopted the surname of Ignacio Allende, a native son, or *sanmiguelense*, who was a hero in the Mexican War of Independence. As the nineteenth century ended, San Miguel was a sleepy, dusty pueblo, practically a ghost town, but fifty years later it had become popular with Mexican artists and entertainers such as José Mojica and Cantinflas. Then foreigners "discovered" San Miguel, founding cultural and art institutes. GI's came to study. Living was cheap. The town became a destination for writers.

When we arrived, San Miguel still felt like a small town, without traffic lights or stop signs. This wasn't a problem for local drivers, including taxis, since they were used to waiting at intersections and took pride in their good manners. Many of the cobblestoned streets were so narrow that two cars couldn't pass side by side. There was no posted speed limit, but drivers didn't go more than five miles an hour. Not only were the streets slow going, so were the sidewalks. Laid with flat stones, yet still uneven, they measured about the width of a person, so pedestrians constantly made adjustments to accommodate each other. You had to learn the unspoken system: men ceded to women, everyone ceded to older people. And with the buildings at most two stories tall, slow and low was the scale.

During our second week the town feted its patron, St. Michael, with Concheros dancers in the main square, known as the *Jardín*. Unlike the *Sanmiguelada*, which drew teenage boys from as far away as Mexico City, this was a local party. Middle-aged men in loincloths and giant feathered headdresses assembled each morning in the *Jardín* to dance and drum in front of the pink parish church, the *Parroquia*. Up the hill, two blocks away at Alma's, we could feel the heavy pounding of their instruments in our heads.

Every day I took to the streets to call my mother, searching out working pay phones, using prepaid cards. One morning from a booth near the Churrigueresque church of San Francisco, I described to her the feast of St. Michael, with its scantily clad Indian dancers. "Why, they're always celebrating something there, aren't they!" she said, as a truckload of enormous puppets passed by. She was happy for our Mexican adventure, but then she'd been supportive of all my "foreign" escapades, whether I was going out of state to college or out of the country on vacation. And how was she? Nothing was new, and she was "doing fine." Whatever might be going on with her, she retreated again behind her reliable standbys.

We'd landed in San Miguel during its month of high holidays—the *Grito*, marking Independence Day, the *Sanmiguelada*, and St. Michael's feast day. We would skirt the frenzied dancers on our way to do errands or to visit the bank, where the ATMs generally ran out of money by noon. One day as we sat sipping *limonadas* at an outdoor café, a parade of horses made its way into the *Jardín* from the city of Querétaro, forty miles away. All this celebrating reached a climax with a huge fireworks display known as the *Alborada*, which started at four o'clock one morning and lasted until daybreak. On the first of October, when we could finally move into our rental, the dancing and fireworks and parading ended. Alma came to our aid one last time, by hiring a small truck to carry our four suitcases across town.

—

The little pink house had an arched wooden window that spanned two stories and a white bougainvillea that stretched like a knitted roof over its back patio. But within hours of moving into the house we both got sick. I blamed the insecticide our landlady had sprayed on the patio, until a few days later, when we got a call from a fellow lodger at the pension. Everyone there was infected with salmonella, and an elderly man had nearly died.

Fall continued that way, with almost daily ups and downs. In the mornings we wrote, and in the afternoons we studied Spanish. As we strolled through the vegetable-and-flower market on our way to school, we passed sun-wrinkled women with babies slung in shawls on their backs, selling *nopales* and squash blossoms; slow-moving men leading patient burros with sacks of dirt or bundles of sticks piled high on the animals' skinny backs; and throngs of chattering schoolchildren in muted checked uniforms, fresh from their own classrooms, waiting on corners for the lumbering *urbanos* to ferry them home.

We studied Spanish in a cubbyhole of a classroom, in a rabbit warren of a building. It wasn't easy, acquiring a new language. Gerry and I were squeezed into wooden desks made for people much shorter, listening to the *maestro*. Enrique sat before us in a throne-like chair. Over his left shoulder, a ray of white light shot through a narrow windowpane. He looked otherworldly, our young teacher, and though his dark, handsome features were blurred in the room's brightness I could see his mouth moving in the dance of his language. Talking, always talking, Enrique. But what was he saying? I wondered aloud how I could learn Spanish if he conducted our class entirely in Spanish, but he shrugged off my concern. There was only Gerry to hide behind. It was just the two of us in the twice-weekly private class.

It was our second lesson, and Enrique was about to break some major news. He stood in front of the blackboard with his chalk poised. Spanish had two forms of the verb *to be*, he said, and his tone seemed withering toward those of us who'd managed all our lives with only a single form. In one column he wrote the word *ser* and in the other *estar*. Then he added the present-tense conjugations and examples of when to use each verb. *Ser* was for permanent conditions, *estar* for temporary ones, although if someone died *estar muerto* was used to describe their state, which certainly seemed permanent. We left carrying paper diagrams of the conjugations, which I taped on our bedroom wall for us to memorize.

Late afternoons, when we left Enrique's classroom, I would see the pinks and reds and yellows and oranges of San Miguel's shops and houses, which appeared fused together by the sun to fit tightly into the hillsides. On many afternoons I would see an orange glow in the darkening sky, the reflection of sun in the swirling clouds, and a hint of occasional lightning. The end of the rainy season in San Miguel. I'd come to Mexico to write about the hurts and doubts of a troubled upbringing with an overbearing father in a deep southern town, during a time when the world demanded change. Not only did I need to understand, I needed to find a voice. I had to find my own language and try to make it dance.

—

As November approached, we were having a hard time adjusting to life in an unheated concrete house shared with hairy black spiders the size of my hand. Though the days were still warm, the nighttime temperatures were dropping, and it felt downright cold in the mornings. But nobody in San Miguel had central heat. Over breakfast we huddled in the dining area around a portable propane space heater, which always seemed to be running out of fuel. As for the spiders, they nested in the pretty white bougainvillea over the patio. Maybe this was why the landlady had sprayed so enthusiastically before we'd moved in?

We struggled with the language, often leaving Enrique's class-room bewildered. Not because he wasn't a good teacher—he was, though his formal education, like many Mexicans', had stopped at age eighteen. He loved languages, the when and why of gram-mar, the fine points of vocabulary, and he drew on his extensive knowledge of Mexican literature and music to teach us. I left his classroom bewildered but in love with Spanish—with Jaime Sabine's poems about everyday Mexican life and Octavio Paz's essays about Mexican culture and the whimsical music of Crí-Crí and the romantic songs of Agustín Lara. I memorized conjugations as easily as I'd once learned my times tables, but I had trouble using the verbs correctly. Gerry had more of a feeling for putting sentences together, though for a while he went around saying *descuento* instead of *desculpe*, asking for a discount instead of pardon, when he bumped into somebody on the sidewalk. With its fourteen tenses and four subjunctives, Spanish was supposed to be "easy." How could we learn the language in six months?

Enrique declared that there weren't two more dissimilar coun-
tries sharing a border than the United States and Mexico. This was
true, he said, for differences big and small. Some were welcome,
such as doctors who made house calls, and some were oddities,
such as eggs sold at room temperature in clear plastic bags. It
became our mission to arrive home from the grocery store with
them intact; we longed for the humble egg carton. We had to pay
all our bills in person because the mail service was so inefficient.
Once a friend sent us a postcard from across town and it took a
month to arrive. There was also the Mexican bureaucracy. Even
returning empty beer bottles proved a challenge. If a register receipt
couldn't be produced, the store wouldn't take back the empties. It
became easier to toss them.

By Thanksgiving I had a lingering case of bronchitis and Gerry
was struggling with a spreading infection in his thumb he'd gotten
from gardening without gloves. The English word *debridement*
entered our vocabulary, and for a while he had to visit the local
dermatologist's office every day to have the skin around his wound
scraped. (We joked that in New York everybody was taking antidepressants, but in Mexico it was antibiotics.) We spent the holiday
by ourselves, eating turkey roll at a New Orleans–style restaurant.

All these weeks, I'd kept up the phone calls to my mother.
But one morning she sounded incoherent. She wasn't making
complete sentences, and her words were slurred. After we hung
up, I remembered how, first thing, she would prick her finger to
monitor her blood sugar. Had she forgotten? I called her back,
but there was no answer. Panicked, I reached Willie Belle at the
sheriff's office, and she and a deputy sped out to my mother's
house. When she didn't answer the door, Willie Belle called for an
ambulance. Mama had hooked her screen door, and the deputy
had to wrench it off its hinges. They found her slumped near the
refrigerator, with an unopened orange juice carton in her hand.
Once the EMTs got her to drink some of the juice, she recovered
quickly. After checking her vital signs, they assumed she'd had

an instance of hypoglycemia and left. But the episode was a fresh warning of how risky it was for her to live alone.

In mid-December we flew back to Mississippi—whether for a visit or en route to New York, we didn't know. What had I learned? New York gave you the illusion that you were in control; Mexico, the certainty that you weren't. New York meant business and go-getting; Mexico taught you humility and patience. In New York life coursed predictably, the commuter trains running nearly on time; in Mexico the unexpected happened every day. In New York there was order and the rule of law and fair play. In Mexico the solution to a problem came unexpectedly, often through the people you knew—you needed to have friends with *palancas*, people said, or "levers." In New York the risks involved money, prestige, power; in Mexico a black widow spider might live under your desk, but if you were lucky it didn't do you any harm. In Mexico there were many Virgin Marys to give yourself over to, the main one being Our Lady of Guadalupe, whose radiant figure adorned paintings, house mosaics, even shopping bags; you had only to accept her and her protection was yours.

Living in Mexico for three months had been like falling headlong into a love affair, with all the magic and misery, excitement and danger, and ups and downs of the heart. But I wanted my mother. On Christmas I lay on her loveseat and fought off a low-grade fever. I thought about seeing an infectious disease specialist, but before I could make an appointment I developed a tooth abscess. For the first time in my adult life I visited the dentist for a major repair and had no insurance. That Christmas I no longer knew where home was, or where I belonged. But at my mother's side, with a real gas (not propane) heater in nearly every room, I came to believe that the new-old duplex was indeed a very luxurious place.

Eight

A Housewife and All That Entailed

Three freight trains had lumbered through town in the last hour, blasting their horns at the railroad crossing two blocks away. These days the once melodious locomotive whistle had been supplanted by the new air horns, which sounded a strident note. Except for the trains, the January morning was still, and a light frost kissed my mother's St. Augustine grass. By this hour she would usually be settled in her yellow recliner, sipping Maxwell House and watching CNN, but she was huddled under the bedcovers. She hadn't had another fall or health scare, but we had a trip planned to see a dermatologist in Jackson about the growth on her scalp. She'd scraped the lump recently on her car door and finally consented to have it examined. But she wasn't looking forward to it, and so she dawdled in bed.

When my siblings and I were teenagers, my father had dragged us to this same specialist, when dollar-store acne soaps hadn't cured our skin eruptions. Dr. Wise, who spoke in a voice edged with humor and irony, had been born in Yazoo City. A century ago the Wise family had owned a department store on Yazoo's Main Street and a fine home around the corner on Mound. Dr. Wise seemed aptly named, exuding gentlemanly courtesy and wisdom as if these qualities sprang from his bones. Here was a doctor who quoted Mark Twain to his patients and probably knew the strategy of every Civil War battle ever fought.

Mama and I managed to find seats together in his crowded waiting room, but when another chair opened up a few feet away she moved to sit next to an older couple. "Mrs. Davis and me grew up together out in Midway," she explained. From time to time my mother would cover her mouth and pantomime a chuckle at something Mrs. Davis said. They gossiped so quietly about schoolmates they'd known that I had to strain to eavesdrop.

In the examination room, Dr. Wise offered an immediate diagnosis: "the barnacle of old age." He admitted that this was the term for the harmless growth before it became politically incorrect. We laughed, and he froze the "barnacle" with liquid nitrogen. It was a relief to be seeing a doctor with my mother about something as simple as a common skin problem. Dr. Wise tarried with us long enough to reminisce about his hometown, especially about the legend of the Witch that Yazoo-born writer Willie Morris had embellished in his children's book *Good Old Boy*. "You know," he said, "Willie liked to make things up."

After the appointment my mother was anxious to get home. She said no to a stop at a big-box store and no to a meat-and-three plate lunch. All the way to Yazoo City she slumped in the front seat of the Crown Vic with her chin on her palm, staring out the car's side window. During the drive—the flatland between Jackson and Flora interminable and the hills between Flora and Yazoo even more so—she said, with unmistakable longing, "I could have been in my chair all day." And then we were back in Yazoo, at Four Points intersection and that commercial stretch of Highway 49 known as Jerry Clower Boulevard.

I asked myself: what made this home for her? How did this small town become so deeply my mother's place in the world? She seemed to have found that place so easily, and so early on, while I, having sold my house in New York, flailed about in a foreign country looking for mine. What old intractable memory came to her, as we traveled that length of highway bordering the town? On the eponymous Jerry Clower Boulevard, did she conjure the local fertilizer salesman who'd made a name for himself as a comedian and a regular at the Grand Ole Opry? Did the storefront advert for Just Horsin' Around Western Wear remind her of the shop's owner, Debbie's best childhood friend? How the two little girls used to roam Grand Avenue toting toy guns, pretending to be cowboys?

In this small town, settled so long ago and isolated for so many years, accessible only by hilly, two-lane roads, all kinds of close connections existed among people. It was a place where, in a sidewalk conversation, you might learn that the person you just bumped into used to work with your father or went to high school with your mother. It was a place where the elderly saleslady in the jewelry store was delivered by your grandmother, a country farmer pressed into service as a midwife; where a stranger in McDonald's might sidle over to reveal that he has stored in his barn the overhead fan from your grandfather's old hotel, for nigh on thirty years, and would you like to have it back, ma'am? Where in any of the town's seven restaurants you might not know everybody, but everybody knew somebody.

I'd thought of New York as home, but now I didn't know where I belonged. Not any longer. But I'd succeeded in getting what I'd wanted: my world turned upside down. A neighbor in Mexico, an older lady from Puerto Rico who'd lived there a long time, had summed it up one day, when she'd said, "Oh, look, the first robin of fall."

The trick would be to find my bearings. Because in a week, despite our difficult beginning, we were headed back to Mexico. After all, it was only for three more months.

—

But we had one more short trip to make before leaving Mississippi: to visit Bossie Niven, another childhood friend of my mother and still a resident of Midway. Meeting Mrs. Davis in the doctor's office had sparked the trip. Afterward Mama admitted a hankering to see her old friend and their shared birthplace. We agreed on driving out to find Bossie.

On a bright weekend afternoon, during a warm-up in the latest cold snap, we collected Willie Belle and set out in the Ford Crown Vic. Gerry drove, with Mama as usual riding shotgun and Willie Belle and me taking up the rear. During the ten miles to Benton I chatted with my aunt, scarcely noticing the passing landscape of gentle hills and huddled wintry trees. I asked Willie Belle what Bossie had done all her life.

"Why," she said, glancing out the window, "Bossie was a housewife and all that entailed."

Gerry stopped at a crossroads with a ramshackle convenience store. We were entering Midway, Willie Belle added.

"How can you tell?" I asked. I was entering Midway and knew almost nothing about it. Not even where it was. Midway, my mother and aunt agreed, was just "a dip in the road" between Benton and Ebenezer. It was rich pastureland and farm fields, hilly country, though the hills topped out at three hundred feet.

Bossie lived off a two-lane road named after her husband's family. Niven Road was new asphalt, well-kept and clean, and so isolated that we hardly passed another car. Nearby were other roads named for other families—Swayze, Fouche, Pearce—and the inscrutable Chew Forks, where my mother's ancient aunt Lula Saxton had lived. Bossie's modest house was set back, and even in full-bore sunlight looked a little tumbledown.

We slammed the car doors, the noise reverberating in the quiet, and Bossie appeared at her front door. The visit had surprised her. She reached up to hug my neck, though we'd never met. She hugged my mother and Willie Belle and shook Gerry's hand. A heavy odor hung inside her living room, maybe from frying oils left too long in the skillets on her stovetop, and a fine layer of dust speckled the furniture and family photographs. Bossie, petite but round-waisted, retook her recliner while my mother and Willie Belle sat opposite on the couch. How young my mother looked with the soft winter light on her face.

Bossie began to hold forth. After she married Bud, she said, they raised three sons and farmed. She still owned 90 acres off Niven Road that her sons hayed. During any lull in her monologue, Gerry peppered her with questions, which she answered in whole paragraphs. Both she and my mother had been born in 1924 around Midway. They had both left as youngsters, when their families moved north to the Delta to try farming there. Both families had returned to Midway in '29, Mama's for her father's funeral. My mother and Bossie had been friends since they were ten years old, and they had still other connections: Bossie's aunt Nal had married my mother's uncle Will; and Bossie had been my uncle Lawrence's girlfriend, before he'd met Willie Belle.

Bossie's speech, like my mother's, moved in unhurried cadences and featured the off-key pronunciations of her upbringing, with "Delta" becoming "Delter" and "sister" becoming "suster." She spoke about her family, her father's early death from cancer, about her childhood spent in the cotton fields and farming for shares, about the boll weevil and hog-killing days and cleaning chitterlings.

"They used to have a store up at Midway, and everybody that sharecropped—the folks you rented from wouldn't let you have the money—you'd go up there and borrow your money to make a crop on, whatever you had to give for collateral. We had to have some mules and a wagon and things like that, you know. And by the time you paid what you had borrowed—"

"And the interest—" Mama added.

"You might have a little bit to do you until March again."

"Very little," Mama said.

"You know you'd have to pay a fourth to the landowner," Bossie explained. "I think you paid a third of corn, a fourth of cotton. Back in those days, like I say, a one-horse farmer, you couldn't hardly save any money unless you was lucky enough to make three or four good crops."

"And you couldn't hardly do that," my mother said.

Gerry asked, "Do you remember the boll weevil?"

"It was a mean little dude, wasn't it, Sister?" she asked, using my mother's nickname.

My mother bobbed her head. "He was a little tiny black bug with a horn. And he'd puncture all the cotton bolls."

"That's right. And that's where he'd mess up your cotton. Back then people didn't know what fertilizer or poison was."

"Planted the crop and it was just sight unseen," Mama said.

"That's right," Bossie said. "You'd make it or you didn't make it."

"What was picking like?" Gerry asked.

"Backbreaking." Bossie gave a hard laugh. "I was out there, but I never could pick no whole lot of cotton. I picked just as hard as anybody, but when we got to the scales, mine didn't weigh as much as theirs did." She and my mother laughed and then were quiet.

"Did you go through the fields more than once?" Gerry asked.

"Oh, yeah. We used to scrap it all till it wasn't no more to scrap."

"My mama sent me out to the fields to pick cotton for quilts," Mama added.

Bossie said, "A lot of times, you know, they would wait till the last scrapping, and they'd make you go through there and scrap it, and they'd make beds out of them."

"What were the houses like?" Gerry asked.

"Some of them was in bad shape," Bossie answered. "Uncle Will's when we first moved in it, you could lay there in the bed and see the stars out through the roof. And Uncle Will finally got some old rough lumber and instead of tacking it on the rafters up there, just laid it on the rafters, you know, where it would help keep the heat down, 'cause you didn't have nothing but a fireplace."

"Do you remember hog-killing days?" Mama asked Bossie.

"You'd have to wait till you got freezing weather almost. Well, you couldn't very easily wait till it was freezing, 'cause your meat would freeze before, you know, you could get it salted down. You'd have to wait till it was cold enough so the flies wouldn't get to it 'fore you got through with it. Daddy loved chitterlings, and he'd always save all of them out of the hogs, and Mama'd soak them for a week before she cooked them. I can remember having them setting around in the kitchen, change the water every day. Do that for about three or four days before she'd cook them."

After a pause Mama said, "Well, we survived it, didn't we?"

"Yeah. Yup," Bossie answered. "That's what I say, we knew we was poor, but everybody else was too, so we didn't think too much about it."

"We didn't have a good time," my mother said, and laughed.

"It wasn't a whole lot that we want to remember, was it, Sister?"

"But we remembered it," my mother said.

Bossie had talked for an hour, though not about life as a "housewife and all that entailed." Her childhood memories had overtaken her that afternoon. Mama's family, with its nearly parallel circumstances, had endured similar hardships. Listening to Bossie's stories, delivered in her intoxicating accent, I'd felt pride in their survival of those hardships and in their laughter in the face of them. They had qualities that mattered, these hill-country people: endurance, acceptance, humor. What had taken me so long to realize?

Late in the day, when we climbed back into the Crown Vic, the winter light was full of shadows. As she fastened her seatbelt, Willie Belle said, "Once you get Bossie started, you can't hardly get her to stop." But what talk it had been. My mother had surprised me when she'd said she remembered. Surprised me, since the times I'd asked about her childhood she'd said she didn't remember anything. I promised myself to ask her again and to write down her story. But in Yazoo, in the duplex, inertia took over. Then it was time for Mexico.

Nine

Magic and Mystery in San Miguel

January mornings dawned cold in the pink concrete house, but afternoons finished warm due to the plentiful sun, which made outside more temperate than in. During the first week of February it suddenly seemed as if somebody threw a giant switch in the central highlands, ushering in spring. Six days a week I was working on my manuscript and on my Spanish. I felt us settling in, Mexico finally taking hold. But the spring equinox, the deadline for our return to New York, was fast approaching. The time had gone by so quickly. The weather was so beautiful. Without thinking about it much, we decided to finish out the year's lease.

All that spring in Mexico, I was overcome. We both were, but not by the euphoria of life there—by the heat. April and May were the hottest and dustiest months in the highlands. Except for a shower in January, it hadn't rained since the previous September, when Gerry's laptop perished and was resurrected. Now the entire town anticipated the daily downpours. All the talk in the markets and squares was about when the yearly rains might start.

In late April we found out that another pink house—another of the thirteen condos built into the stables of the hacienda—had come up for sale. No one had lived in it for nearly twenty years. More big black spiders nested in the doorjambs; tiny brown scorpions clung to the walls. On the ground floor, a concrete partition divided the living room from the dining area, where an ungainly arch took up too much space. There was a dismal galley kitchen, two bathrooms the size of closets. Even the bedrooms lacked sunlight. But the price was low.

"I can't do it," I said to Gerry, after walking through the rooms. "I can't live in a dark house in Mexico." After all, one of the attractions of these mountains was their light.

"If we buy this house, we won't ever have to work in publishing again," he countered. "We could live in Mexico and write, and we'd only need to bring in a fraction of what we made in New York."

"I'll never live in it," I said. "That's final."

A week later, we signed the contract.

We'd realized that we could gut the house, also for very little. Everything was in scale—low real estate prices and construction costs, as well as property taxes. In the New York suburbs we'd worked months to pay our local taxes. Here the bill would be negligible.

On an exceptionally hot afternoon in May we walked two blocks to a lawyer's office with a new friend who was about to become our next-door neighbor. A bilingual Mexican journalist, she'd agreed to translate at our closing. A fine gray dust flew in the streets, and the sun beat on our unprotected shoulders. I stopped on the sidewalk. Buy a house in Mexico!

"You can always live in it awhile and sell it," our neighbor pointed out.

A half-hour later, sitting before the lawyer's big wooden desk, after our friend had translated the contract out loud, Gerry and I wrote a check on our New York bank and left with the keys to the house. Our love affair with Mexico had turned into a hasty marriage.

The next step was to find someone to renovate. A few days later, he presented himself in the condominium. Jesús was an engineer who worked in tandem with his son, an architect, and they'd recently begun overhauling another condo on our grounds.

He drove an ancient yellow Volkswagen and displayed Old World manners—stiff-postured, sporting a Panama hat, he was a man ready with his *buenas tardes*. Jesús didn't speak much English, and our Spanish hadn't improved enough that we could carry on a conversation; besides, we lacked any construction vocabulary. No matter: we met regularly over the dining table in our rental, where Jesús drew quick, confident sketches of his proposals. We were seduced.

In late May our Spanish school decided the time had come for us to graduate. Enrique had taught us the entire curriculum, the director, Angélica, informed us. The afternoon of our last class we stopped by her office to pay our bill, and I couldn't even ask in Spanish how much we owed. How was I ever going to learn to speak the language?

"Don't worry," she answered, also in English. "Now it's just a matter of practice." I recognized her reply as a paraphrase of a lyric from the children's composer Crí-Crí, about a goat learning to ride a bicycle: *Todo es cuestión de practicar.*

We went to say goodbye to Enrique. When I repeated Angélica's comment, he offered a solution. "I'll come to your house Tuesday and Thursday afternoons, at the same hour of your old class," he said, "so you can practice your Spanish."

"Well," I told him, "we'll pay you what we paid the school."

He sounded put off. "Nobody pays in Mexico to have a conversation," he said, but maybe our *reuniones* would also give him the opportunity to speak some English? He began coming to our house two days a week, and we never spoke much English. The language of our friendship became Spanish.

By June, in the condo, we still honeymooned high. The renovations were progressing without major problems. We made the kitchen bigger and moved it into a portion of the back patio, raised the ceiling in the downstairs bathroom, added a Juliet balcony and French doors in the upstairs master bedroom. Jesús inspected the site twice a day and improved on our suggestions. A tiled fountain in the patio? Good, but over there, to form a visual axis with the French doors. A *boveda* ceiling in the kitchen? Fine, but add a cupola to let in more light. We were determined to possess every cliché of traditional Mexican architecture.

For those months life in Mexico seemed to be about magic and mystery. Minor difficulties had a way of sorting themselves out given a little time. The country didn't operate so much on logic as it did on luck and coincidence and, some expats believed, the miraculous. This inexplicable enchantment soon spread to our work. Gerry finished a draft of his manuscript, and I achieved that elusive writer's goal: a contract with a literary agent.

Then in July, at her home, my mother fell for the third time.

The preceding January, shortly after we'd left her, she'd fallen a second time. She'd driven herself to the emergency room, where they'd diagnosed a urinary tract infection. After that Lisa began visiting her every two weeks and writing detailed emails to Debbie and me. Mama wasn't sleeping well and often got up at three a.m. to read or vacuum. She wasn't walking well, and she wasn't calling in her blood-sugar readings to her endocrinologist.

Lisa was disturbed by the bloody smears she often saw on Mama's clothes, from rubbing her fingers on her shirtfronts after checking her blood sugar. After her heart surgery she'd been pre-scribed the blood thinner Coumadin, and she was supposed to see her local doctor frequently so he could control the level of the powerful drug in her system. She assured Lisa she was doing this, but if so, why was she bleeding so freely from the finger sticks? One day she knocked a scab off her leg, and Lisa was surprised by the amount of blood. But my mother wasn't bothered. Whenever she and Lisa went out, to dinner or for shopping, she didn't even think to change her bloodstained shirts.

The day my mother fell for the third time, I started, as I did first thing every morning, by calling her. Her voice sounded feeble, but she insisted she was "doing fine." I knew from her emails that Lisa was also alarmed by the tone of my mother's voice, so much so that she'd asked Willie Belle to check on her, which my aunt had done by telephone from the sheriff's office. My mother had also reassured Willie Belle that she was "doing fine."

But early that morning, she'd walked over to the front door to peer out the fanlight. Her blood sugar must have been especially low, because as she turned back toward her recliner, she fell and struck her head on the door hinge. When she came to, she crawled across the carpet to her chair. She got up once to clean the gash but left the bathroom with the water running. Sitting in her chair, she imagined hearing Debbie's voice, reminding her about the Coumadin, warning her that the bleeding wouldn't stop on its own. Only then did she call Willie Belle, who managed to get her into the car and drive her to the emergency room.

She was so caked with blood that the ER doctor couldn't find the wound. "He bandaged her head right quick like a mummy," Willie Belle said, so he could attend to other threats. My mother's blood pressure was near zero, her pulse over 160, her blood sugar hazardously low. Once he stabilized her, he admitted her to the hospital.

After Mama's hospitalization, Debbie sent an email she called *veritas et ratio*—"truth and reason." In a stunning summary, she outlined the facts about our mother's health as she saw them. During the last year, she began, "Mama has fallen three times and has not called for help." She has refused to "truthfully detail her condition and/or situation when we telephoned her." Her medications and complex medical problems were "consistently out of bounds." Her home was "unsafe, not old-age proof." She had "no mechanism for emergency personnel notification and wouldn't use one if she had it." She was "at risk for significant errors which were potentially lethal due to cooking, cleaning or ironing, and removing garbage." This made me cringe. I hadn't told Debbie about the previous Christmas, when Mama had struck a safety match near an open cabinet over the stove and caught the paper products on fire. Fortunately, Gerry and I had been with her in the kitchen.

She required close supervision, Debbie went on, either by a "qualified personal living companion or in an assisted living facility." And, she added, Mama's ability to drive safely was questionable. Debbie acknowledged that we couldn't realistically be responsible for her well-being from the distances we had to travel. Financial planning was imperative, given my mother's meager funds. If she were to fall again, or "suffer another event" and become an invalid, no retirement facility would accept her, and she would be forced into a conventional nursing home—exactly what she feared the most. "If a safe environment is created for her then she probably has years of nearly independent living left," Debbie concluded.

We began looking into assisted living facilities. But the closest ones were an hour away, and my mother didn't want to leave Yazoo City. My sisters and I talked to her about how, if she were to stay at home, she would have to be more forthcoming. How she would have to learn to ask for help, and not just from Willie Belle. We arranged for home health care: an aide for bathing and light housework, a nurse for monitoring her vital signs and keeping her prescriptions filled. We bought an emergency alert system, and my mother practiced pushing the button on the rope necklace to call trained operators in northern states, her southern accent undoubtedly sounding as foreign to them as theirs did to her.

After this, Gerry and I volunteered to live with my mother four months a year, a month each season. As with the decision to stay in Mexico, we agreed to do this without thinking much about it. After all, she'd nearly died. Along with Lisa's regular visits, I hoped this would be enough to keep Mama safe and at home. Debbie viewed the plan as a stopgap but didn't protest. And so I became my mother's caregiver, one of them at least. She'd lived alone the nine years since my father's death. Never again would she be so alone.

There would be no safety net for Gerry and me, no salaries and company health insurance, but there would be time to write. We would have to rely on Mexico, on its low cost of living and on its supposed magic. Just as the house in Mexico had taken on a new shape, a new life began to take shape for us. During our visit with my mother the previous Christmas, when we'd driven out to Midway and Bossie's, I'd realized I hadn't known where home was. I still didn't, but now I had two places to move between. One was in Mexico, in a pink house on a dusty street, and the other in Mississippi, in the duplex, in my mother's presence.

Ten

So Began the Years of Back and Forth

It was late November, and we were navigating our silver station wagon through the bleak Chihuahuan Desert of northern Mexico. On the second day of our trip, in the Sierra Madres south of Monterrey, we came upon a rainbow, the biggest end-to-end I'd ever seen. Crossing into Texas, we practiced Spanish verbs and listened to Spanish-language radio, pretending even after leaving Mexico that we were still there. Along Highway 59 we pulled into truck stops and noticed the sad and desolate, gray and overweight faces of the locals. As we turned east on I-10, the afternoon sunlight fell on our shoulders. In Louisiana's Cajun country we stopped for a late lunch. A young woman in a gas station recommended a restaurant, which we found tucked into a neighborhood of slab houses, many with corrugated roofs and broken-down sofas and refrigerators on their front porches. Hungry for a taste of the South, we ordered so much food that it wouldn't fit on our trays: oyster po'boys and shrimp gumbo, hush puppies and slaw, and iced tea served in containers as big as boots.

On the third day, after Baton Rouge, we turned north on I-55 and into Mississippi. Now the sunlight washed across the car's front windshield, and the temperature topped 85 degrees. Soon the land turned undulating and lonely, punctuated by stands of russet trees and circles of muddy ponds. Finally we reached Highway 49 and pointed the car north toward Yazoo City. We listened to public radio for the last thirty miles, our Spanish conjugations fading and the Mississippi accent taking over, with its stretched vowels and lazy diphthongs.

In July, after Debbie's *veritas et ratio* email, I'd promised we would live four months a year with my mother, spread out through the seasons, but by November we hadn't yet started the new routine. Right after her fall Gerry and I had flown to New York, sold off half our furniture, downsized our storage space, and collected our station wagon for the twenty-five-hundred-mile return trip to Mexico. On the way we'd stopped off in Mississippi, then rushed back to San Miguel to check on our house renovations. In early October, just over a year after arriving in Mexico, we'd finally moved in. The little house was no longer pink, at least not entirely. The façade was coral; the front patio walls were crimson, with yellow accents; and the back was a shade of amber. During that fall, while we were still settling in, Lisa wrote with regular updates: my mother was sleeping and eating well, she was paying her own bills, washing and folding her clothes, and making her bed. She'd even remembered to renew her car's inspection sticker. I'd reneged on my promise and postponed visiting.

That November afternoon when we pulled under her carport, my mother bounded out the door, barefoot. There was no question she was better, but there was also no denying that in July she'd nearly died. With my makeshift plan I'd contended she could live at home, but was this really the best thing for her? Assuming I kept my word, were my periodic visits, along with Lisa's, enough to keep her safe? The rational answer was no. Why was it so important to me that she live at home? That was what she wanted, but why did I let her take the risk? With all the changes in my life, did I need for hers to stay the same as always?

That night the weather turned cold. We had a short rain, straight down, no lightning. We slept. I heard one train, around five o'clock, breaking the otherwise quiet night.

—

A year had passed since our visit to Midway and Bossie, and I hadn't asked my mother anything about her childhood. Over Christmas I made an attempt. On a temperate afternoon in December we drove the dozen or so miles to Midway so she could show me where she and her family had lived. Thirty years ago, this landscape had been dotted with Depression-era shacks, but now they were falling down, and soon the remaining lumber and cheap roofing would be gone, borne away by time and scavengers. We stopped near a large field that my mother thought looked somewhat familiar. Surveying the wrecked chimneys, I asked, "Which one was yours?" She glanced around before giving this halfhearted response: "Over yonder in that direction, I guess."

On our way back to Yazoo, she asked to stop at the Primitive Baptist Cemetery. Known as Shiloh, this remote cemetery sat next to a small church. This iteration of the building—the sign said the congregation had been established in 1843—was built of yellow brick and lacked a steeple, but a grove of pecan trees graced its grounds. My mother's parents' grave lay close to a narrow, unpaved road. We parked the car and walked to their double tombstone, but Mama kept her thoughts to herself. Then she said she wanted to "walk a ways." Other Hoods lay buried nearby, most born thirty years on either side of the turn of the twentieth century, with unfamiliar names: Albert Lee and Harleen and James "Boss" and Leslie Callie. My mother bent to read an old marker, her shock of white hair contrasting with her blue fleece. Again she stayed quiet: if this graveyard held any of her family stories, she kept them to herself also. She seemed to have nothing to share.

The next morning, a Sunday, I woke up thinking about my paternal great-grandmother and her homeplace, which I'd last seen in about 1966. Both sides of my family, the Hoods and the Nicholases, had been poor, but in Mississippi to be poor is to parse degrees: growing up, the Hoods had no homeplace, no house that had been a long time in the family's possession, accumulating memories, whereas the Nicholases had the good fortune of having two. My Nicholas grandparents' bungalow was one, and the other had belonged to Vashti's mother, Tennerlee Long Pettus. I wanted to see it again.

Known as Mugga, my great-grandmother had been a tall woman of right angles, all jutting knees and elbows. To me, her house had represented frontier Mississippi—a simple cabin with few furnishings, a kitchen with a pump and a deep sink, iron kettles and butter churns and an array of oil lamps, and an outhouse down a dirt trail. Mugga's cabin had been built in a deeply wooded area, in a county adjacent to Yazoo, Holmes, near a bend in the road where the trees grew close and thick. A gravel path bordered with white-painted rocks had led up to the cabin, and two robust cedars had grown near the porch.

On the December afternoon we set out to find it, the weather reminded me of childhood days: the air felt heavy and moist, the light looked soft and yellow. Thunderstorms were forecast for the evening, and that meant it would soon turn cold and we would have a stretch of clouds before it warmed up and the cycle repeated itself. Winter in Mississippi.

My mother wanted in on the excursion, so after dinner we three climbed in her car. Gerry drove the Crown Vic north on Highway 49 and in a few miles made a right at Eden. My father had called Eden a "cowboy" town, maybe because it looked so rough. We headed east past rundown buildings, traveling along the edge of a cotton field where the stalks of last season's crop fanned in rows to the horizon. When we came to the end of the field we faced a choice: take the gravel road left or continue on the paved road up a hill. I had a flash of memory, of sitting in the cramped backseat of my grandparents' Opel, their tiny white car fishtailing up this hill on what at the time had been a dirt track. We took the paved road.

We spoke little, seeing few houses or cars, though an occasional pickup passed us. This was one of the season's prime deer-hunting weekends. Most men were already in the camps, and those who weren't seemed in a hurry to get there. We were trying to find Coxburg, the unincorporated community near where Mugga and Vashti had lived.

Finally my mother said, "You could get lost in Holmes County."

I said, "Mama, we are lost in Holmes County."

We drove on. Exasperated, my mother tried directing us south, back to Yazoo. All the roads were smoothly paved and clean of debris, gleaming on this sunny day, but they led us in circles. My mother was navigating by memory, and memory isn't always linear.

Gerry said, "We should call somebody on the cell phone for directions."

"And say what?" I asked. "We don't know how to tell them where to give us directions from." Besides, I failed to say, there was no signal on the flip phone.

At the next crossroads my mother declared that she was finally sure of the way. When we reached the country store in Zieglerville, I saw a sign pointing toward Coxburg.

We came to a modest church at the top of a hill. *Coxburg Methodist Protestant Church, Established 1894.* Surely here we would find Mugga's grave. The winter sun was disappearing fast, but we strolled through the headstones, reading out the names, until my mother exclaimed, "Why, this is where all the Killebrews are buried!" She'd stumbled on her sister Ethel's marker and realized her mistake. My paternal great-grandmother wasn't buried here; members of my mother's family were. It was all mixed up, one family's past with the other's.

Leaving the cemetery, we came to another four-way stop, but the road my mother chose led to a dead end. Whenever a stray vehicle passed she said pitifully, "Ask that man in that truck," but Gerry never stopped. Back at the four-way, we headed off in the opposite direction. Soon the land, with its gullies and woods, was full of memory. When we rounded a bend I saw a weathered clapboard cabin on a ridge and knew we'd found Mugga's.

Gerry sailed by, and I yelled, "Turn around!"

He made a U-turn in the driveway across the road, which displayed a giant-size Frosty the Snowman in the yard and a notice in the window, *Beware of the Dog.* This had been a simple country house belonging to Vashti's brother, Hop, his wife, Janice, and their son, Eddie. I suspected that cousin Eddie still lived in this new brick house with the Frosty inflatable. He would be in his late fifties, and I hadn't seen him in thirty years.

While I climbed over the barbed wire fence to Mugga's property, Gerry and my mother stayed in the car. Four horses grazed nearby, one raising his head to neigh as if he were a guard dog. I picked my way past the horse heaps to a weedy path and found the two cedars that had loomed over Mugga's porch. I made my way around to the back, where I hoped to discover an unlocked door, but the rear porch wasn't passable due to the appliances—a washer, refrigerator, and stove had collapsed the floorboards. The cistern and two derelict buildings remained, including the outhouse where Mugga had possibly caught the chill from which she'd died, on December 27, 1966, my father's forty-first birthday.

I walked back around to the front porch. There were two hand-lettered signs posted near the door's sidelights: *Cowboy house* and *Take off your spurs before you enter.* Mugga's house was functioning as a private hunting camp, and though a rusted padlock hung from a metal plate, a good shove would have opened the door. I cupped my hands to peek inside. On the one hand, I wanted to walk the jumbled, forgotten rooms, to discover what memories they might evoke. What waited inside to be stirred into consciousness? Would there be something of my great-grand-mother and grandmother, those two indomitable ladies, and their lives in the cabin? Would there be something of my father and the boy he'd been on his summertime visits? But I couldn't bring myself to enter. What if, instead of reviving memory, my present vision of the homeplace supplanted the way it had looked back then?

I picked my way back through the horse heaps, retook the fence, and climbed into the car. "It's Mugga's, all right," I said. "I remember the old cedar trees. Scraggly now."

My mother suggested we stop across the road, odd for some-one who generally didn't go in much for visiting. But as a second cousin, Eddie was family. This time Gerry and I stayed in the car, on account of the dog, while my mother knocked, a hunched-over, gray-haired lady in a blue fleece. Eddie emerged from the carport, along with a dozen swishy-tailed cats. He looked to be about six-five and three hundred pounds. I could tell he didn't know who my mother was, because he was exchanging too-polite greetings with her.

I stepped out and said my name, and he let loose a big grin: Eddie still had most of his front teeth. He said, "Y'all come on inside." I protested, but he insisted, and I told him, fine, but we couldn't stay long because we had to find Mugga's grave before dark.

Eddie had several more cats inside and two large, doe-eyed dogs that liked to nuzzle. All around his living room, including on the tops of the furniture, electric-powered trains motored quietly by. He cleared off some chairs for us. A brightly lit holiday village on the dining table entranced my mother and especially Gerry, who exclaimed several times, "I like your village." Eddie assured us that his electricity bills weren't too high.

We stayed long enough to ask a few questions and for me to develop an allergy attack from his cats. I asked Eddie if his father and Vashti had been born in the cabin.

"Naw," he replied, "they was born in Belmont and worked as sharecroppers 'til they got the money to buy this place."

Belmont was apparently another unincorporated community in Holmes County. The "place" that Eddie referred to had consisted of two hundred acres near the cabin and thirty more near his house. Vashti had disparaged this land as worthless "hills and hollers," where the family had been able to farm only the bottomland, growing what cotton they could. I wondered out loud how they'd accumulated enough money to buy any land, if they were sharecroppers, but Eddie had told us all he knew. Except he told us where to find Mugga's grave, and he gave us directions to get home. "Do y'all want the most direct route or the one that'll get y'all there?" he asked. We assured him, the one that would get us there.

We found Mugga in the Oak Grove Baptist Church cemetery, a few miles north in Tolarville, another unincorporated community Vashti had often mentioned. Her tombstone read *Tennerlee Long Pettus, Jan. 22, 1879–Dec. 27, 1966*. Next to her were her husband, Elma, and her son and Eddie's father, Herbert O., and other, unknown (to me) Pettus relatives. Who was Ida Vassie Pettus (*1888–1935, Thy Trial Ended, Thy Rest Is Won*), and what had her trial been? The Pettus clan lay in this remote county, in this remote cemetery, on a hill overlooking a small lake and pasture where lazy cows grazed. Not a bad place to lie for all eternity. I was glad Mugga's grave was near a cedar tree, like those in her front yard.

What had I learned? If Eddie was right, that my grandmother's family had been sharecroppers. Sharecroppers, the lowest rung on the white social ladder. All my childhood, most of my life really, I'd seen Vashti put on polite airs, just as she'd put on her fine feathered hats and church-going eight-button gloves. But according to cousin Eddie, she'd also grown up in a poor farming family, in a poor farming community not so different from my mother's. What I learned that Sunday in Coxburg also had to do with geography. I hadn't realized where my mother and grandmother had lived relative to each other. On the few times we'd visited Midway, we'd approached from the south, toward Benton; we'd approached Coxburg from the north, through Eden. These little communities, consisting of at most a church, a store, and a crossroads, had seemed worlds apart, but now I saw they were separated by only a few miles. Seemingly worlds apart, like my mother and grandmother, yet they traced a circle from Yazoo City to Midway to Coxburg and back to Yazoo. I had to get lost in Holmes County to realize what they had in common.

My mother, when she'd spoken at all about her upbringing, had emphasized the harsh, deprived, I-don't-want-to-remember nature of it, while my grandmother had been about rootedness, about longing to return to her homeplace. I'd seen them as opposites, my grandmother as a prim southern lady who seemed to regard my countrified mother as a less than adequate match for her elder son, while my mother kept her distance, calling her mother-in-law, if she called her anything, "Mrs. Nick." But they'd both been raised in deep country, and not far from each other. Apparently they'd even sprung from similarly strapped backgrounds. Had my perception of their relationship also been mistaken?

And then there was cousin Eddie. He'd been right about the best way for us to get home. It wasn't the most direct route, but, as he said, it was the one that got us there.

—

So began the years of back and forth between Mexico and Mississippi. I kept my promise. We would spend two months in San Miguel, long enough to contract a stomach ailment, then head back to Mississippi to recuperate and check on my mother. But after her third fall, when she'd nearly died, we embarked on a spate of quiet years. Three, to be exact.

It had taken half a century, but my mother and I finally had the calm and close years that we hadn't been able to have when I was a child. Nights we watched old movies on TCM, as she sat in her recliner and I lay curled up on the loveseat, practically at her side. These years I was working through our past, finally getting beyond our half-formed mother-daughter relationship. Was it my deep need for this closeness that had driven me to support her wish to live at home? Probably. Had I created this opportunity? Yes, by volunteering to live part-time with her. As a child I'd written a deadly serious note addressing her as "Mrs. Nicholas" and begging her, my all-caps "MOTHER," to be nicer to me. I'd been barely conscious of my resentment for her taking me away from my grandmother Vashti, my mother in practice if not reality. Now my own mother became my mother. Became Mama.

Her company during those years gave me another definition of home. Home was where she was; she was the smallest unit of home. But where would home be for me? I knew it wouldn't be New York again. But surely it couldn't be Mexico; surely Mexico was a temporary head-over-heels madness. Like the south, Mexico was a place obsessed with the past. But I had no past in Mexico, as I did in the south, no history with the language, and so in Mexico I was able to change. I hadn't liked to talk, but there I talked more often. I'd written secretly; there I started calling myself a writer. In Mexico even my laugh got bigger.

In the memoir that I'd been writing for so long I grappled with my father and our quarrelsome past. At odds with him, I'd seen words, even writing, as weapons to cause pain. If I could get beyond my father and our past I might come to understand where I belonged. I'd thought of myself as part of that generation of southerners Willie Morris had written about in his autobiography, *North Toward Home*, expatriates "in the European sense," who couldn't live in the south but couldn't get it out of their imaginations. If I could come to grips with my father, then something akin to acceptance might emerge, a state beyond anger and disassociation. Only then, I thought, could I live in Mississippi again. In 2006, our last quiet year, I finished the memoir and sent it off to my agent. The title: *Buryin' Daddy*. But though I'd finally finished it, I still didn't know where I belonged.

Eleven

In and Out

I was in Mexico when Mama fell for the fourth time. Who would have thought the cause would be a book? It was the middle of May, the weather cool for Mississippi. Mama hunched in her recliner, knees crossed man-style, dressed in a T-shirt and pink sweats. It was just past five o'clock when Willie Belle called her. Though my aunt lived next door, they spoke more often by phone than in person. As they said goodbye, Willie Belle suggested they meet at the property line so she could return some books she'd borrowed. Both liked to read and would try anything, but they adored detective novels, which they traded back and forth like baseball cards.

There was no fence. For years the houses had been separated by a waist-tall privet hedge, the same hedge that had supplied Mama with the switches she'd used to mete out our whippings. But the hedge had been cut down decades ago, and the only remaining barrier was the hackberry tree and its circle of purple iris. The two met at the iris patch, and Willie Belle handed off the volumes to my mother.

Mama made her way back to her house holding the books in the crook of her left arm, but when she swung open the screen door she lost her balance and landed on her left elbow. With no railing to help break the fall, she hit the concrete step hard. How long did she lie there, blinking back the pain of bone protruding through skin? Finally she managed to pick herself up and stumble back to her recliner. But once there she didn't push the emergency alert button on her necklace, just as Debbie had predicted. She called Willie Belle instead, and my aunt drove her to the emergency room. Mama traveled by ambulance to a Jackson hospital, where that night she had surgery on her arm. Then she had a stroke.

A few days later, when I got to her hospital room, I found her lying on top of the sheet, wearing her gray-and-white hospital gown, clutching the fresh cast on her elbow. She'd wriggled her bare right leg off the bed so that her big toe touched the floor.

"Mama, what are you doing?" I asked.

"They're waiting for me downstairs," she said.

A nurse had been by earlier that morning to tell her that a van had already been requisitioned. The hospital planned to discharge her to the same rehab center where she'd been treated four years before. Unassisted, Mama was doing her best to vacate the premises.

I rang the nurses' call button. An aide finally came and draped a shirt over my mother's hospital gown and got her situated in a wheelchair. The short trip to the rehab center, only a few blocks away, wore out her weakened body, and she slept all afternoon.

Each day in rehab she was bathed early, dressed in sweats and white sneakers, and set up in her wheelchair. In the mornings she saw an occupational therapist, and after lunch, a physical therapist. She had almost constant pain in her left arm, and on and off she ran a low-grade fever. At times she got confused and couldn't speak. She also had no urge to pee. Rather than insert a bladder catheter attached to a drainage bag, which would have limited her mobility and slowed down her recovery, the staff performed an "in-and-out cath" on her several times a day.

After a week the rehab center sent her by van to a follow-up appointment with the orthopedic surgeon. He ordered her arm X-rayed, and while we waited for the results in his examining room my mother shivered under the full-throttle air conditioning.

I asked that she be given a blanket, which we wrapped around her shoulders and pulled up to her eyebrows.

When the surgeon joined us with the X-ray results he got straight to the point. The operation he'd performed had failed. The bones had re-separated. He needed permission to operate on the arm again, right away, or there would be a "reduced prognosis."

The surgeon, a slight man with dyed jet-black hair, had hardly glanced at my pitiful mother, his patient, frozen and huddled under her blanket-tent. I didn't know how to respond. Finally I asked, "My sister is a doctor. Would you talk to her?"

Later, after their phone call, my sisters and I discussed what Mama's reduced prognosis might mean. She wouldn't be able to bear weight, or lift heavy objects, with her left arm, and she might have residual pain. While we were still deciding what to do, the orthopedic surgeon consulted with Mama's cardiologist, who recommended against the operation for fear of her having yet another stroke. The surgeon decided a redo wasn't a good idea. I was relieved and rationalized that at least my mother's right arm still worked.

For three weeks Mama remained a patient at the rehab center. And she was patient. She kept up a grueling schedule, bearing everything, even the surgeon's unfortunate news, with equanimity and without complaint. But I knew she was ready to leave, past ready. She appeared stronger. But then her chest became congested, and the rehab doctor in charge of her case started her on breathing treatments. And there was that other snag, the recalcitrant bladder. For her to be discharged, the nurses told me, I had to find someone who could perform the in-and-out cath at home. Failing that, I would need to learn to do it myself.

—

It was easy, they said. When I heard that, a frequent saying of my father's popped into my head: "Easy as P-I-E." But I didn't want to think of his old catchphrase in the same sentence with catheterizing my mother. I didn't want to learn how to do it, easy or not. I started making phone calls, trying to find someone else to do it. Someone qualified.

Home health services said they could perform the procedure, but the nurses in the rehab center catheterized my mother two or three times a day. Before the accident, home health nurses had visited her at most two or three times a week. Even after the accident they would call on her only once a day, less often later on. There were rules about the number of allowable visits, inflexible rules dictated by Medicare and insurance companies. A daughter's desperation didn't enter into it. I could hire a private nurse, home health services suggested. But exhaust my mother's savings with a private nurse?

I made these phone calls from behind the white curtain in my mother's room, as she was stretched out on her bed on the other side of it, getting catheterized. The procedure was quick, and then the nurse would zip past me on the way to the toilet with her little container, announcing the milliliters of urine. She would dash back to her patient, pull up her sweatpants, and help her into the wheelchair. There my dazed mother would wait for her next therapy session, her white tennis shoes resting on the linoleum floor.

It never occurred to me to protest that my learning to cath Mama wasn't the solution. It never occurred to me to suggest that she needed to see a doctor to figure out why she couldn't pee. She was already in a hospital. I accepted their premise that temporary catheterization was needed and that Mama's bladder would eventually rebound.

My mother was the sort of person who always wanted to use her own bathroom. If we happened to be out of town for the day, maybe visiting Jackson, and she had to go, she might declare, "I have to go home." Not even "I have to use the restroom." She could hold it for a long time to make sure she got home—without commentary or foot tapping. This is not to say that she never used a public bathroom, but home was a clear preference.

I'd never seen my mother's naked body. Except for her arms and feet, my mother's body was strictly out of sight. I'd never even seen her in a bathing suit. As far as I knew she couldn't swim and hadn't ever owned a bathing suit. She didn't wear shorts either.

Once, when I was in eighth grade, she'd taken me to our local movie theater for a revival showing of *Gone With the Wind*. I'd found the movie interminable, made more so by my tight undergarments. At intermission I'd visited the ladies' room off the lobby. When I'd reclaimed my seat, I'd whispered to Mama, "My girdle is killing me."

The response? Her short, trilling laugh. She never took her eyes off the screen. Her girdle was probably killing her too, but she hadn't complained about it, and she hadn't gotten up to adjust it. For that matter, she also hadn't gotten up to use the bathroom.

Several more days passed at the rehab center, along with more phone calls about who I might hire to catheterize my mother. Then something unexpected happened: Mama felt the urge. She rang her call button, and a nurse escorted her to the bathroom. A small miracle had occurred at the needed moment, and now she could go home without catheter tubes, sterile gloves and drapes, and cleansing solutions.

But then a conscientious nurse decided to catheterize my mother *after* she'd paid a visit to the toilet. We received this unsettling news: Mama was retaining too much urine. This could lead to further health problems, such as bladder infections, said the nurse, who showed my mother how to gently press her lower abdomen to squeeze out the last stubborn drops. But still Mama retained too much. A urologist was finally consulted. He agreed she could go home, but that she would need to be catheterized regularly. Daily.

By this time the rehab staff seemed past ready for my mother to be discharged. There was nothing more they could do for her, they said. I begged the doctor, a tall woman with honey-brown skin and fluffy, golden hair, to keep her a few more days until I could find somebody in Yazoo City to perform the procedure.

"It's easy. We'll show you how, step by step," she said, shaking her head. Then she added, "She could do it herself if she had two good hands." But I knew my mother would never do it herself, no matter how many good hands she had. The doctor promised to return that afternoon with the conscientious nurse. Together they would teach me how to catheterize my mother.

During these weeks Mama had enjoyed a double room all to herself. The bed closer to the door had remained vacant, its sharp white sheets unmolested except by the nurse, who'd used it as storage for her cath supplies. Mama had slept on the other side of the white curtain, next to the windows, in the bed that looked out over the hospital's rooftop.

The nurse decided to use the empty bed as a teaching platform for the in-and-out cath. She helped my mother up onto the bedcover and wriggled her out of her pants. While I hung back, Mama lay as patient as a biblical figure. She and I hadn't talked about what was happening, but I felt sure she knew. I was learning this procedure so the staff could discharge her without compunction.

"Time to glove up," the nurse said. She snapped on a pair of latex surgical gloves.

I was reminded of the semi-threatening tone used by the Sisters of Charity at St. Clara's Academy when they taught us something new in grade school, such as how to diagram a sentence. The tone implied you were going to stand at that chalkboard in front of your classmates until you'd diagrammed at least one sentence successfully. Maybe inserting a catheter into your mother was similar to diagramming a sentence: you simply broke the process down into its components. After all, this was supposed to be easy as P-I-E.

I snapped on a pair of the gloves and stepped forward until I stood about a foot from my mother's private parts. The nurse wiped my mother's vulva (her word) with a cleansing solution. She separated the labia (again, her word). I was suddenly reminded of something else, of sitting in a circle with my women's-libber college girlfriends, a plastic speculum in one hand and a small mirror in the other. (This had been the seventies, after all.)

The nurse wiped the area again, making a smooth motion from front to back. I allowed myself a glance at my mother's exposed midsection: her stomach shone like yellow porcelain. I looked at her face: her eyes were squeezed tight behind her glasses.

"You guide the catheter," the nurse said, "through the urethra into the bladder." She started the movement but stopped. "Here, you do it."

I took another step toward my mother, keeping my eyes on the tubing.

"You push a little," the nurse said. "Gently, gently." I placed my gloved hand on hers and felt the catheter slide into position. Urine started to flow.

I'd complied with the rehab center's wishes, and I felt oddly pumped. Afterward the nursed analyzed the odor, color, and clarity of the urine, the health import of which, I had to admit, I'd never considered. I nodded with each description. Finally she showed me how to measure the urine before depositing it in the toilet. All the while the doctor hovered in the background. "Easy, wasn't it?" she said, before gliding out the door.

I helped the nurse pull up my mother's pants and settle her back in the wheelchair. Her silky hair formed damp silvery waves around her forehead. She didn't look at me, and from her quiet, remote bearing I imagined what she might be feeling—humiliation, maybe despair. Her body had always been terra incognita, as inaccessible to me as her inner life. Now I had infringed upon this other secret part of her. And with this, a continuum had been completed: I'd gone from not knowing her to knowing her all too intimately. But she would have undergone anything to get out of rehab, and probably in her mind she just had.

Mama was discharged the next morning. But soon we would learn that she had much bigger problems that needed tending.

Twelve

Home Again

It was June, and it was hot. The air felt thick with humidity, making it hard to breathe, especially for my mother. To discharge her, the rehab staff dressed Mama in her pink jogging suit and white sneakers. They moved her into a spanking-new wheelchair, which they were sending home with her. A burly attendant pushed her to the curb cut under the hospital's main pavilion and effortlessly "transferred" her into the front seat of the Crown Vic.

During my mother's stay in rehab I'd often overheard therapists use this word to characterize a patient's self-sufficiency. There were those who could transfer themselves and those who needed minimal assistance, such as a stabilizing hand, and then there were those who needed somebody, often a burly attendant, to lift them up and over into another seat. After all these weeks in therapy my mother still resided in this third, disadvantaged group.

We began the hour-long trip from Jackson. Mama wasn't feeling a chill from the car's air conditioning blowing right on her, she wasn't thirsty from the extreme outdoor temperature, and she didn't want to stop for a plate of catfish—or so she grunted in answer to my questions. As we left the bustle of Jackson behind, she gazed out the side window, taking in the often-seen places along the highway—the tree-covered Indian mound at Pocahontas, the busy crossroads at Flora with its big grocery store, Ramey's, and the long, high curve outside Bentonia. She took in the summer cotton and the distant bands of woods. She stared out the window and appeared content. I stared at her and worried.

Finally we were home. In Yazoo City. When we pulled under her carport, we faced the first dilemma. How was she going to transfer herself from the car seat to the wheelchair? The rehab center had thoughtfully provided us with another appliance, a folding metal walker, which Gerry extricated from the Ford's capacious trunk. My mother waited in the front seat, with the car door open. Gerry positioned the walker next to her. He asked, "Mama, can you push yourself up and grab hold? We'll steady it."

She inched her long legs out, placing her white sneakers on the concrete. When she tried to stand, though, she fell back, blowing out a puff of air. She would need all her strength to stand up. But Gerry pushed the walker aside, took her around the waist, and shifted her into the wheelchair. She blew out another puff, her lips pursing and loosening.

Minutes later he and I stood contemplating the front porch. The second dilemma. She had to go up three steps to reach it. But there was still no railing, because we'd never gotten around to installing one. With me on one side and Gerry on the other, we boosted Mama up out of the wheelchair by her armpits. She grabbed the walker's handlebars; we steadied her. We moved the walker against the bottom step; she placed one tentative foot on it, then the other. It wasn't textbook, but she made her way up the steps and across the porch. In the living room, she dropped into her recliner and exhaled another big puff. The ancient air conditioner issued a tired whine from the dining room.

Once in her chair, Mama wriggled out of her tennis shoes. Her stomach spread across her hips: she looked like a pink-clad Buddha in a jogging suit. She stared out the front screen door into the yard. With this faraway look in her eyes, she assessed her physical state, or so I imagined. By this time, Mama and I had become a "we" in my mind. "We" had to eat something. "We" had to drink water. Did "we" have to go to the bathroom? This "we" was even starting to encompass Gerry, as if "we" had become a trio. But Mama didn't want to eat, drink, or go to the bathroom; she only wanted to sit in her chair. She'd been parted from that chair for a month, but at last they had been reunited.

Then I realized: Mama had attained her personal therapy goal. She would eat in that chair, and sleep there too. She had no plan beyond life in her chair. My second realization had to do with her white sneakers. They were too tight. She'd worn them for weeks in rehab without complaint to prove to her doctors she was fit to be discharged. They'd been her symbol of normalcy. But she had no intention of putting them on again, ever.

Mama was still in her chair when the home health aide came and brushed her hair into wispy bangs. She was in her chair when the home health nurse came to take her vital signs—and running a slight temperature. She was in her chair when I served her a tuna sandwich for supper, and then she fell asleep in her chair. Around nine o'clock, Gerry and I crawled into Daddy's double bed, a few feet down the dark, narrow hallway. I could see her in the yellow light of her table lamp, her chin sagging toward her chest.

We'd gotten her home. She was in her chair. But now what? How would we take care of her? Never mind the faulty bladder, the nagging fever. Never mind her smashed left arm and her most recent stroke. How would we ever get her out of that chair? Weeks of rehabilitative therapy hadn't prepared her, or us. Our lives would become about transfers, about moving my mother from one place to another, from her chair to the wheelchair to the bathroom, if she ever had to use it again. The reproachful wheelchair, with its stiff navy canvas and shiny steel wheels, took up too much space in the duplex's tiny living room. Even if we removed the cocktail table, we wouldn't be able to maneuver the wheelchair around the loveseats. Our lives would become about transfers and bad backs and managing my mother's medical condition, or as Debbie had labeled it in her seminal email, her "out-of-bounds" medical condition. Not to mention managing her fifteen prescriptions. Something else I hadn't considered: Mama hadn't been ready to come home.

In case she might need me during the night, I'd given her a tiny replica of the Liberty Bell that I'd found in the recesses of the china cabinet. In Daddy's bed, as I drifted from worry to worried sleep, I anticipated hearing that tinkling bell, which never rang.

But a few feet away, down the dark, narrow hallway, bathed by the yellow lamplight, my mother was worsening. How can a person's health go so bad so quickly? Her cough was my wakening bell, a gasping, juicy cough that seemed to come out of nowhere, topping the whine of the ancient air conditioner. She couldn't stop coughing. I crawled out of bed and took her temperature. It had climbed to 101 degrees. What to do?

As Gerry slept in the warm dark of Daddy's bedroom, I crumpled to the floor and dialed Debbie on my cell. "Mama can't breathe," I whispered to my doctor-sister, states away from us. "Plus, she hasn't peed all day." I didn't add that I'd been trained to, but had failed to, catheterize her. And I hadn't remembered to broach the topic with the nurse either.

"Take her to the ER," Debbie said.

I stayed on the floor next to the bed awhile. Go to the emergency room? But we'd only just gotten out of the hospital. I dialed the home health nurse's supervisor. Even at ten o'clock at night she came and put a stethoscope to my mother's chest. She was another Yazoo connection, my long-deceased brother's sister-in-law. "Take her to the emergency room," Pam said.

———

It was around eleven when Pam left. I'd wanted her to stay until we got my mother into the car. Really, I'd wanted her to stay so I wouldn't feel so alone. Gerry and I threw on clothes—Mama was still in her pink jogging suit—and he lifted her into the wheelchair.

We helped her put on the white sneakers. She went as limp as an old doll. Her hair, which had gone flat and greasy, was matted against her skull. Even her skin and lips were gray, and her eyes were blacker than normal, without so much as a pinprick of light. All of a sudden my mother had wrinkles everywhere on her face, left and right, up and down, forming narrow circles around her eyes. She breathed in gulps. It came to me: she might be dying.

We were outside. Somehow, we'd gotten her as far as the porch. It was hot and still. How could it be this hot at midnight? Across Calhoun, a brightly lit sign at St. John's advertised the church's weekly worship schedule. We shuffled with my mother to the edge of the porch's top step and looked down: it was as if a gully opened before us. We stood there, not speaking. She went to try the step, but her knees folded, and Gerry caught her. We supported her arms. Once on the sidewalk, she plunked down in the wheelchair. Gerry pushed her to the car, and with huge determination she transferred herself to the front seat. But Gerry couldn't fit the wheelchair in the trunk. While Mama and I waited in the dark and heat, he struggled with the ungainly chair. Finally he threw off the footrests and in it went. He drove slowly the six blocks to the emergency room at King's Daughters Hospital. Or perhaps time itself had slowed. From this I would learn the efficacy of dialing 911.

We got out, Gerry and I, at the rear of the hospital, at the emergency entrance. Nobody was around except for a wary guard in a glass cubicle. We cleared the double doors with Mama in the wheelchair, sailing along the fluorescent hall toward the examining rooms, past the command center for doctors and nurses, past the poster of poisonous snakes of Mississippi, past trauma rooms one, two, and three. In five minutes they had my mother's clothes off, and she was gowned, catheterized, and wearing what looked like a stubby clothespin on her right index finger. An IV line was attempted and failed; another inserted, only to fail as well. Clear plastic tubing was looped around her ears and oxygen administered through blue prongs in her nostrils. Mama, lying on the gurney, registered no response to what was happening to her, except perhaps resignation. By two a.m. they had finished checking us over, started us on an antibiotic, and moved us to a floor. That night I slept in her hospital room on the vinyl loveseat, which we pulled out into a single bed.

The next morning Mama was weak, sleepy, and hardly able to speak. I sat with her and filled out the rest of the hospital paperwork. A nurse asked me to sign a form saying she didn't have a living will. Was this routine, or did she also think my mother might be dying? I refused and told her I'd get the directive. Lisa had been searching for it these last two months, and she'd recently found it in my mother's safe deposit box. At noon, when Gerry got to the hospital, we ate some barbecue sandwiches, and I left to retrieve it.

I decided to drive Mama's car to the bank. As I slipped behind the oversize steering wheel, I got a fresh whiff of the Crown Vic's sweet-sour interior. In a flimsy plastic tray under the dashboard lay my mother's stretchy black gloves, the dark wraparound glasses she'd worn after her cataract surgery, a cheap dangly earring, and the receipt for an oil change. I drove toward downtown. All the trees were summer green, and tiny magenta flowers hung in clusters from the crepe myrtles. The crepe myrtles were in bloom, and I hadn't noticed. In the shimmery heat and white sun everything— the two-lane street, downtown's century-old brick buildings, the lush vegetation—seemed to stand in high relief.

On Main Street, there was no parking space near the bank, so I circled the block. I started to turn right on Madison but stopped: the street was signed one-way. Had it always been one-way? We used to park here in front of Mr. Thibodeaux's house to attend Sunday Mass at St. Mary's. I continued onto Mound Street. The hulking wooden icehouse was still standing, and momentarily I envisioned how on summer days its patrons had tarried, the young boys with their legs hanging from its high porch. I made a right on Powell Street. Lissa Henry, Vashti's best friend, maybe her only friend, had lived on this block. But the window screens of her former home were rusted and ripped, the doors askew. The house seemed off-kilter, and an idle young man stared from behind a shadowed porch.

I made a right turn and found myself back on Main. I had a strong sense that Mama was with me, and Daddy too, and their whole life in this place. With me, but compressed, the years jammed together, the *was* of time becoming *is*, the *is* becoming *was*. And it was so real, this feeling of Mama and Daddy and the town and our lives, the realest memory I'd ever had. I thought I knew what it meant: he'd come for her. Daddy for Mama.

I walked into the bank. I took the safe deposit box key that my mother kept on her key ring, along with her discount card for the Sunflower grocery, and handed it to the teller. She located the strongbox, but it was too heavy for her to lift, since it was full of Daddy's coin collection. I grabbed one end, and together she and I carried it to a cubicle. There, on top, lay Mama's birth certificate; underneath, Daddy's death certificate. "Probable cause of death: heart failure. Time: +/- 3 a.m." Under these, Mama's burial policy and her living will. I scanned the form but kept my head tucked so the bank's security cameras couldn't capture my reaction. When I'd collected myself, I removed still more papers. Old stock certificates; an envelope labeled in Daddy's handwriting "Clippings from the day Jimmy Carter came to town," back in '77; another envelope with his writing—"Fifty-nine two dollar bills." I put everything back, minus the living will, closed the box, and heaved it into its slot.

Outside again, my earlier presentiments seemed to have vanished. I turned to look north toward the tree-lined canal and thought I'd never really looked in that direction before. I'd never taken in the fullness of the trees, the leisurely arc of the street. We don't really look at things. Not at each other. Not at places. We don't see what we see. And then there are all the little things that go unnoticed: how the nurse takes my mother's blood pressure and moves the glass of water inches out of her reach. All the things that go unnoticed.

I drove slowly back to the hospital. When I got to my mother's room the nurse came to find me. She'd been waiting. As Mama dozed and dreamed, lost someplace, the expressionless nurse asked me again if I'd sign her form declaring that my mother had no living will. I opened my bag, pulled out the document, and handed it over. It stipulated no heroic measures. For the rest of that long afternoon I stayed in Room 132, sitting at the foot of the bed in a straight-backed chair, my feet flat on the floor, watching my mother drift in her lost place. Later the doctor came. Not her regular doctor, who was on vacation, but his stand-in, an athletic-looking man in his sixties with a trim white beard. He pulled a chair close to my mother and asked me some questions about her. If she'd eaten anything, if she seemed to be in pain. His name was Will Thompson, and before leaving he said, "I think she will be okay."

Thirteen

The King

The following January, at the Martha Coker Convalescent Home, Mama was hunkered down in her "private room"—a converted storage closet, where mops and brooms stood piled off to one side, covered by a thin white sheet. Just back from lunch, she slouched in a stiff leather chair, while her nursing assistant, Ernestine, perched on the hospital bed. Each day at noon this odd couple moseyed down the nursing home's practically block-long hallway to the dining room: my pale mother bent over her walker and the dark-skinned Ernestine by her side, dutifully toting my mother's water bottle. Ernestine was a big proponent of hydration.

The Martha Coker Convalescent Home, known as "Martha Coker," shouldn't be confused with the Martha Coker Green Houses. Built in the early sixties, Martha Coker was Mississippi's first nursing home and, for its time, one of the most advanced. You can find it mentioned in the letters of Eudora Welty, whose mother, Chestina, was a resident in the mid-sixties. Welty described Martha Coker as "a new facility run by a hospital, by hospital staff, in a nice new spacious building with patio, beauty parlor, bath-tubs that the hydraulic lift will let you down into, real splashing baths—all kinds of special things." She visited her mother there several times a week, for years, and while making the solitary drive from her home in Jackson she would jot notes for the novel she was trying to finish, despite her role as caregiver. (She would title the novel *Losing Battles*.) The Martha Coker of my mother's day bore the same orange-brick façade as Chestina Welty's, but with its unkempt patio and nicked walls and scuffed floors it seemed not just outdated but downright tired.

Dr. Thompson had been right about my mother: she'd recovered from the pneumonia she'd contracted in rehab. On his recommendation, while still recuperating, she'd transferred to the hospital's swing-bed program, which meant she'd stayed in the same room and received daily physical therapy. After a month, when she went home, Ernestine went with her. Short and broad-shouldered, with a wide and ready smile, Ernestine had stood out among the half-dozen applicants for the job. Trained as a certified nursing assistant, or CNA, she was probably in her early forties. One day she hoped to study nursing, she told us, but now she would work for minimum wage, any hours we liked. We hired her practically on the spot. She put in twelve-hour days, five days a week, helping my mother bathe, cooking her meals, and driving her to the beauty shop, grocery store, gym, and doctor (including to the urologist, who last September had pronounced my mother's bladder normal). But Ernestine was more than the sum of her duties. She was Mama's friend. Their favorite afternoon activity was watching reruns of *The Golden Girls* and mulling over salient plot points.

Now, in the nursing home in early January, the duo bent their heads conspiratorially, Mama's wispy, silvery hair touching Ernestine's stiff black locks. Martha Coker's January newsletter and activities calendar had just come out, and my mother was mentioned prominently as a new resident. She'd been given a rousing welcome in print, and when Ernestine told her she smiled, despite her ambivalence about being in a nursing home. Then Mama noticed an "Elvis Day" was on tap for the King's birthday, January 8. She looked worried. She'd lived alone for so many years that it was hard getting used to the exigencies of group living, though she'd learned that she liked some of the proffered social activities.

She looked forward to the Saturday afternoon bingo games and besting her rival Mr. Waters, raking in Hershey bars and packs of Nabs as spoils. She enjoyed Louise's exercise classes too, which she participated in from her wheelchair, bending her arms and lifting her feet in time to Broadway show tunes. But an Elvis Day? What would be required of her for that?

She rested the paper handout in her lap and sighed. Then she turned to Ernestine and asked, "Does this mean I have to dress up like Elvis?"

My mother had moved into the converted-broom-closet-cum-private-room out of necessity, on a rush basis, but not because of any illness. Things at home had gone bad so quickly, and she'd wound up in the broom closet because there hadn't been any regular rooms available at Martha Coker. Last November, my mother's house had become uninhabitable due to a plumbing mishap. Both the hot- and cold-water pipes in her bathroom had developed leaks, which had gone undetected, damaging not only the bathrooms but also the two closed-off bedrooms on the duplex's south end. The damp rooms had grown a smattering of mold on the carpets, Sheetrock, and window frames, and so now Mama was in Martha Coker with no other place to live. And there she had to stay, until we could put the duplex back together.

I'd heard about this latest calamity in Mexico, during an anguished phone call from Lisa. The second person Lisa called: Arcell, my mother's plumber. Arcell drove a battered pickup and possessed a demeanor perhaps best described as "don't mess with me." "AR-cell" was how Mama said his name. They enjoyed a friendly relationship, partly due to her two sycamores. These trees with their riotous roots tended to penetrate her drainage pipes, causing them to gurgle in a deep-throated way and, if left untreated, to back up. Arcell was summoned at least yearly to the property with his special machine. Mama took pleasure in Arcell's "visits," as she called them. And they were visits, because after he reamed the pipes he would sit and chat awhile with my mother in her living room. Then she would write Arcell a check and present him with a jar of homemade fig preserves "for his mother."

Soon after Ernestine discovered the plumbing fallout, Lisa met with Arcell. "You should have seen the mud on him when he crawled out from under the house," my sister reported. As children, possessed with both fascination and revulsion for that narrow crawlspace, with its soft dirt floor, we'd snuck under the duplex to eavesdrop on our parents. My mother had forbidden us to go under there, and when that hadn't worked, she'd tried threats of a brown recluse spider bite, every southern child's nightmare and every southern mother's weapon of persuasion. Tough Arcell was immune to such ordinary fears—it was the state of the plumbing that horrified him. Since Daddy's death, Mama had done a lot to improve the duplex, but its sixty-year-old infrastructure hadn't been touched. Who could blame her for Sheetrocking and painting first? Lisa tasked Arcell with updating the pipes.

It was hard to think of this as being just about plumbing. As silly as it sounds, and it was silly, it was hard not to think that the duplex was exacting some kind of systemic revenge. Was the troublesome house reminding us of its traditional place in our lives, as the embodiment of our feelings of shame, despair, and helplessness? When we were young, we'd struggled to find ways to surmount those ingrained feelings. Now, once again, Lisa and I had to tackle the emotional challenges the duplex presented, not to mention the practical ones.

After calling Arcell, my sister broke out the cleaning supplies. She scrubbed the walls in the bathrooms and the two damaged bedrooms. But the mold and mildew hadn't stopped there. In Mama's bedroom, she took the hanging clothes out of the closet, dividing them into piles to wash and piles to throw away. She bought and assembled a new shoe bag for the closet door. Even my mother's prized Singer sewing machine, in the aptly monikered Junk Room, farthest from the leak, was suspect. Lisa decided expert help was required. She found a restoration and cleaning company in Jackson specializing in mold remediation and touting the slogan "Faster to any size disaster." These mold hunters advised taking the south-facing bedrooms down to their studs. After the demolition we would have to hire a construction company to put the duplex back together—lay flooring and carpet, Sheetrock walls, and paint. Lisa argued with the insurance adjustor about whether our claim was due to mold (with a policy cap) or water (in which case they might pay close to total costs).

Gerry and I bought airline tickets to Mississippi. But before leaving San Miguel we had our own disaster. On a crisp and sunny December morning, the kind that makes you believe nothing bad can ever happen, we were exiting a parking lot when a taxi stopped to let us make a left turn. As we inched beyond him, a motorcycle policeman roared up, without lights or siren, and brushed the hood of our station wagon. He wasn't badly hurt—the bridge of his nose was bleeding slightly. But the scene was chaos, with the flashing lights of the ambulance, the heavy presence of the police, the mounting traffic, and the reporters from the local TV station with their microphones and cameras. Later in the prosecutor's office we refused to accept responsibility for the accident, and our car was impounded.

The next day we learned that Gerry's mother had died suddenly of heart failure. We arrived in Yazoo City during the second week of December. Though we planned to drive to Florida for Marion's memorial service, we would take over the frontline management of my mother's calamity. Lisa temporarily retreated to Picayune, a victim of duplex fatigue.

While Mama languished in the broom closet at Martha Coker, we lived at Willie Belle's. Every morning I got up early and strolled next door to the duplex to make sure that nobody had made off with the furniture. Anybody (a trim anybody) could have shimmied under a gap in the foundation, popped up like a jack-in-the-box in one of the floorless bedrooms, and walked along the floor joists to the living room, where Mama's possessions were heaped. Then they could have opened the front door and carted off whatever they liked.

One morning I got to the duplex extra early and found Arcell already parked in her driveway. I wanted his advice. The mold was nearly abated, but I felt confused about which contractor to hire: the slow-moving local man who seemed meticulous or the Jackson-based company that promised to finish the job fast. Unlike the local man, who employed one helper, the company laid out a detailed schedule, including when the "rocker" would come to Sheetrock, the "mud men" to spackle, and the "trim man" to finish up. Arcell led me through the pros and cons, and when he saw I leaned toward speed, he nodded. After all, Mama was waiting in the nursing home, wearying of Bingo games and Broadway show tunes.

Then Arcell said laconically, "Y'all really should rip out those walls in those bathrooms too. Those bathrooms are full of mold."

He walked me to an outside wall and effortlessly jimmied off a clapboard with a crowbar. We peered inside, first Arcell, then me. Furry pastel streaks marked the interior.

"Get your insurance man out here to look at that," Arcell said, wagging his finger, pointing out what nobody else had noticed, not the mold hunters or the contractors. Visions of fresh bathrooms, with standing showers instead of 300-pound cast-iron knee tubs, danced in my head—paid for, in part, by insurance. It was nearly Christmas, after all.

A few days later, the weary insurance adjustor visited my mother's house again, this time to take a look-see at those furry pastel streaks. Thanks to Arcell, Mama got approval for repairing the bathrooms. But on our way to buy the white beadboard vanities she'd picked out from the Lowe's catalog, Gerry and I encountered another unexpected problem.

It was a Saturday morning, and we were meandering along Highway 16, a quiet two-lane back road bordered, like so many rural Mississippi roads, by lovely fields and forests. I was admiring the poetry of a vast cotton field, the stubby dried plants backlighted in the early morning sun, when my mother's Ford Crown Vic began decelerating, as if it too wished to pause and admire these remnants of last season's harvest.

I turned to Gerry, who was in the driver's seat. "What's wrong?"

"I don't know," he said, staring at the Ford's dash. "It's losing power, that's all."

Sure enough, the heroic old car had decelerated until it could muster a top speed of only fifteen miles per hour.

"It's dying!" I wailed.

Gerry made a U-turn, and we slunk back toward Benton. We stopped at a gas station on the town's outskirts to check the transmission fluid, but that wasn't the source of the Ford's slowdown. We crawled the final eight miles to Yazoo City while camouflage-clad hunters in mud-splattered pickups, many trailing four-wheelers, passed us with aplomb.

Later, from the comfort of Willie Belle's den, I commiserated with Lisa by email. We'd been doing a lot of commiserating lately. "They say problems come in threes, but we're up to at least four," I wrote. "Whoever invented that superstition, anyway?"

"It certainly seems that everything that could possibly go wrong is. Maybe we need to rub an armadillo on our head," she joked. "I tried to buy a good luck cabbage, but there wasn't one available anywhere in Picayune." This was New Year's. I guessed she preferred eating cabbage to the traditional black-eyed peas.

"Just remember, you can't solve all the problems that are crop-
ping up in the house," she continued. "Let's just try to get it put back
together so Mama can move back in. Try to keep your spirits up."

She had the advantage of distance, and therefore perspective,
while I felt humorless, mired in the battle-zone muck. Then I
pointed out that, despite the insurance money, Mama was running through her funds quickly. We might not have money to fix
the Ford.

"Maybe Mama and Ernestine can creep around Yazoo City in
very low gears," she suggested.

The next day I capitulated and slow-drove the Ford to Cotten's
repair shop. Not surprisingly, the car needed a complete transmission overhaul. To pick up the new bathroom vanities, we borrowed
Willie Belle's big blue Buick.

Mama's luck did change. Not long after Elvis's birthday, Arcell pronounced the reconstructed duplex "good enough" (high praise from
him) and finished installing the new bathroom fixtures, including
"comfort-height" toilets—just another little way he looked out for
my mother's well-being. A week later she checked out of Martha
Coker. At an age (eighty-three) when many old folks were moving
into nursing homes, she moved back into her own home to live by
herself, though with Ernestine's excellent ministrations.

Gerry and I had already returned to Mexico, more or less
sanguine that things were working out. In Yazoo City Lisa took
over—vacuuming and dusting the remodeled duplex, arranging
the furniture, and washing and rehanging the window sheers. The
fresh Sheetrock had been covered with two coats of China Doll,
still my mother's favorite color, with crisp white for the trim and
ceilings. We'd even wrangled enough money from the insurance
adjustor to repaint the outside of the duplex a warm beige, erad-

icating the "Chia Pet" appearance that the clapboards had taken on due to some streaks of black and green mold.

That year my mother's health improved under the aegis of the competent, smiling Ernestine, who could sound like a drill sergeant when it came time for Mama's daily strengthening exercises. Sometimes I felt niggling guilt and even anxiety about Ernestine replacing us as caregivers. But Ernestine wasn't put off by seeing my mother's naked body, while powdering and creaming my mother's skin after her shower. She wasn't squeamish about monitoring my mother's trips to the bathroom and helping her on and off her comfort-height toilet. Our real problem wasn't that Ernestine was replacing us as caregivers. Our real problem was that Ernestine was applying to nursing school and would be leaving us soon. A race began to take shape: would we lose Ernestine to her schooling or to my mother's funds running out? To augment Mama's dwindling savings, Lisa proposed we take out a reverse mortgage. Now we were pinning all our financial hopes on the duplex.

Mama's luck turned that year, but ours didn't. Gerry and I continued to be mired in legal problems from our car accident in San Miguel. The motorcycle policeman who'd hit us was claiming to have sustained permanent injury to his left pinky. And not even to the entire finger, only to its top joint. He'd refused the settlement the insurance company had offered him, the peso equivalent of eight hundred dollars. The case had dragged on for months in the country's tortuous legal system, until finally our personal lawyer called to inform us that everything was settled: the policeman would give us his official "pardon." We would be legally forgiven for something we had never admitted was our fault.

Then on a Friday morning in October, as we sat working in our study, the condominium's gardener knocked. Without expression, the young man said in Spanish, "The *Ministerio Publico* is waiting at the front gate to arrest *Señor* Gerardo." Gerry panic-called the American consul, but he didn't pick up. He panic-called our lawyer, but she didn't pick up either. After an hour, the insurance company's lawyer arrived at the condo. The reason for Gerry's arrest: he'd failed to show up in court, she informed us. But we'd never received notice of a court date, which the insurance company was supposed to have passed on to us. Rather than the official at the gate dragging Gerry off in handcuffs, she had arranged a deal. She would escort us to the state prison outside San Miguel, where Gerry would turn himself in.

At the prison, Gerry was strip-searched, fingerprinted, and given a medical examination. "Is your blood pressure always so high?" the doctor asked. Gerry was placed in a tiny cell with four other men. By now his Spanish was fluent enough that he could have a conversation with his fellow prisoners, some of whom had been in jail for over a decade. They offered to share their doughnuts and *atole*; they were kinder than the guards, who didn't offer so much as a glass of water. In the late afternoon Gerry was led to a courtroom and made to stand handcuffed behind bars for two hours while the charges against him were read in front of a judge. Enrique, our Spanish teacher and friend, was also present. He'd come to the prison to wait with me but got conscripted to translate the Spanish legalese into everyday Spanish for Gerry's benefit. Occasionally Enrique would have trouble too, and ever the grammarian, would halt the proceedings to complain about the state's choice of verbs. The insurance company lawyer sat mute, except to counsel Gerry, before the judge, to plead guilty. He refused, and after an eleven-hour incarceration, was released on bail.

On Saturday we huddled in bed and thought about fleeing the country. But then some English expat friends recommended we hire their personal lawyer, a former judge from the nearby city of Guanajuato. We called her cell phone on Sunday afternoon. The next morning she met us at the courthouse, where the policeman was having a medical examination. She sat beside him, gently manipulating his pinky and soothingly relating how she herself had once suffered such an injury, which had turned out to be only minor. Four days later the judge dismissed the charges against Gerry, the policeman accepted the insurance company's original settlement, and the case was closed. As soon as we could we left for Mississippi, uncertain whether we would return to Mexico. Misery had replaced the magic and mystery, misery along with disenchantment and plain old fear.

—

I wondered if this would be our last Christmas with Mama. There, in the twice-renovated duplex. The carpet pile still stood rigid on the new beige wall-to-wall, and the fresh-from-the-can smell still clung to the China Dolled-up Sheetrock. There we were, preparing a scaled-down Christmas dinner, just for us, on Christmas Eve: roast turkey and baked-outside-the-bird cornbread dressing and broccoli casserole with, yes, Cheez Whiz. Only the favorites, forgoing the giblet gravy, green beans, sweet potatoes, even the deviled eggs. My mother got up once from her chair and shuffled to the kitchen in her navy slippers to doctor the dressing with her blend of seasonings, so it would taste as it had always tasted, with just the right predominance of black pepper. Only the favorite Christmas foods, but they had to be memory right. She leaned on the kitchen counter to taste and stir. I noted that, and the breathlessness that followed. We set the table using the red holiday tablecloth, along with my mother's Syracuse china and her Candlewick crystal and her good, heavy silver, and posed for the commemorative photo. Would it be our last Christmas together?

There we were, in the living room. On Christmas morning, Mama in her yellow recliner, wearing her purple bathrobe, Gerry and I on our flowered loveseats. Opening presents. We'd forgone the cedar Christmas tree (and the artificial one) and had piled gift boxes on the "Christmas chair," an upholstered green slipper chair that had once belonged to Vashti. This was the Christmas of red and pink: Gerry and I got red velour shirts from Lisa, and Mama pink slippers, delicate moccasins with orange ties. She put them on, along with a pink T-shirt and tan pants and warm-up jacket, and we went next door to Willie Belle's for Christmas dinner. On the way we paused on the front porch for two photos: Gerry with Mama next to the mailbox, with its dangling plastic Christmas bell and holly, and then me with her. With him, she smiled an elfin smile, her belly protruding slightly; in our photo, she put an arm around my waist and inclined her head toward mine, as I did mine toward hers. She smiled, but less broadly. Months later when my friend Carlos painted those images he would capture the sadness of that smile, not the bit of gladness it held.

We did know it would be our last Christmas with Ernestine. Nearly a year had passed since she'd huddled with my mother at Martha Coker and plotted their Elvis Day observances. She'd given notice and would be leaving in January. As we made the turn to 2008, it was impossible not to feel foreboding, and not only for Ernestine's departure.

What would the year bring? During the fall the stock market had reached an outrageous high, but there were troubling signs for anybody who knew how to read them. (I didn't.) Other setbacks loomed. My agent hadn't sold my manuscript. We'd made no headway in securing a reverse mortgage for the duplex and believed the likelihood slim to none. Gerry and I had about decided to buy it, and not only to help my mother. We would return to Mexico, but warier. Never again would we see the country so naively. We needed not only a place stateside to run back to in case of calamity, but a place that could become home. But buy my nemesis? Well, at least the duplex was twice renovated. That Christmas, none of us knew if this would be our last holiday in the duplex with my mother. But with my belly Christmas-full from Willie Belle's congealed salad and cheese spaghetti, her family's memory foods, I lay on the stiff carpet in Mama's spiffed-up living room and fretted that it might be.

Fourteen

All the Hospital Rooms

On March 1, 2008, my mother was admitted to King's Daughters Hospital. To Room 132, the same one she'd been in twenty months before. All the furniture surfaces, so hard—the narrow hospital bed, the mauve vinyl loveseat, the straight-backed leatherette chair, the straight-backed wooden chair. There was an outmoded TV mounted on a wall, a scarred-up bedside table, a hanging sink. On another wall, the ubiquitous sofa-size painting. Room 132, we would come to find out, was like all the other hospital rooms.

As Gerry and I entered, fresh from Mexico, how smoothly the room's blond wooden door glided open. My mother was lying on her back, with the bed's metal sidebars raised. Staring at the ceiling. She was pale, swallowed up in a faded hospital gown. When she saw us, she raised her left arm in greeting. I bent to kiss her cheek.

We sat on the loveseat, with Lisa opposite us. "Here are Mama's toiletries," she said, holding up a Ziploc bag. "I brought her clothes from home and put them in the closet. I picked up after the EMT guys. You know, the gauze and plastic they leave behind."

This was Mama's second hospitalization in two weeks, the first having ended a few days before. Lisa had stayed with her throughout. "She's doing great, considering," she'd emailed us. "This will be a short one, for her." In total Mama had been in the hospital for five days, with pneumonia. She'd seemed healthy when discharged, but within hours she'd relapsed, and Lisa had called 911. We were here to take over for round two.

At five o'clock a nursing assistant brought supper on a tray, and I leapt up to feed my mother. I cut off a hunk of canned peach, flew it around in a circle, and winged the spoon toward her mouth. She laughed when the fruit slipped onto the sheet. She wasn't saying much, but her black-dark eyes were taking everything in, without giving much back.

Shortly afterward we kissed her goodnight, and the three of us headed off to the Mexican restaurant, a low building with a wavy concrete exterior that resembled hardened meringue. On its front wall the owners had draped a large red sign in Spanish, advertising that for a fee they would wire your paycheck to Mexico. The service was yet another testament to Yazoo City's small but growing Mexican population, like the Spanish Mass at St. Mary's and the bins of *serranos* and *poblanos* at Sunflower grocery.

El Palenque was deserted on that chilly night, except for a few young Mexican men gathered at the bar. Manual workers dressed in heavy boots and tattered jeans and plaid shirts, on their way to lonely digs, stopping off for a beer and some chat. Our waiter, slope-shouldered and balding, the rare Mexican with a comb-over, showed us to a booth. He returned with a basket of uncommonly yellow chips, along with chunky tomato salsa in what looked like a small plastic vase. We poured the salsa into our individual bowls.

"She asked me about her funeral clothes," Lisa said, dipping into her well of salsa.

"Oh?" I asked, dipping into mine.

"She'd already chosen an outfit, which she'd kept in the back of her closet, but the skirt got ruined in the mold."

"Oh," I said.

"I told her we could go to the Marylena Shoppe and buy something else, once she started to feel better," Lisa went on. Founded in the forties by Lebanese sisters Mary and Lena Thomas, this chic shop on West Broadway had once supplied everything from sportswear to formalwear for the fashion-conscious Yazoo matron. Mama had kept a store account, but she'd rarely been able to buy an outfit. Nylons and girdles, maybe.

"Or she could order something online," Gerry said, unaware of the Thomas sisters' ageless hold over us. He wrapped his fingers around a bottle of Mexican beer.

"The Marylena Shoppe would be better," Lisa said. "Everything's been there forever. What better place to find something for all eternity?"

Our orders came quickly—shrimp quesadillas for Lisa, chicken fajitas for us. As we ate, the restaurant's corn tortillas kept disintegrating into papery shreds, reminding us that we were no longer in Mexico. We finished and drove straight home through the dark night.

Lisa had been staying in the duplex for the last week, but its hushed and damp interior felt bereft of life. Gerry lit the gas space heaters in the living room and bathrooms. There was junk mail scattered on the cocktail table and medicine bottles and insulin needles on the dining table. The duplex seemed like a public space perfunctorily kept by the nursing assistant we'd hired to replace Ernestine. After making my mother lunch, the young woman didn't sit companionably with her in the living room, watching *The Golden Girls*, but stayed at the dining table, thumbing through magazines and gossiping on her cell phone, whose rap ringtone would cause my mother to jump. Mama had reported these transgressions in disbelief, with hurt in her voice, but she was powerless to address them herself. Lisa and I had spoken with the young woman, walking the tightrope between giving her feedback and alienating her, but our pep talks had only seemed to increase her dark-cloud demeanor. We also felt powerless, because if she were to "up and quit," as my mother put it, who would we replace her with? It wasn't as if this time there had been a lot of other candidates for the job.

The wall clock over the TV chimed eight, still too early for bed. Gerry got down on the carpet to start his nightly stretches. Lisa rocked in the recliner, a faraway look in her eyes. "Do you think Mama wants a funeral Mass?" she asked.

I glanced over at her from the loveseat. "I can't talk about her funeral. And I don't think it's good to talk about it with Mama either."

"Well, I didn't bring it up," she said. "Mama did."

From where he lay on the floor, Gerry asked, "Am I the only one who thinks Mama's going to live? I think she'll be home by her birthday."

Her eighty-fourth was in three weeks. I'd been hoping she'd be home before that. "I haven't decided," I answered. "I'm waiting until we speak to Dr. Thompson."

We all went to bed early. The freight trains sounded all night, sorrowful and insistent, because the wind had picked up, blowing the horn blasts toward us. I had a fitful sleep punctuated not only by the trains but also by my aunt's metal garbage can top rolling around under her carport. Before first light, I finally got up. Mama's empty recliner, her red T-shirt draped on a hanger in her bathroom, the pillows on her bed imprinted with her form—these ordinary things, usually so imbued with her presence, mocked normalcy. The house was like a public space because she wasn't in it.

The day dawned falsely warm for early March, with long threads of brown pollen flying through the air like dirty snow. Storm warnings were forecast through the evening, and the hospital staff's chitchat was all about the impending bad weather. Mama felt better: she'd fed herself breakfast and brushed her teeth. She was also engrossed in the storm news, though her agitation was hardly noticeable.

"Are you afraid?" I asked her, as she stared out the venetian blinds.

"Naw, what for?" A friend of Willie Belle's had called from the nearby town of Thornton, I told her, because she'd seen a tornado pass overhead "plain as day."

"Ain't nothing I can do about it," she said, and went on watching the weather.

That night, as we hunkered in the living room against the wind and rain, against the lightning strikes and threat of tornadoes, there was no more discussion about funerals or burial outfits. In the flickering lights we watched a thriller that Lisa had to explain every few minutes. Spooked by the scary movie, we thought we heard a strange noise in the yard. I turned off the lights to look out. Not a single car traveled the dark, wet street.

"Told you it wasn't nothing to worry about," Mama said the next morning.

Lisa stayed with us through Dr. Thompson's early rounds. For the first time, he used the word "malignant." A spot, less than an inch long, had been found on my mother's last lung X-ray. We could do a needle biopsy—I appreciated how he used the inclusive "we"—but better to wait and repeat the X-ray, he counseled. He delivered these words without fanfare and went on to his next points. The pneumonia was clearing. My mother's blood counts were normalizing. Her bladder wasn't working, but we would also wait and see on that.

After he left, Mama took a sip of coffee from her breakfast tray. "It's spoilt," she said of the milk. She slipped on her pink moccasins and hobbled over to a chair, dragging her half-full catheter bag across the linoleum. Lisa was dismissive of the spot on her lung, saying, "They found that before, and it cleared up." By phone, Debbie said, "Oh, I hope they don't want to do anything about it."

"What are you looking at, Mama?" I asked, trying to follow her gaze.

"At the sunshine," she said. Sure enough, a few rays had broken through the clouds.

Lisa left to go back to Picayune, and I went home to fetch my mother's special conditioning shampoo. A little later, as she sat in the sun, towel-drying her hair, she said of the spot, "Well, that's bad news." Taking a page from her book, I urged her not to look for trouble. "Not about something you can't do nothing about," I teased.

—

After nine days of antibiotics, breathing treatments, and chest massage with a machine that looked like a cross between a spare tire and a giant mushroom, my mother left the hospital. "My chair," she sighed, as she sank into the recliner. With her home, the duplex came alive again. She watched TV, napped, and ate supper in her chair. Then she couldn't speak any longer and made sounds like a kitten mewing. We helped her into bed, and I checked her blood sugar, blood pressure, pulse, and temperature. She had a slight fever.

"Bring me . . ." she said. She lay on her right side, her back as round as a basketball.

I waited at the foot of her bed. "Bring you what, Mama?"

"Bring me . . ." she said again, and sighed.

I was alarmed but began the guessing game. Was it in the bathroom? Dining room? Living room? She nodded at the latter. Was it big? Little? Another nod.

"Bring me a . . . dang!" she shouted.

"Dang? That's good, Mama, you got out another word. Bring you what?"

"Bring me a piece of hard candy from the living room!" she blurted, pointing to her bedside table. She wanted a peppermint nearby in case her sugar got low during the night.

In the living room, I worried to Gerry. "Is she having a stroke? Why can't she talk?"

"Maybe she's just tired," he said. He sat very still. It occurred to me that he must be tired too. That we were all tired.

"But most tired people can talk," I said. "It's got to be more. What should we do?"

He shrugged. I dialed Dr. Thompson's office and reached the on-call physician. He laid out our options: take her to the emergency room or wait and see how she did in the morning. So cut, so dried, so devoid of emotion—the dread of another trip to the ER versus the fear of keeping her at home. I dialed the home health service and after relating the symptoms to the night nurse, decided to keep Mama where she was.

The next morning her speech was better, but she didn't want to get up. "It's so nice and warm in bed," she said. After some cajoling, which I later regretted, she tried to eat breakfast at the table. We put her in the recliner and wrapped her in blankets. Within the hour she worsened with chills and fever, but still I kept her home. Thirty minutes later she changed again, changed so that she couldn't focus her eyes, changed so that she drooled, and the nursing assistant who wasn't working out told me what I already knew. The "EMT guys" came promptly, with their gauzes and their plastics and their gurney.

And so began round three, starting with ten hours in the emergency room. The staff doctor ordered a CT scan of the brain, a chest X-ray, blood work to check for sepsis, urinalysis to check for a bladder infection. At four o'clock my mother was assigned a room—144, not our old stand-by—but because patients couldn't "go to the floor" between five and seven, she stayed in the ER four more hours, her breaths coming ragged and fast.

In Room 144, I bent over my mother, watching her chest rise and fall. Debbie had told me, "Count the breaths." When the night nurse entered, I said, "I think my mother is dying." She looked stricken, nodded, and left. She came back and hung clear plastic bags, little oceans of antibiotics, first one, then a stronger one, because Mama's white blood count was three times normal. That night she slept, or drifted, waking every few minutes with a snort, lifting her head off the pillow, ripping off her oxygen mask. I kept leaping up to put it back on. I watched her closely, as if through watchfulness I could keep from happening to her whatever might be happening. Keep it from happening to us. At three o'clock her breathing eased, became softer and slower, and I knew the crisis had passed.

At dawn Gerry came and we waited for the doctor, not Dr. Thompson but a colleague, and then we were off again on a regimen of two antibiotics and an antifungal agent and breathing treatments and chest thumping with the black-tire-mushroom machine, and there wasn't any humor in it, only exhaustion and stress and the near constant leaping up to assist with something—eating or drinking or hair brushing or adjusting the blinds or the TV's volume or winding up her toy bug, a blue plastic fly Lisa had given her. When I wanted to feel self-pity, I thought of myself as Lenny with the shrunken ovary, self-sacrificing Lenny, the oldest of the three Magrath sisters in Beth Henley's play *Crimes of the Heart*.

My sisters and I voiced the question: should we put her in Martha Coker? "Put her," assuming she were to survive the hospital stay. "Put her," as if she were an object, without will, to be moved from one institution to another. I wanted to scream, *Do the math!* I scribbled figures on the backs of envelopes, room rates and drug costs. Martha Coker was private pay. Even with the money she was getting for the duplex—from us, its appraised value in twenty easy installments—she couldn't last longer than a few months, financially speaking. But I wanted Mama home, where she'd always been. Only when she was in her place could I be assured of my place. The place of child, albeit adult child; of second (not oldest, like Lenny) daughter, recipient of my mother's wholehearted looks of approval, of her unquestioning love. If necessary, to maintain that order of mother and child I would take care of her myself, nurse her as Lenny with the shrunken ovary had nursed Old Granddaddy.

On Mama's birthday, the first day of spring, Lisa arrived at the hospital early, trailing a bouquet of helium balloons. When the breakfast tray came, she positioned the over-the-bed table and placed the tray in the center. With a flourish, she lifted the metal lid. On a white plate lay a pink Popsicle. Mama giggled. Lisa giggled. Was this a bizarre birthday tribute from the hospital's food service? A pink Popsicle for a woman who wore pink moccasins, who was becoming known among the staff as "Pink Shoes"? No, she'd mistakenly been put on a liquid diet. The Popsicle was removed, grits and eggs and bacon delivered.

At lunchtime, we threw a small party for Mama in her room. Ada, my mother's sister, drove up from Jackson with her husband, Lou. The nursing assistant who wasn't working out came, along with Willie Belle, who brought a square white cake decorated with a plaid fabric bow. Mama had gotten dressed and sat in one of the straight-back chairs, holding court with her visitors. We ate the pretty cake and drank Cokes. We laughed. The nurses drifted in and out, and we fed them cake too. We took photographs, and Mama looked healthy; she was getting better. Then Lisa left for Picayune, Ada and Lou for Jackson. Late in the afternoon, when only I remained, Mama said wistfully, "I had a nice party."

A few days later Lisa returned, because Gerry and I were leaving. The next morning we woke up at four o'clock for our flight to San Miguel. My mother was newly out of the hospital. I paused at the doorway to her dark bedroom, trying not to disturb her. She lay on her right side, facing away from the door.

"I love you," she said, as if to the air.

"I love you too," I said, moving to kiss her warm forehead.

The visit had ended well. But the next day she was back in the hospital. Not in Room 132 or 144. One by one, she was trying all the hospital's thirty-five rooms.

In San Miguel, I thought about her constantly. If I hold her in my mind, I thought, I hold her in the world. So went my magical thinking. But it wasn't enough.

We bought tickets to Mississippi for round four. We'd stayed in Mexico one day.

Fifteen

Don't Spill Your Beans

This time when Gerry and I got to Mama's bedside, she sighed and said, "I guess I'm in it for the long haul." I held her hand, stroking her thin, tired fingers. Their skin felt fine as tracing paper, except for the tips, which after thirty years of diabetic sticks had formed into dark calluses.

"Oh, Mama," I groaned, knitting her fingers with mine.

What were we to do? How were we to take care of her? What did she need? How would we provide it? Daddy had gone clean, but Mama's exit was proving messy. Barely a month ago, she'd worried she might have lung cancer. Now she worried she would tarry.

I worried she wouldn't tarry. Not only did I not want her to die yet, I wanted to be with her when the time came. How to manage that with my back-and-forth existence?

Over the next few days Dr. Thompson called in a speech therapist to evaluate my mother's swallow reflex. (Swallow reflex: fine.) He ordered a chest X-ray. (New spot: no change.) On Friday morning during rounds Lisa and I tried out our possible diagnoses on him, which he patiently entertained and then dismissed one by one: stroke, meningitis, mastoiditis. (Mastoiditis?) My sister and I fell silent, trying to absorb what he'd told us. Then Lisa said, "Perhaps the duplex is the culprit." She related its recent moldy history.

"No, it isn't the house's fault," he said. "You can't put these pneumonias off on it."

When Mama was last admitted, he pointed out, she'd spit up a foamy substance. His diagnosis: aspiration pneumonia. She needed another course of antibiotics and treatment for acid reflux. She needed to sit upright after eating and to sleep with her head elevated.

Lisa went right out to a medical supply pharmacy and ordered a large foam wedge that would raise Mama's head to a 30-degree angle while she slept. This prompted Gerry to observe how fragile life could be: we were pinning our hopes for Mama's recovery on a piece of foam. The wedge would deliver in a few days, the following Tuesday. But Dr. Thompson had also mentioned that he would release Mama on Monday. If she got out of the hospital on Monday and the wedge didn't deliver until Tuesday, how would we prevent a fifth relapse and hospitalization before it arrived?

That Saturday for lunch we went to the Pig Shak, a tiny barbecue joint at the crest of Broadway hill. In the Shak's galley kitchen there was just enough room for two good-size ladies to prepare food side-by-side. We stood at the order window and asked for barbecue plates with pulled pork sandwiches, coleslaw, buttered corn, and baked beans.

In front of the kitchen a few picnic tables were grouped under a low roof and snugged by lattice walls. While Lisa and I claimed some benches at one of the tables, Gerry waited at the window for our food. He stood next to a wire rack of bagged pork cracklings, chatting with a server. I heard her mention that she was an acquaintance of my mother from "way back" and then ask about her health. Being Catholic, Mama wasn't on the First Baptist Church prayer list, but word of her repeat hospitalizations had spread around town.

I asked Lisa what we should do about the wedge and the dangerous day's lag between Mama's anticipated release and its anticipated delivery.

"I don't know," she said, throwing her red sunglasses down on the table. "But one thing I do know. We have to get Ernestine back." We'd shelved the idea of Mama going to Martha Coker, for now, to see if Dr. Thompson's latest treatment plan would cure her.

I turned toward my baby sister. "But isn't Ernestine in school?"

"Weekends. She's free weekends," she said, picking up her glasses and twirling them. Before, my mother had employed CNAs only on weekdays, but now she needed help 24/7.

Good old Ernestine, I thought, good old hardworking Ernestine. She would solve that problem, and we would only have to worry about replacing the nursing assistant who wasn't working out. I'd gotten friendly with one of the hospital's nursing assistants, a sweet young woman named Vicky. I asked Lisa, what if I approached her about working for us?

"Good idea," Lisa said. "I like her, and I think Mama does too."

Gerry came to the table carrying three stacked Styrofoam containers. The server lady he'd been talking to hollered after him, "Hold it even and you won't spill your beans."

"That's good advice," he called back.

While he'd waited, he'd figured out the wedge problem. "Let's elevate Mama's bed until it comes," he suggested.

That afternoon we poked around in her backyard and found four bricks near the storage shed. We slipped two under each leg of Mama's wooden headboard.

She was released from the hospital as planned on Monday. When she got home and into her propped-up bed, she slid down the sheets until her toes touched the footboard. We pulled her back up. She slid down again. We pulled her back up again and banked fluffy pillows at her feet.

"Don't spill your beans," Lisa said as she kissed Mama goodbye, on her way to Picayune.

What were we to do? How were we to take care of her? What did she need? How could we provide it? Every day we asked ourselves these questions.

Tuesday, when the wedge finally came, Gerry took the bricks out from under the headboard. We positioned it on my mother's queen four-poster on the right side where she liked to fall asleep. We didn't have a pillow slip big enough to fit, and the raw orange foam clashed with the red, pink, and white squares of the hand-made quilt.

"What's that for?" Mama asked, as we gathered at the foot of her bed to stare at the strange new acquisition.

"It's to keep you from getting pneumonia again," I explained without explaining.

"What?"

"That's right," I said. "The wedge is to prevent pneumonia." But as I said this, it seemed unbelievable to me too.

"We're pinning all our hopes on it," Gerry added.

Mama looked at him. Until now she'd appeared to be taking things in stride, without questioning what her trio of caregiver crazies had devised for her. But things were taking a comic turn. And there was something humorous about it, slapstick humor, dark humor, giggle humor, humor crucial to keeping us sane— or in the words of the Shak server, keeping us even. Usually my mother took whatever Gerry said as gospel—he was recognized as the evenest among us—but about this I had the impression (from the tilt of her head, the narrowing of her eyes) that maybe she had doubts. At the same time, I suspected she could see the humor too, see that it allowed us to meet the predicament head on, with some perspective. She turned back toward the living room, slowly pushing her walker.

That night, as she got into bed, she said, "Well, I'm glad that at least y'all took them bricks out." But the wedge sloped more than the bricks, and Mama slid down even deeper in the sheets. We piled more fluffy pillows at her feet. An hour later I looked in on her, only to find that she'd rolled off the wedge entirely and was snoozing placidly.

"Mama," I said, shaking her shoulder. "Please get back on the wedge."

"What's that?" she asked, rousing herself and glancing around the room.

"Get on that wedge!" I pushed it toward her.

An hour passed before Gerry and I went to bed. From our room, I could hear her fumbling in the dark for her walker. "I'm going to sleep in my chair tonight," she called out.

The next day she dozed off and on in the recliner. She went to bed that evening with her head uncomplainingly on the wedge, but after an hour she got back in her chair. We were still up, watching TV. My mother asked plaintively, "What about the Toy Room?"

This had been Daddy's nickname for the spare bedroom that he'd used as a playroom with his granddaughter, my brother's child. "No, Mama, you can't sleep in the Toy Room," I said, not bothering to explain. She spent another night sitting up in her chair.

The following morning even her hair was lifeless. I conference-called my sisters. What were we to do? Clearly, even if she hadn't said so, Mama hated sleeping on the wedge. And who could blame her? We decided to put the bricks back under the bed. That way if she wriggled off the wedge during the night, at least her head would still be elevated.

"But," Lisa mused," if we put the bricks back under, and she stays on the wedge, will she slide right off the bed onto the floor?"

"I tell you what," Debbie said. "Let her have a good night's sleep. She's going to get sick again from exhaustion. We'll worry about it tomorrow."

We let her have an unelevated night's rest. The next day Gerry devised a more-or-less permanent solution. He shoved the wedge under the mattress, where it made a gentler incline. Mama went back to sleeping in her bed.

Spring had rushed in after the last storm, and summer, though not yet on the calendar, followed. The daffodils, azaleas, and irises in my mother's yard gave way as the sycamore and hackberry trees leafed out and the grass turned stubborn green. As the weeks ticked by and we stayed with Mama (Mexico becoming memory), she remained, if not exactly well, with low-grade fevers, well enough to remain at home. On the weekends Ernestine restored us like a tonic. But the idea to replace the nursing assistant who wasn't working out hadn't worked out. Vicky hadn't shown up for the interview.

Then Mama's fevers worsened. One morning Lisa called to say that she'd been in touch with the director at Martha Coker, where a rare, truly private room had become available. A day later Gerry and I walked through the nursing home's double doors and stepped into the director's office. Julie still resembled the classmate I'd known in grade school at St. Clara's Academy; tall and blond, she exuded confidence and calm. She spoke of the good care they would provide my mother and explained the fees. But there was more. In six months, Martha Coker would move into new buildings and become the Martha Coker Green Houses. Three houses were already under construction, with three more planned, each with ten private bedrooms and baths around an open living space. Martha Coker would go from the oldest nursing home in the state to one of the newest-concept eldercare facilities in the country. If we contracted this private room, Mama would be assured of her place in the new Martha Coker. And the new Martha Coker would accept Medicaid. It was magic, Mississippi-style.

Julie took us down the long hallway, past twenty-odd rooms, most housing two people. At the last room on the hall, next to the emergency exit, she swung open the door to where Mama would temporarily live. It was a square room, with a hanging sink but no toilet, and with a big window overlooking the patio. I thought of Eudora Welty's glowing description of the facility when her mother had lived here. But I couldn't get past the room's institutional green paint and worn linoleum floor and the idea that my mother would be living in one room. Gerry slid open the closet doors; he paced off the room's length and width, calculating which pieces of her furniture might fit, because Julie had agreed she could bring some with her. But still I couldn't get over the idea of my mother in one room, away from the other residents, and so far away from us.

As we were saying goodbye, I told Julie we would think about it. She said we had to hurry, because there was another candidate. The pressure felt high because the stakes were high—we were deciding not only for this room, but also for one in the new Martha Coker, which by taking Medicaid would solve our looming financial problems.

We went home and I phone-reported to my sisters. Then we sat down on the loveseat next to my mother, who rocked in her recliner. We described the room. She sat quietly, looking occasionally at me, occasionally out the open door into her front yard.

Finally I asked her, "What do you think?"

She stared off, her dark eyes narrowing. Then she asked, "What does Lisa think?"

I answered that Lisa seemed, reluctantly, for it. That it might be the best care.

She blinked rapidly. "What does Debbie think?"

I answered that Debbie believed she should decide.

After a while she asked, "Well, what about the money?"

"You have enough," I said, though I was unsure if her funds would stretch.

She asked, "Well, what do you and Gerry think?"

I glanced at him. He was starting to tear up. Before I could say anything else, she invoked a reliable standby. "Well, I might as well go on and get it over with."

When I heard that, I decided for her, against the green room at the end of the long hallway. We would take care of her at home for another year. In the spring, when Martha Coker opened the next three Green Houses, well, maybe she would go live there then.

At five o'clock Mama asked for help putting on her pajamas. That night I dreamed the three of us traveled to Antarctica, where we rode in a sled that looked like a long pink sock. Mama was admitted to a hospital, and I couldn't find her. The next morning Gerry said I'd talked in my sleep a lot—I'd been doing that lately—and over the drone of the air conditioner I'd yelled, "Hospital!" When I was a girl and my mother had been in the hospital, I hadn't wanted to visit. Now I was developing a waking and dreaming life around her hospital stays.

Sixteen

The Green Room at the End of a Long Hallway

Several weeks passed. Mama continued taking antibiotics, continued spiking low fevers. One Sunday after we finished dinner, as we relaxed in the living room, Ernestine asked her if she wanted to "porch walk." Six years ago, after her heart surgery, Mama had been able to walk two blocks on our street to therapy, but now she could barely cover the twenty-foot-long porch. She shuffled, stopping near the steps to catch her breath. She spotted a tiny lizard, the color of a spring leaf, resting on an azalea sprig. She studied it. Then she asked Ernestine, "Can we go riding?"

Sunday riding. It's what we'd always done, as a family, as a town. You ate, you drove. You drove the streets you'd always driven—up and down Grand Avenue, up and down Main Street, up and down Broadway, but you did it without purpose. You cruised the houses of the people you knew and those you didn't. You waved at families on their porches, sitting with their paper fans and funny papers. On Main Street you slowed to examine shop windows. "Going riding" reinforced our love of the town; it reinforced our clannishness.

My mother would stare out the car window and ruminate. My father would drive and jabber, his monologues pure nostalgia. Remember the electric trolley that ran from Goose Egg Park to downtown? (It had been the second oldest municipal railway system in the country.) Remember the Soapbox Derby race down Broadway? (He would have won the competition in 1938, but his wheel fell off.) Remember the two-story Santa Claus at the foot of Main Street (and when that boy painted him a black eye)? Remember the dark, chilly evenings of the Christmas parades and the holiday windows at Henick's Auto Supply, decked out with animated displays? My father's reminiscing would often commence with the town and his childhood but come around to the holidays, with their idyllic, simple wonder.

That Sunday in April when we climbed into the Ford, Gerry and Mama sat in the front seat, Ernestine and me in the back. A new family group. Gerry drove south on Grand, past Goose Egg Park and the all-too-familiar hospital, past the majestic Victorians near the canal. Too many of these fine old homes were beyond repair, their broad clapboards rotting, their aged roofs sagging. At Main and Broadway, Mama asked Gerry to park at what had been Anderson's Drug Store, where she and Daddy had met, she told us, sixty years before. That was all she said, and then she sat staring at the empty storefront. I wondered what her memories were, separated from mine by a generation, by a world of change. Did she see the patrons at Anderson's sidling up to the soda fountain? The kids' matinee line at the Dixie Theater and the elegant clientele at the Lamar Hotel? Saxton Hardware, with the country folk squatting out front on a Saturday, exchanging stories and smokes? Or did she see Main Street in its current state of abandon, the same buildings but largely vacant?

We meandered south on Main and north on Washington until we came again to Grand Avenue. Mama pointed and said, "Gerry, drive out this-a-way," and he knew she meant Grand Avenue Extension, so she could check on the progress of the new Green Houses. Nobody spoke; it was as if the car held its breath. As we passed the three half-formed buildings unfolding from the cotton field, she was thinking about it. Living there.

When we got back to the house her fever was up. I called Debbie, and we speculated about other causes—urinary tract infections, drug allergies, the suspicious spot on her lung. Then Ernestine took her smile and went home, and that slow Sunday came to a close.

I felt fatalistic about everything. Fatalistic and very tired. Dragged down, spent, wiped out, gone. Every day I got up early, got my mother to the table, got her breakfast, got her settled in the recliner. I tried to write something, anything, starting when the nursing assistant arrived. At five o'clock each day I fixed my mother's supper. I worried constantly about her medications, especially the four daily shots of insulin timed with her meals. The nursing assistant often drew the Lantus to the wrong amount, so I decided to prepare the syringes myself. But I noticed I didn't always fill them properly either. Administering the insulin posed another dilemma. It needed to be given before eating, but sometimes Mama came to the table and lost her appetite. I worried about causing her to "bottom out," to lose consciousness due to low blood sugar. Everything was complicated.

Some days she would wake from one of her chair naps, and I would see her blank expression and the drool on her chin, and I would hear her weak voice, unable to pronounce a word, even one word, and I would wonder, now what is going on? Has she worsened during her nap? Once she seemed not to know me, but the next morning she was better, flashing me a grin. Some days I had trouble remembering why I'd wanted to be with my mother. Could I last eleven months, until next March, when the three more Green Houses would open up? (Not could she. Could I?) I deserved a separate life. (Didn't I?) Gerry, who might have had conflicting feelings about staying with my mother so long, didn't. Not his nature. He kept busy writing, a new book about cotton farming in the Mississippi Delta.

To escape, some days I went to Ricks Library, as I'd done when I was a teenager, paying a Saturday visit to the periodical corner while Mama sat under the hair dryer in the beauty parlor across the street. I took to furtively reading the obituaries of eighty-four-year-olds in the *Yazoo City Herald* to see what they'd died of. For comfort, at times I thought of Emily Dickinson and her poetry, of her minute observations of the ordinary and the eternal. When I was outside hanging up our wash on the clothesline, I thought of the wind, the clouds, the birds. Those spring days were lovely, with their sharp blue skies, their cool northern breezes. Notice that, I thought.

Then my mother got worse again. The wedge wasn't working. "Mama's care is too complicated to handle at home," Debbie emailed. "We'd wanted to temporize, to wait until next March. But I've felt for some time that she needed to be in a professional environment." My sisters and I debated what to do: Should she stay at home with CNAs (and with us)? Be admitted to the hospital and transfer to its swing-bed program? Go directly to Martha Coker? We consulted with Dr. Thompson and with Mama's home health nurse. In this Bible-minded place, they would not offer advice but would pray for guidance.

We decided to contract the green room at the end of the long hallway. It did seem the best way to get her the best care. It would be affordable long-term, thanks to Medicaid. I don't recall what we said to each other, Mama and I, at the moment of decision. After everything, we slipped quietly to the next step. But on that morning, I made Gerry call Julie.

Then I spent the afternoon curled up on my bed. This was the third week of April. My mother would have to stay only five months in the old facility, I told myself, and she would have a spanking modern room in the new Green Houses. But would she live that long? I'd read the studies. The median length of stay in a nursing home was five months; over 50 percent of patients died within six months of admission. I told myself my mother would be different. She was strong. She had always pulled through. But would she this time? What about the unceasing pneumonia? The suspicious spot on the lung? Would she ever get to the Green Houses? Could she endure what she had to endure to get to a better place?

The day after Gerry phoned Julie, Mama spoke more than she had in months. She would take her recliner with her to Martha Coker, she said, along with Daddy's double bed, the green "Christmas chair," a small bookcase, an end table, her chest of drawers, and her telephone number. She wasn't in the habit of making demands, even simple ones, but she did now. She wanted the canary-colored recliner re-covered. It wasn't good enough for Martha Coker. She wanted new black stretch pants. Her everyday sweats weren't good enough for Martha Coker either. And she wanted a white pleated skirt.

"Y'all threw away my old one because it had mildew on it," she said reproachfully.

"Mama, you never wear skirts. Why do you want a pleated skirt for Martha Coker?"

"It's not for there. I want to be buried in it. That and a navy-blue blazer."

"Okay, Mama, we'll buy you a white pleated skirt."

"And the navy blazer." She wagged her pointer finger.

"Yes, that too."

She didn't feel up to going downtown to the Marylena Shoppe, so that evening frantic catalog shopping ensued—L. L. Bean, Land's End, Lane Bryant—but we didn't find anything. Around eight o'clock, the latest she'd stayed up in months, she asked me sweetly, "May I have a honey bun? Or would that be against the law?"

"What? Would what be against the law?"

"Would it be against the law if I ate a honey bun?"

"No, it wouldn't be against any law, Mama."

During Lisa's last visit, Mama's blood sugar had registered fifty-four one morning, and my sister had practically run the two blocks to the corner grocery to buy twenty dollars' worth of sweets, including a whole carton of honey buns.

Mama ate a honey bun. We increased her Lantus.

The next day depression replaced elation. She refused breakfast. Said she didn't want to go to Martha Coker. But admittance had been slated for the end of April.

"Should we hold off on paying?" Lisa asked. "What should we do?"

"We go on with our plans," I said. "We pay Julie."

Except that Mama's foot was down. Finally she was able to explain that she wanted to be home for Debbie, who was due for a visit in a few days. We agreed with Mama that she would go to Martha Coker a little late.

Anyway, there were things to do. Cancel Mama's gym membership. Dismiss the nursing assistant who wasn't working out. Everywhere I went people seemed judgmental—an old friend, the receptionist at the gym, the server lady at the Pig Shak. Too bad, they said. Mysteriously, Mama's health improved. She was sleeping well, eating well, speaking better. Were we making a mistake? Could she live at home? Gerry and I would have to leave Mexico to help her full-time. But how would we have a life? I began to weave a fantasy. We would rent an apartment in the historic Yazoo downtown and work there in the mornings. We would hire a new daytime CNA. We would sleep at the duplex, except for two nights a week, when we would sleep at the apartment. But how long could we keep that up? What effect would it have on Gerry and our marriage? And what about Mexico? I was more and more confused about which was my "real" life—here, or there. There, or here.

One night Mama's spirits seemed especially ruffled. As I was flipping TV channels, I landed on a Lawrence Welk rerun. Her attention settled on the flamboyant dancers, the corny singers, the champagne orchestra. When I was young my Nicholas grandparents had watched this show, and so had I, from their laps, in the bungalow. Looking at that rerun with my mother, I could pretend that not much had changed over the years. My grandparents hadn't died, Daddy and Sol either. The bubbly music lulled us, took us back. Mama was calmed.

—

The next Saturday Debbie roared up in a metallic-red Mitsubishi convertible. She parked on the grass catty-corner to the driveway, the nose of the shiny car pointing toward the street. As she sat fiddling with the rental car's controls, I stared out the door at my petite big sister in the too-bright red car against the backdrop of a too-bright day; she appeared encircled by blue sky. Mama waited beside me, smiling shyly, her head tilted, her chin tucked. We visited all that afternoon and into the evening, then ate supper and called it an early night. Debbie looked a little older and a little softer, and I was glad to see her. Mama was especially glad.

We were building to Monday, when Mama would go to Martha Coker. Sunday also dawned bright, and Ernestine came to us. She spent the morning ironing labels into my mother's new black pants. Debbie and I fixed a batch of cabbage rolls, boiling the cabbage, separating the leaves, and filling them with meat and rice. About noon, after church let out, Willie Belle joined us and we ate together, the six of us crowded around our small dining table. In the late afternoon, Lisa and her husband, Joel, came in from Picayune.

"What's the plan for tomorrow?" Joel asked, sitting cross-legged on the living room carpet. As a lifelong cyclist, he was the most athletic among us. As a physical oceanographer, he was also the most methodical.

It was a good question, but I hated hearing it, hated admitting why we'd gathered. I said, "Eloise will come at nine to get Mama bathed and settled in her chair." We'd recently hired Eloise, an older lady who drove a vintage Mercedes-Benz, a present from her son. Mama liked her because every afternoon, around four o'clock, Eloise massaged her feet. The plan was for her to visit Mama in the nursing home every day for a while to ease her transition.

"And then what?" my brother-in-law asked.

"Then we're going to use Willie Belle's truck to move Mama's furniture," I said.

"I cleaned it and covered the back with a flowered drop cloth," my aunt added. Since this white GMC truck, circa 1985, had been first my brother's and then my father's, it felt as if they too would be escorting my mother and her belongings to Martha Coker.

The next morning began as planned. While Mama and Eloise waited in the living room, we disassembled Daddy's bed and loaded it with the other furniture into the truck. Minutes later we were at Martha Coker's back gate, and minutes after that we'd finished piling everything into the center of my mother's room, Number 108 in the west wing.

Debbie was seeing the space for the first time, Lisa and I for only the second. The walls weren't green, as I'd remembered them, but the color of putty, and all scarred up.

"We've got to paint it," Debbie said.

"Paint it?" Lisa asked. "When?"

"Now, before she moves in," I replied.

And I knew the color. Gerry went off to ask Julie's permission. Minutes later, he returned. "She said no problem. Asked if we'd like to paint anything else."

Painting the room would make it seem less like a hand-me-down, more like my mother's. But it would delay her coming, and secretly I was glad. She would get to spend one more night at home, one more night with Debbie, which was what she'd wanted all along.

We reconvened at the house to talk it over with Mama. As the five of us gathered in a semi-circle in front of her chair, Eloise politely excused herself and stepped into the kitchen. Debbie explained the situation. Did Mama want us to paint her room?

"I want it," she said.

"What color, Mama?" I asked.

"China Doll," she affirmed.

Debbie and I drove the red convertible with the top down to the Sherwin-Williams up the street, and in twenty minutes they mixed a can of the favored paint. We returned to Martha Coker, where we met up with Gerry. At eleven o'clock Debbie started taping, Gerry and I painting, and in two hours we'd finished a complete coat. Meanwhile, Lisa and Joel visited the dollar store to buy picture frames for some family photos. For an hour we all lounged in the sun on the duplex's porch, lunching on giant barbecue sandwiches from Ubon's.

The painted room looked fresh. Another coat of China Doll wouldn't be needed. While Debbie cleaned paintbrushes and I met with the director of nursing about my mother's diet and medicines, Gerry, Joel, and Lisa positioned Mama's things: Daddy's double bed, with its rustic quilt, against the center wall, and the newly framed photos above the headboard. Next to the bed, the chest of drawers. In the corner by the window, they added a surprise: a Med-Lift recliner in a soft blue fabric. With the push of a button this new chair would boost its occupant to standing. There was only one thing left to do—visit Black's to buy muslin for the curtains Willie Belle had promised to sew that afternoon. In a few hours we had transformed Room 108 into a near replica of Mama's own bedroom.

The next morning after breakfast, after Eloise helped Mama with her bath, we were still postponing the moment. Mama ate an early lunch, and only then did we escort her to Martha Coker. Did she ride in the white Ford Crown Victoria? Or in the shiny red Mitsubishi convertible? Or with Lisa and Joel? I can only remember another blindingly bright blue day.

When we walked through Martha Coker's double doors, we found Julie right there to meet us. "Would y'all like to join us for the employees' tea?" she asked.

My sisters and I looked at one another. My mother leaned heavily on her walker. "No, thanks," I said, "I think we'll take Mama to see her room."

She swapped walker for wheelchair, and we pushed her down the hallway. We opened the door to the room, and she went in. She surveyed the China Doll paint, her furniture, the photo arrangements. "I like it!" she said, pronouncing the word the way she did, *lak*. We pointed out the new chair in the corner, and she exclaimed, "Oh!"

"Careful," I told her, as she tried it out. "Don't push the buttons too fast or you might tip out."

She shot me her sternest *young'un, quit-your-worrying* look. Then she glanced out the window toward the patio, where Joel had hung a cylindrical birdfeeder that swayed under the weight of a dozen greedy sparrows. Again she exclaimed, "Oh!"

And that was all. The world didn't crumble and spin out of control. The dramatic came down to the mundane. With her hard-knock history, my mother could accept whatever fell her way, even living in Martha Coker, the oldest nursing home in the state of Mississippi. It was just another disappointment in her long life. But she was making it easy for us.

After Mama had inspected all the dresser drawers, after she'd peered into the recesses of the dark closet, we stopped by the employees' tea. She ate chicken salad on saltines while we hovered in the background. Soon it came time for supper, and a nursing assistant showed us to the long communal table where my mother would take her meals. Again we hovered behind her. "Mama's not like the others," Debbie whispered. "She doesn't need a bib." But in the days ahead Mama would prove that she was like the others. At least, she did need a bib.

Since arriving Mama had been eating practically nonstop. "It's what we do here," her tablemate said. "We eat." Lisa and Joel had to leave after supper, but Gerry, Debbie, and I stayed with Mama. Debbie and I stretched out on her double bed, Gerry sat in the green chair, and Mama took a seat in the Med-Lift recliner. We watched an old movie. I dreaded leaving her, but by nine o'clock we were exhausted, and unlike her, we three hadn't eaten. Debbie and I helped her into pajamas. We tucked her into bed. We kissed her goodnight.

The duplex looked a wreck. Stuff scattered everywhere on the floor, like storm debris. In my mother's bedroom, eight-track tapes, an old radio, and a VCR. Even the lamp lay on the carpet, because we'd taken the end table to the nursing home. The living room seemed empty, with no TV, no TV stand, and no bookcase. We ate something quickly and went to bed. Gerry and I slept in Mama's bedroom, in her beloved four-poster. I had the experience, for the first time in a long time, of crying myself to sleep. It was grieving for what we'd lost—her at home, her independence, a phase not just of her life, but of ours.

Seventeen

Homecoming

The next Sunday was Mother's Day, and yet another sunny day. This long run of luminous weather seemed out of sync with the dark mood brought on by putting my mother in the nursing home. For the holiday I wanted her back, so we arranged to check her out for a visit. It was easy, the protocol. We just had to sign for her at the nurses' station, get her into the Crown Vic, and drive four blocks to the duplex. It was easy, except it was impossible.

When we arrived at Martha Coker, at eleven o'clock, she was dressed and waiting in the Med-Lift chair, halfway eyeing an old movie. Did she feel like walking out to the car?

"Better put me in the wheelchair," she said.

Invoking the indomitable Ernestine, I asked, "Are you sure you don't want to try?"

"Naw," she replied. (But Ernestine would have cajoled her into doing it.)

I pushed her down the hall, out the front door, and to the curb, where Gerry idled the Ford. After I locked the brakes on the wheelchair, she managed to transfer herself over to the front seat. Gerry heaved the wheelchair into the trunk, and we started for home.

In the living room, she plunked down in her old yellow recliner. "Hunh, the TV's at the nursing home," she said, sounding surprised, though she'd just left it there. She surveyed the boxy room, with its gaps instead of furniture. She knitted her brows and stared out the front door at the sycamores. It was obvious that, in only a few days, all this had become foreign to her. For dinner I'd prepared a Lebanese dish, imjadra, with lentils and rice, and we dutifully went to the dining table. She took her customary place, at the end closer to the living room. Though a favorite of hers, imjadra didn't whet her appetite.

"I'm visiting y'all," she said, but then after that nothing.

After clearing the dishes, I went next door to borrow Willie Belle's spare TV, a portable Sony like my mother's. We no longer had cable, so we watched a cassette of *Holiday Inn*. Despite the familiar cheeriness of Crosby and Astaire, the afternoon ground on. At five o'clock I asked if she would like to stay for supper, homemade pizza, another favorite. She nodded. But after she'd eaten one slice she announced, "I'm ready to go home."

It hadn't occurred to me she wouldn't think of the duplex as home anymore. I wasn't past thinking of it as her home. Though I'd agreed to hand over her care to Martha Coker, I'd been pretending she wasn't all the way theirs. But she knew there was no going back to her old home, which was fast becoming my de facto new one. And she never did again.

———

The personalities of the nurses at Martha Coker slowly began to emerge. Stiffly coiffed but softhearted Eleanora, the director of nursing. Missy, the perky young nurse with the spiky red hair. Steadfast Donna, whose uncle, Mr. Rochester, had bought my grandparents' bungalow. Then there were the nursing assistants: no-nonsense Evelyn, who'd taken care of Vashti during her years at Martha Coker, and Daisy, brassy and fun, who threatened to call the "PO-lice" whenever my mother eschewed her help.

Slowly Mama adjusted. She did seem at home. She enjoyed sitting in her corner, in the Med-Lift chair, monitoring her bird feeder and keeping up with her classic movies. Still she struggled—to walk, to finish her arm and leg exercises, to prettify herself. "My hair's a fright," she sometimes said, lamenting that she didn't yet have a standard appointment with the in-house hairdresser, though she'd long ago given up going to a professional salon. Now that she resided at Martha Coker, a public place, she felt she had to look her best, and so she had her nails painted for the first time in probably forty years. She "loved" her new electric-powered chair (her "favorite thing in the whole world") and her new Keen sandals (all the rage from San Francisco to San Miguel and now Martha Coker) and her new pink chenille bathrobe, fluffy as a cloud. She even admired the shine on her new walker. If she felt sadness, if she felt loss, she kept these to herself. She lived with her standbys at the ready, including "Ain't nothing I can do about it" and "Ain't no need to worry."

Mama's first week in the nursing home wasn't a good one for Martha Coker, with two deaths and a visit from the fire department. It turned out the truck wasn't needed. A resident had opened an emergency exit and wandered the patio briefly before the staff had been able coax her back inside. During my mother's second week I had to clear up a misunderstanding with the dietician. I'd noticed how Mama's dinner plate—with baked chicken instead of fried, plain salad instead of buttered vegetables—looked less savory than her tablemates'. "My fault," I confessed. On the admittance papers I'd checked a low-fat diet. "Food is one of the few pleasures they have," she said kindly, relieved at the reversal.

"Putting" my mother into Martha Coker, I struggled with dislocation so profound as to cause grief, but I also adjusted. I came to accept (more or less) not finding her at home in the canary-colored recliner, though strong bursts of emotion could still hit me at times. When I visited Mama I no longer experienced the longness of the long hallway or noted the vacantness in the faces of the residents, who smiled or waved as I passed. The rundown-ness of the facility, one reason Martha Coker was moving, no longer registered either.

My mother was steady in spirit, but unwell in body. For one thing, she had a loose tooth. During her third week in the nursing home she had it pulled, and the dentist gave her a course of antibiotics, one of many she'd been prescribed all that spring. She iced her jaw and swallowed some Tylenol, and in a few days she seemed recovered.

Then one rainy Friday afternoon, my mother felt worn out. I did too. Sometimes it seemed I'd moved into the nursing home along with her. I lay on her bed, and we tuned into a western starring Henry Fonda, with the prescient title *Welcome to Hard Times*. At five o'clock we made our way down the hall to the yearly barbecue, which, due to the cloudy weather, was being staged in the lobby, on tables set up near the nurses' station. We donned bandannas and funny western hats—Mama a tiny porkpie, which made her look like Buster Keaton, while her bingo rival, Mr. Waters, sported a tiny red cowboy hat. We ate hamburgers and potato salad and baked beans and listened to a live bluegrass band. We had our photograph taken. After the party Mama repeated that she was tired, and Daisy got her into pajamas. Still, when she sank into her bed she giggled as she settled down to sleep.

The next morning she suffered what the nurses described as a "soft fall," her legs collapsing like matchsticks. I'd cajoled her into walking the length of the hallway to the barbecue—was that why? But her vital signs were also poor. We gave her sips of Sprite, and Eloise visited and rubbed her feet. She seemed a bit better, though she drooled, and her eyes were glassy, her face wooden and gray. The nurses hoped she just had a stomach bug.

But the next day she was admitted to the hospital, where they diagnosed *Clostridium difficile*–associated diarrhea, a potentially life-threatening infection caused by extended use of antibiotics. Known among doctors as C. diff, the bacterium was notoriously hard to get rid of, and the drugs they gave for it (there were only two) were harsh. The disease was also highly contagious, and strict hygiene protocols had to be observed. The hospital used disposable plates and cups for her meals and collected her trash in hazardous waste bins.

I wasn't there, because right after the barbecue we'd left for a short break in Mexico. Lisa drove up and slept in the duplex, camping out in the hospital and running errands for Mama during the days and trying to do her editorial work in the evenings. She said that one day shortly after her admittance, Mama asked for help sitting up in a chair, but after only an hour she felt exhausted and had to be escorted back to bed. Still, that day her color was better and her appetite stronger. At lunch she was served a sweet potato pudding with whipped cream, and Lisa told me, "I'm surprised she didn't eat the foam container it came in." Afterward Mama put on her glasses and promptly fell asleep. She napped with a toothpick hanging off her lower lip, until Lisa managed to pull it away.

At one o'clock the nursing assistants knocked to change Mama. Lisa was waiting in the hall when two middle-aged ladies ambled by and introduced themselves. "I'm evangelist Mary and this is evangelist Ruby. Does she [pointing to Mama's door] want us to pray on her?" When Lisa told them that my mother was getting her diaper freshened, evangelist Ruby replied, "Well, tell her we are going to pray on her on the way out to the car." Maybe their ambulatory prayer worked, because Mama was discharged before Memorial Day.

Two weeks had passed in Room 147. All spring she'd suffered from stubborn bouts of pneumonia, the repeated infections coming on her like waves on a beach, and we were afraid the same thing would happen with the intractable C. diff. Dr. Thompson warned us she might need several more treatments to be free of it. I felt fatalistic about this too. Fatalistic and still tired. To take my mind off things, in San Miguel I signed up for a Spanish literature class at a university, along with some other gringos. Gerry and I had been trying to put our life in Mexico back together, getting to know more Americans, fashioning an expat support group to help cope with any future calamities that might well befall us there.

We visited Mama in late June, and she was well enough to attend a sing-along in the dining hall at Martha Coker. We visited her again in late July, and she attended another sing-along. With physical therapy she learned to walk again, even to walk the length of the long hallway. But the return of her well-being could no longer be taken for granted. Something fundamental had shifted, and not only with my mother's health. That summer almost everything—the personal, the professional, and the public—started syncing up in a bad way. My agent abruptly ended her representation of my unsold manuscript. Stock markets fell and big banks collapsed, shattering faith in the economy and replacing it with more financial worry about the future.

In July we paid Mama the final installment on the duplex. The money went into her bank account and right back out to Martha Coker. We had one other expenditure. Since Medicaid allowed its beneficiaries to prepay burial costs, we handed over to Mr. Haymer, the funeral home's representative, payment for Mama's service. I finally bought her burying clothes, which we stored in Willie Belle's closet to keep them safe from any mold spores that might be lurking in the duplex. Soon my mother's funds fell below the legal limit, and we began the process of applying for Medicaid. All we needed now was for the Green Houses to open.

We visited Mississippi again in September. The days were again bright and blue, and my mother appeared free of C. diff. She'd had many ups and downs, but for now she was up, though the next down might be just a bend away. During my afternoon visits I sat on Mama's bed and pleaded with her to tell me her life story. It seemed a good moment to start an exploration of her past. Besides, there was something nostalgic and reflective about late September in Mississippi, when the long season of heat finally began to wind down. We had nothing but time together, though it also seemed our time together might be running out.

"Mama, tell me about growing up," I said, on the last afternoon of that month.

She glanced out the window at the scattering of dusty leaves on the patio pavers, at the busy metallic birdfeeder, at anywhere but me. "Don't nobody want to hear nothing about that mess," she replied. How often she'd said that. Another reliable standby.

I assured her that somebody did. I didn't want her one-room tar paper shacks to fall into the past without a description from her, her hard-knock farming life to disappear without an acknowledgment, and her inimitable sentence constructions to go unrecorded. I didn't want her to die without hearing her talk about herself and her past. This is the story she told me, and what she might have told me, if she'd had the words and time.

Eighteen

Mama Speaks

My mother sat straight up in the blue Med-Lift chair, her feet flat on the floor, her gray head bowed. I had come to her room prepared with my red schoolgirl's notebook and fine-point pen. Years had directed us to this moment. The years of feeling we weren't close; the years of separation; then these last years of changed circumstances, when I'd longed to know more about her past life but had learned less about her than about the anatomy of her illnesses. How to elicit my mother's reluctant memories? How to explore her silences?

During her young adult years, whenever she'd visited with her seven brothers and sisters in Grandma Hood's house on Dunn Avenue, they'd sat around smoking and reminiscing about old hard times. As a child I'd heard snatches of their stories as I'd run in and out of the living room, racing around with my cousins. My mother's siblings slapped their knees and shared full-throated laughs at the hard knocks they rehashed. They were not criers. Rather than complaining about the past, they enjoyed the camaraderie it provided. But Mama, more of a face-palmer and mm-hmmer, assumed the role of onlooker.

So how to begin? I would conduct an interview. Did she remember her grandparents? Did she remember her father? "Naw, naw," she answered, fluttering her long fingers at me. Perhaps it was true after all, what she'd maintained—it wasn't that she didn't want to remember her childhood, she just plain didn't remember. We sat in silence awhile. *Don't nobody want to hear nothing about that mess.* Then she raised her head. She'd made a decision to tell me what she could, the best way she knew how. To go on, get it over with.

———

"The first thing I remember was my daddy dying. I was sitting in the kitchen and he was out in the yard, leaning on the chicken house, and he slid down dead. We was living up in the Delta. It was August and hot, hot, and we traveled for what seemed like days to get the body back to Midway for the funeral. We buried him at Primitive Baptist." John Wesley Hood had died on August 27, 1929. He was forty-three years old.

"I can recall the church service," she said after a pause. "I fell asleep on a wooden bench, and my aunts low-rated me for it. But I wasn't but five years old."

She'd spoken these first words haltingly. She hadn't looked at me, sitting on her bed, but at the floor, the sharp light falling across her tired face. These must have been her deepest hurts, which she'd hung on to for decades: the death of her father on a hot August morning and an undeserved scolding at his funeral by her many aunts.

She added: "I don't remember Daddy except for when he died. We wasn't close."

He had been married before, she said, and had brought with him two young children, Johnny and Annie, when he married Nettie Lee Gilmore. She was fifteen the day of her wedding in December 1913. She and John Wesley quickly had four children together, all born before 1920: Wilmer, Ethel, Otis, and Lucille. Then the twins in 1924. They had been named to rhyme, Florence Adele and Lawrence Odell, but they were always called Sister and Brother.

"When Brother and me was born, I come out first. That's what they said," Mama continued. "I come out first and was bigger and stronger. After us come Ada and J.W. When Daddy died, Mama was pregnant with J.W." She'd laid out the whole family, all her siblings.

"Where were you and Brother born?" I asked, though I believed I knew the answer.

"We was born in Midway. At home. Those days, nobody went to a hospital."

"How long after you were born did your family move to the Delta?"

"We went up there sometime after that. Things got bad and people wasn't making any money and Daddy had heard there was work up in the Delta. We went up there and hoped to do better. It wasn't just him that went. One or other of his brothers went with him. In the Delta we was like gypsies. Every year a new place. Well, sometimes we stayed on two years in the same place. We was in Indianola, Arcola, Shaw, and Greenville, but we always lived out in the country. We farmed cotton on other people's land. We moved around to get work. We lived in raggedy houses." She sighed, letting out the air with a *whoosh*.

"What else do you recall?" I asked, afraid she might stop just as she was beginning.

"Like I told you, I don't remember much of my childhood. And it ain't important." She hung her head and studied the linoleum floor.

"Mama, tell me what you remember. What were you like, you and Brother?"

She sighed again, but more quietly. Then she continued. "I was a timid child. So shy Mama said I didn't even know to get in out of the rain. Brother was sickly. He had asthma something bad. Mama would build a tent with a blanket and put Brother in there with some Vicks salve in hot water. They would set up all night with him."

She added, glancing toward me, "I know a little story I might could tell you."

"Sure," I nodded.

"Johnny, my half-brother, was setting up with Brother one night trying to let Mama rest. He was rocking Brother in front of the fireplace, and he got so sleepy he couldn't hardly stand it. Daddy had some moonshine whiskey in a quart jar, and he got on to that and sat down in front of that fire, rocking Brother all the time, and he got to sipping on that whiskey and drank near the whole jar of it. He said it was the first time he ever got drunk, and he never done it again."

Perhaps this little story had been one of those rehashed in the Hood family gatherings. Perhaps that was why she'd remembered it. Or perhaps the story had stayed with her because she considered it off-color. What struck me was the existence of her half-brother in her remembered life. I'd rarely heard her speak about him or her half-sister, Annie. Had I ever met them? They'd been like phantoms, unlike her full siblings.

I asked, "Did they ever take Brother to the doctor? For his asthma?"

"We didn't go to any doctor. We did not know what a doctor was. The only time I can remember going to see a doctor was when I had to go for my eyes. We had to ride several miles in a wagon. Some people named McQueen took us to Greenville to see a Dr. Davis. A skin came over my eye. He gave me medicine, and it cleared up."

She added, "But that was the only time."

"Okay," I said. "What happened after your daddy's funeral?"

"After Daddy was buried, in summer of twenty-nine, we went back up to the Delta so Mama could get the crop out. That was when I started picking cotton. Snakes would dart out from behind the weeds as we walked to and from the fields. It would be hot as blazes, and my hands would get all scratched up. I had to work like thunder to stay caught up with the others. Boys ploughed and planted. Girls hoed and picked. Well, everybody hoed. And the boys picked cotton too. Mama worked in the house cooking our meals and in the fields.

"Teresa, I know a little story on Grandma Hood. If you want to hear it."

I assured her I did.

"Well, one day a traveling salesman passed the house and threw out a box of snuff. Mama didn't drink or smoke, but she tried it and got drunk as a Cooter Brown. She lay on her back under a big pecan tree and kept looking at a cloud off in the distance. She told us children, 'We won't go back to the field until we see what the cloud does.' I was tickled to death, but the little cloud cleared out, and we had to go back to picking cotton anyway."

"That doesn't sound like Grandma Hood," I said.

"That night she saw the stove dance," Mama added, and smiled.

"Did you ever get to play as a child?" I asked. "Or was it all hard work?"

"I played mostly with Brother," she said. "They would put the cotton in the shed, and we would play on it. Dig a hole in the cotton and put my head in like I was standing on it. We would go out into the woods, rake leaves, and make houses out of the leaves. One time Mama went to town, and we got us a ball. We played ball, but we wasn't any good at it. And another thing," she said. "Our house was a dump. Wherever we lived. Once we lived in a shotgun house—one room after another. It had a tin roof, and when it rained it played like a drum. We slept three deep in iron beds. There would be a room full of beds."

Now her memories were coming faster. "Mama slept with Lucille. She was a tattletale. Ethel slept with Mama too. I slept with Ada. In the summertime the house was hot and in the wintertime it was cold. We hugged the fire. The house was heated by a fireplace and a cookstove, and we slept under quilts Mama made by hand. Old scrap quilts with flour sacks for the backing."

It was something we'd shared—shame about the houses we'd grown up in. But at last I saw why she had more patience for the duplex's shabbiness than I did. At least the duplex had been hers, a house she didn't have to run from every year or two.

"You want to know what kind of furniture did we have?" she said, though I hadn't asked. "We had a beat-up old table for eating off of. Some old hard benches to sit on. No couch. No refrigerator. No running water." She shook her head.

"What did you do for water?"

"We had pumps up in the Delta. You'd pump that pump until you got it primed and water would gush out. Or you would get you a big barrel and put it under the edge of your house and let rainwater collect. We was always toting water."

Out of necessity the Hoods were subsistence farmers, without knowing the term. "We had us a vegetable garden. Had to have a garden to live. We all worked in the garden. I didn't like working in the garden because it was a lot of work. We grew potatoes and green beans and peas and turnip greens. We had a sweet potato patch, and we would bake those sweet potatoes in the ashes and eat them. They tasted so good. Mama would put up vegetables for the winter. We ate pretty good because Mama had the garden."

The family also furnished their own meat. The boys hunted squirrel and deer. "Mama killed a hog every year, a big one. He lasted a long time. Mama would make chitterlings, but I hated that mess. We made souse out of the head. Cooked it with salt and pepper. We would pick the meat off the head and congeal it. We ate it with biscuits and corn bread. We didn't know what a cracker was until we got growed up. When a cotton bale was ginned, we would get to buy some sausages packed in cottonseed oil. But that was our only store-bought meat."

She stopped to stare out the window at the birds at her feeder. She'd taken me with her to the Mississippi Delta, to the years right before and during the Great Depression. Her father had died two months before the financial crash in October of '29.

"Teresa, I still don't know why you want to hear all this."

"Mama, I do. It's important to me. Please don't stop."

"I hope you don't want to write about it," she said.

"I can't promise that."

"Well, I didn't tell you about going to the one-room school," she went on. "We lived in Greenville in two places. One was a two-story house. Imagine that. We had to walk a country mile to get to the one-room schoolhouse. We would go to school after the crop was put up in fall and before we begun planting in spring. For a time I didn't have any shoes, and Wilmer toted me piggyback all the way to school. Seemed like a long way. Everybody else had shoes. Like I told you, we lived out in the country, and finally when Mama went to town she bought me some shoes." She added, "You know, Teresa, somewhere there's a photograph of me in front of that little schoolhouse."

As she said this, I thought of another September day a few years ago, when she and I had gone riding together. It had been another drawn-out afternoon, with the heat of the sun still strong, with the sky an immense surrounding blue. All that day we'd hung around her living room, the humidity sticking to us like paste. Let's go for a ride, I finally suggested, and she readily agreed—anything to get out of that house. We meandered through the familiar territory south on Highway 49 toward Jackson. While my mother looked out her window, studying the kudzu-wrapped hills and telephone poles, I drove the Crown Vic at low speed. There was little traffic, and what traffic there was passed us without fanfare. Near the town of Bentonia the hills leveled off, and tucked among the stands of trees were snatches of cotton fields, newly picked of lint. My mother didn't speak, but I thought she seemed pleased about something. In downtown Bentonia I drove us past the Blue Front Café, where a few elderly Black men had come to sit on the run-down porch. Then I made a U-turn to the highway. Bound for home, Mama said, "Lazy days, after the crop's been put up."

I couldn't have guessed what she'd been thinking—that she'd taken in the fall landscape and remembered a string of uncommon, lazy days. Days of loafing in the warm sun, of smelling the acrid, omnipresent wood smoke, of hearing the stabbing cries of the blue jays, of dawdling on the dirt road to school. "Lazy days, after the crop's been put up." I couldn't have guessed, because I'd hardly heard my mother speak, and certainly not ever wistfully, about the early years of her family life. But perhaps I should have known, because it was the land, and our relationship to it, that defined so many of us here. Mama was no exception, and as poor farmers, she and her family had epitomized this. Small example: Brother and the gardens he tended as an adult. Every year he planted a huge vegetable garden, complete with melon patch and cornfield. A lot of the produce he simply gave away.

In the duplex, during the evenings, I dug around in bookshelves and bureau drawers for old family Bibles and photographs. In an early baby photo, tiny and overexposed, the twins Florence and Lawrence lay bonneted in a dresser drawer lined with an old quilt, shoulder to shoulder, their legs extended, with his right touching her left, his head inclined toward hers. Mama had told me that she "came out first" and was "bigger and stronger." She was also darker, her complexion tending toward olive, while her brother's skin was paler and suggested frailty. In the photo a bedspread has been draped on a clothesline for their protection from the sun, while behind them stand the leafy stalks of June-high cotton.

In a photograph taken about five or six years after their birth, Brother's right side still touches his twin's left, and he still appears paler and slighter. Yet more cotton grows in the background. Another photo from half a dozen years later shows six out of the eight Hood children posing before a tree, including the twins. My mother, wearing a cinched print dress, stands in front of a large branch, along with her older brother and sister, Otis and Lucille; the youngest children, J.W. and Ada, sit on the ground before them. Lawrence kneels in the picture's lower right, still looking less robust than his twin sister.

Searching the duplex also yielded a cache of photocopied documents relating the history of both the Hoods and the Gilmores—yellowed pages written by distant relatives and distributed at long-ago family reunions. The twins' parents, John Wesley Hood and Nettie Lee Gilmore, had each been one of eight children, with three Hoods marrying three Gilmores in their generation. Florence and Lawrence had come into an isolated, deep-country world populated nearly exclusively with Hoods and Gilmores.

The Hoods could trace their histories in Mississippi for five generations. Mama's great-great grandfather, John Hood, had been born in 1775 in South Carolina and had married a woman from Georgia, Mary, fifteen years his junior. Shortly after their marriage, they'd moved to the southern part of the new state of Mississippi. John farmed in Perry County, and when he died at the age of seventy-five he was said to have possessed real estate valued at two hundred dollars. One of his four sons, Samuel, traveled north in the state and when he was twenty-two married Mary Laura, also from Georgia, in Yazoo City. After settling in Scott County, in central Mississippi, Samuel farmed, accumulating a modest estate. He died of unknown causes in 1860, at the age of thirty-two.

Of Samuel's four children, the eldest, John, also died young, knifed at a molasses mill. Only twenty when he was killed in

1875, John thought himself a ladies' man. He kept a little leather diary in his pocket in which he would jot poetry to the women he admired. To one, in his fancy hand, he wrote, "I love you better than anything in the whole world, except fried gosling." But John was also considered by many to be a mean man, and the townspeople drew straws to determine who would get the chance to kill him. So went family lore, and to this day the little diary, in the possession of my aunt Willie Belle, bears the knife lick.

Louis Patrick, Samuel's third son, was the marrying kind, not the wooing kind like his brother, and on August 18, 1879, in Scott County, he wed the stern-faced Temperance Pricilla Warren, who, if her photographs are any indication, had a liking for broad-brimmed, feather-trimmed hats. After their brother John's untimely death, Samuel's three surviving children, including Louis Patrick and Temperance, nicknamed Tempe, moved to Yazoo County. They settled in the Benton-Midway hills, farmed, and raised eight children.

The family Bible provided more detail about my mother and her parents. In 1910, Louis Patrick and Tempe's second born, John Wesley Hood, married his first wife, Allie, and they had Johnnie and Annie and lived for a time in Arkansas, where John Wesley worked in a sawmill. After Allie died, John Wesley married the fifteen-year-old Nettie, the same year Nettie's mother died. They settled in Midway and had their eight children, including my mother. Louis Patrick and Tempe (who had been born twenty-four days apart, in the spring of 1859) died a few days apart in the fall of 1921. On the day of Tempe's death, the mourning, prescient Louis Patrick wrote out his last will and testament, declaring, "After the death of my wife and myself, and my debts are paid, I give, devise, and bequeath all of my estate both real and personal to my children, to be equally divided between them." But what did his estate consist of? Family lore—again, family lore—held that Louis Patrick had owned land, but also that, somehow, he'd lost it. But if L.P.'s land had been bequeathed to John Wesley and his siblings, even just a scrap of land, why would he and Nettie have moved from Midway a few years later, hoping for farming opportunities in the Delta? It was history lost to history.

———

There had also been five generations of Gilmores in Mississippi, but less is known about them. William Monroe Pierce, from North Carolina, had married Mahala Hammons, from Alabama, and by 1860 they lived in Neshoba County, about a hundred miles east of Yazoo County. Their daughter, Melissa Pierce, who was born in Mississippi in 1845, married Elijah Gilmore, a Methodist minister, who served a year in the Confederate Army. According to Elijah's discharge certificate, he stood five feet eight inches tall, had blue eyes and "yellow" hair, and worked as a farmer. When he was released from the 36th Mississippi Infantry Regiment in 1863, due to a scrotal hernia, the Army gave him the grand sum of $8.08. Once discharged, he and Melissa set about having children, eight in all, until Elijah died plowing in the fields one day. Among their offspring was George Hanna Gilmore, who wed Nannie Ruth White in 1894. They, too, had eight children, including my grandmother Nettie.

My mother was a fifth-generation Mississippian on both sides of her family. The Hoods and Gilmores had been some of the earliest settlers in central Mississippi, having come from older states such as the Carolinas and Georgia. Some, like Louis Patrick, had been small-time farmers, owning their land, but others, including my mother and her parents, had resorted to tenant farming or share-cropping. As farmers they had acquired associated skills such as carpentry (they could build a chicken house), farriery (trim the mule's hooves), and butchery (kill the fall hog). They died early deaths from heart attacks and childbirth. Some died violent deaths, and not only the foolhardy poet and ladies' man John. "Died in the early 1920s when team ran away and wagon and load of posts fell on him," one relative noted in her Bible about her unlucky spouse.

In the old photographs, my mother's kin looked stalwart and unsmiling, but it said something about them that they had money and gumption enough to have any photos taken at all. In later generations, in Kodak snapshots, they were overweight and toothless, but they smiled. In one, the middle-aged Nettie poses with her siblings while wearing a loose shirtwaist dress, rolled stockings, and blue scuffs; in the background are scrubby grass and leafy trees, and a stretch of land with dips and rises. In almost all our family photos there is dense vegetation. These were country people, not Delta but hill people, even though those hills might be at most three hundred feet high. I imagined they could tell a story about what had happened a century ago as if it had happened to them yesterday. Out of necessity they were thrifty and cautious and sometimes grim. They compensated for hard luck with hard work. And by and large, with one or two exceptions, hard work had killed them.

Nineteen

Mama Speaks Another Day

It was mid-October and the beginning of a new week when Mama and I sat together again in her room for another interview. That day her memories stemmed from the decade of the thirties. "I knew we lived in the Depression," she told me, "but that meant nothing to us." Their life was already so harsh that a global depression added little to their misery.

Sometime after John Wesley was buried and the fall crop gathered in the Delta, Nettie, a widow at thirty-one, moved her children back to Midway. My mother's timeline about returning to Chew Forks Road was hazy. But she clearly recalled, "Our house in Midway was a dump." Wilmer, at fourteen, became the titular head of the household.

Many of Mama's Hood and Gilmore aunts and uncles lived in the Midway–Benton vicinity. One of them, Will Hood, had acquired some land that was said to have belonged to Louis Patrick and Tempe. Some seasons my mother and her siblings worked for him; Uncle Will paid each child a dime a day to help tend his crops. I asked Mama how it was to be employed by her uncle. "Hard work didn't kill Uncle Will," she answered.

In Mississippi, at the turn of the twentieth century, a third of white farmers were either sharecroppers or tenant farmers. Of these non-landowners, sharecroppers were the most impoverished. They had no resources—no cash, no livestock, no tools; they farmed a plot of land for the owner and received a share of the crops they produced. Tenant farmers fared a bit better. They had some livestock and tools and enough cash to rent a piece of land. My mother told me that some years they gave a portion of their cotton (like Bossie, Mama believed it was a quarter) to the landowner; yet at times they did own some livestock, chickens, hogs, and a cow or two. Whether the Hoods sharecropped or tenant-farmed depended on that year's circumstances. Mama skirted the whole issue by referring to her family as dirt farmers. Their yield would usually consist of one bale of cotton.

The clannish Hood and Gilmore aunts and uncles visited often. "All of them was overweight and wore plain clothes, whatever they could scrape up," my mother said, by way of describing her relatives. During these visits, the adults slept in the beds, while the children camped on quilt pallets on the floor. The adults ate first, while the children made do with chicken feet and doodle gravy, concocted from water, lard, flour, and maybe a tomato for flavoring. "I bet Mama made our house in doodle gravy," my mother said.

If she didn't run and hide from him, Uncle Joe would rub his whiskered face all over hers. "Aunt Myrt and Mattie was the kissing aunts," Mama said. "We would run from them like a turkey." Aunt Myrt visited often after her husband, Andrew, died, and she "would cry all night long because she missed him." But Aunt Lula was sweet. She also lived on Chew Forks Road, and whenever she visited she brought along her twins, Charles and Charlene. Longevity wasn't a family trait. Aunt Addie died young, of cancer. Aunt Florence died young, in childbirth. Uncle Will died young, my mother said, of "meanness."

The Hoods didn't have many close neighbors on Chew Forks Road, though one Black family did live nearby. "We was scared of them," Mama said. "We didn't have trouble, but we was afraid they'd do us harm." She seemed unaware of any irony as she confessed to this. "Sometimes I would hear their hound dogs. I laid awake many a night thinking they was going to get me." One cold snap when the hogs went missing, the Hoods suspected these neighbors. But, Mama said, "There came a big freeze and all the ponds froze up. We looked for the hogs ever'where. Then when spring rolled around, there was the hogs in the pond. They had gone across and dropped in and drowned."

In a 1942 study conducted by the state of Mississippi, only 14 percent of white sharecroppers were found to have radios, and only 10 percent had refrigerators. "In the summer, the iceman came house to house," Mama said. "Still didn't have no refrigerator. We would buy twenty-five pounds of ice and put the milk in the cistern. It was a hole in the ground and usually had some bricks or something up around it. You had this big old bucket with a rope and pulley on it that you let down in there. Get it full, bring it back up. Sometimes the cisterns would go dry if you didn't have a lot of rain."

During farming season, from March until September, Mama and her siblings trailed the sun, toiling in the cotton fields from sunup to sundown, from "can see" to "can't see." In the off-season, if there weren't any regular chores that needed doing, Nettie found them some work, clearing brush or pulling weeds for the hogs.

"She mail-ordered our overalls, but she cut out flour sacks and sewed our underwear by hand. We wore rags. We had a picture of me and Brother, I don't know where it got off to, but you could tell what we wore. I don't think Mama cared one way or the other."

She went on. "I don't remember ever wearing a blouse or sweater. I don't know what we wore to school. Mostly I just put on what I had. I was ashamed of my clothes. When we wore out our shoes, we had to go barefoot. We didn't have enough money for nothing. We was powerfully poor. We didn't have what other people had.

"I wished for clothes out of catalogs. I didn't get a pretty dress until I was practically growed up. It was white on top and blue checked on the bottom and the prettiest dress I ever saw. I wore it ever'where. I was in high school. Mama bought the material, and a colored lady made it for me."

Nettie could seem uncaring in other ways. When my mother grew fond of a baby chicken with a crimped leg, she wasn't encouraged in her attachment. One day she came home to find him floured and fried. "Mama didn't even tell me that she was cooking him," she said. "I didn't cry, but I didn't eat any. But the others hogged him down."

In the Delta my mother had been known by her middle name, Adele, but her youngest sister's given name was Ada Belle, and in Midway, their classmates confused them. Mama decided to call herself by her first name. One day a boy commented to Lucille, "Your sister Florence sure is pretty." To which Lucille replied, "I don't have no sister named Florence." Nothing about school ever came easy to her; she was in her teens before she learned to read. "Well, I guess they did teach me how, but I didn't follow suit. I finally picked it up on my own. Then I read anything I could lay my hands on," she said.

At home the others laughed at her because she would hide in a closet with her book. "They hated school and liked being outdoors, even if it meant picking cotton, because if Mama wasn't looking they could run up and down the rows in a snatched game of tag." She graduated from elementary school in 1940, at sixteen. Afterward the family moved closer to the small town of Benton, where she attended high school. "They had a library," she said proudly. I thought of the books she and I had read when I was a teenager—*Rebecca*, *Jane Eyre*, *Wuthering Heights*. Many with shy, socially awkward, independent heroes and heroines.

Brother outgrew his asthma, dropped out of high school, and in 1943 joined the Marines, while my mother raised a red-and-white calf to pay for her junior ring. She graduated from Benton High when she was twenty years old, on May 29, 1944, one of seventeen in her class. According to the school annual, *The Flight of the Benton-17*, classmate Florence Hood's favorite expression was "Jeepers." The class of '44 had trouble keeping its members together in this town that normally saw little change. They lost male classmates and teachers to the draft and to enlistments. Their superintendent went into the Navy, another teacher to the Air Corps. They lost female classmates who left to marry young and start a family with their sweethearts while they had a chance. All but two graduates were girls.

Social functions were few, and those lucky enough to have cars were urged to save on gas and tires. My mother, dogged by timidness and shame, had few girlfriends, and it was hard to imagine her

at the formal senior banquet given by their class sponsor. The girls wore evening gowns, dined on fried chicken, sang "You'll Never Know," the class song, and later drove to the picture show to see a Bette Davis movie, *Old Acquaintance*. In my mother's school portrait she stared out at the camera, her hair drawn back to expose a sensitive face. She was pretty, with dark wavy hair, almond black eyes, and full lips. But she was going out into the world with hurt in her expression and only the trace of a smile.

After their father's death, the Hoods had stayed together, but soon after Brother left for the war the family began to scatter. Wilmer married his fiancée, Hazel, and they took up farming near Holly Bluff; Otis married Bet while standing on a plank over a ditch, and they also farmed at Holly Bluff; the baby boy who had been born after their father died, J.W., tried to enlist at sixteen; Ethel ran off to live with Auntie Loggins until she married Ches and they began farming at Tchula; Lucille attended Draughon's Business School in Jackson; Ada finished at Benton High and worked as a telephone operator. My mother worked in a Bentonia lumberyard, then in a Greenville meat factory, and then for the telephone company, first in Canton, later on in Yazoo City. (She'd met Mr. Waters, who was now her bingo rival, at the phone company in Yazoo, where he'd been her colleague.) She had her first boyfriend in Canton, a college student. But she didn't much like him, or any boy. "I didn't trust them," she said.

Finally Brother returned home from fighting overseas. He'd been in the Battle of Iwo Jima, and was stationed in Nagasaki after the atomic bomb. "Ever'body sure was glad to see him," Mama said. The day he got off the Greyhound bus in Yazoo City, on August 6, 1946, after serving three years and five months in the Marines, he started as an attendant at the Rose Oil gas station on Broadway. My mother, Ada, and Lucille went to live with him and their mother on Dunn Avenue, in what would become their family's homeplace. Finally they didn't live in a rented shack, a "dump," but in a solid house that belonged to them.

We'd talked all afternoon, and Mama wasn't finished yet.

—

Was it love at first sight? That evening after supper, I went back to the nursing home and retook my seat on Mama's bed to ask her about meeting my father.

"Daddy was my next boyfriend. He was nice to me," she said. "I thought he was handsome." In a photograph taken in the Nicholas Cash Grocery around the time they met, in 1947, my father looked more flesh than bone. Since graduating from Yazoo High, three years before, and posing for his senior portrait, he'd gained some weight. Now his face appeared full, with its high forehead, wide temples, and bell cheeks. His best features were his thick, black, curly hair and his large amber eyes, and his hands with their strong, well-proportioned fingers. What did she think about his being Lebanese? "It didn't bother me that he was Lebanese," she said. "He seemed like other people. He was just half Lebanese anyway."

After high school he'd gone to work at his father's grocery, shelving canned goods, loaves of bread, and bulky cellophane bags of cookies. He'd sliced sandwich meats and cheeses at the deli counter, toward the rear of the long, narrow space. He'd waited on customers from the front counter, many of them elderly Black men who lived beyond the railroad tracks. Though the store was called the Nicholas Cash Grocery, much of what it sold was on credit, and my father would record these purchases in an oversize binder. Sol Jr. kept the books for his father, and one day he hoped to set up a bookkeeping office in the building's loft.

My mother sidestepped my question about whether she felt love at first sight.

"Well, where did you meet him?" I asked, though I knew from our Sunday drive.

"Anderson's Drug Store," she said. "Corner of Main and Broadway." He had the habit of getting together with his pal George Thomas at the drug store's soda fountain, where they enjoyed Cokes, milk shakes, and malted milks. George and he were both Lebanese bachelors, Catholic boys who still lived at home. George's parents also owned a small grocery, but theirs was located away from downtown on River Road, facing the Yazoo River. Sometimes the friends—George was five years older—teamed up with two other young Lebanese men in Yazoo, Armeen Weber and Jimmy Moses, to take George's pretty cousins, Mary and Lena Thomas, dancing in the Delta, as far north as Clarksdale, more than a hundred miles away.

"Every day at five I left the phone company on Jefferson Street. I was shy for an operator," Mama confided. One evening, she stopped by Anderson's. That was unlike her. Usually she went straight home to tend to her homebound mother, who suffered from obesity and diabetes and other chronic ailments. "And there was your daddy," she said.

"While we were courting, we ate out a lot in Yazoo City. Once we went to Primos in Jackson. We would drive to Holly Bluff to the Quonset Hut, where we danced and ate. Your daddy was a good dancer," she said, something I would never have guessed.

"He proposed after a couple, three years. I was still working at the phone company. Living on Dunn Avenue." Growing up around Midway, she'd looked to Yazoo City as her go-to town. If her family shopped on Saturdays, it would be there, not Greenwood, Vicksburg, or Jackson. All her life she'd lived in the country, off isolated roads with their encroaching woods and ankle-deep dust. She'd heard that city folks said they could identify a country hick by the dirt on his eyelashes. Once she lived in town she had no pretensions, but she tried to put the country, and all that it invoked, behind her: her father's untimely death; the casual cruelty of her relatives, including her own mother; the grueling cotton season; the perennial deprivation.

She married my father on May 21, 1950. The announcement in the *Yazoo City Herald*, which ran beside an article about a graduation wiener roast for the seniors at Benton High, was headlined, "Solomon Nicholas Jr. Marries Miss Hood at St. Mary's Church." Their formal wedding took place on a temperate Sunday afternoon at four o'clock. Tall baskets of white gladioli flanked the high church altar. While the guests were being escorted to their seats, Mrs. Helen Cummings played Schubert's "Serenade" and "Traumerei" and Roswig's "Ave Maria." For the wedding processional the pianist segued to Lohengrin's "Wedding March" and for the recessional, Mendelssohn's "Wedding March."

The bride's brother Otis "gave her away." Her five bridesmaids wore white organdy over green taffeta, with a side bow and green streamers, the *Herald* reported. The bride wore "white satin with a lace bodice and lace sleeves ending in calla lily points," and at her neck "a yoke of net formed the high jewel-neckline with which she wore a single strand of pearls." Her "satin skirt was fashioned with points of lace over which she wore a covering of net, ending in a long train." She carried a white prayer book and a single purple orchid with cascading white satin streamers. (Why the prayer book? She'd never been baptized, until she converted to Catholicism, a condition she'd had to accept in order to marry my father.)

Following the ceremony, conducted by Father Charles Hunter, the bridal couple and guests attended a reception at the groom's parents' home on Grand Avenue in Yazoo City. There, in the refreshing cool of the north-facing dining room, the mahogany table draped with a white lace cloth, the couple cut a three-tiered white wedding cake trimmed in green. The wedding party posed for a photograph in the living room, in front of the gas fireplace, and the bride slipped her hand into the groom's. They left for a short honeymoon trip to the Gulf Coast. When they returned, they would make their home with his parents.

"Grandma treated me really well," Mama said about Vashti and the nine years that followed in the bungalow. And I'd thought they hadn't gotten along. That Vashti had held herself above her daughter-in-law, and that Mama had kept her distance.

—

Why was I interested in hearing all this? That was what my mother kept asking.

All my life my father had spoken about his family, about his grandparents from Lebanon, "the old country." How they had come to Mississippi with my toddler grandfather at the turn of the twentieth century and established a general merchandise store on Broadway, next to the railroad tracks. How they expanded it to include the grocery. How they lived over their businesses, raised their children there. How they died, George in 1939, Rosa in 1943. Many times, I'd admired their imposing pink granite tombstone in the cemetery, with its inscription *George Nicholas Family*. Their lives had centered on family, as had my father's.

My father's story became the dominant narrative of our lives. My mother wasn't one to romanticize old times the way Daddy tended to, but did she also dwell somewhere in the land of the past? Now she'd recalled her early years as best she could, its details and its big events, its tone and substance. What was my mother's relationship to the past? I should have known from her stance on living in the nursing home. She'd made the transition from home to Martha Coker and hadn't looked back. There was no returning to her life in the duplex. She probably felt the same way about her mother and siblings. She'd felt ashamed for being poor. What was there about their lives to look back to? So why was she talking about her past life now? Perhaps because she felt time seeping away. Perhaps because of being in the nursing home, because of leaving her own home. Perhaps because she wanted to accommodate me. I'd asked for information, and she'd provided it. This was an act of love.

When I was little, I'd felt ashamed of my mother's past life too. This shadow of shame had lain over our relationship. She was ashamed of being poor, and I was ashamed of her for being poor. I'd cringed over the material and social differences between her family and my father's. Both were poor, but there were degrees, and I'd parsed them. I'd faulted her for staying too close to her country roots. For metaphorically not putting on airs and fine feathered hats and eight-button gloves, and for being plain and simple, and just who she was.

And yet these last years I had come to admire her for being who she was. Whereas before I'd been ashamed of her, now I felt pride. Whereas before I'd felt she was plain and simple, now I felt she was complicated and brave. She could endure much. She had endured much. And she had found a way to live in the present, something I had yet to do. I was either digging around in the past, trying to sort out things, or skipping ahead to the future, wondering, and often worrying, about what was to come. If only I could learn from her.

Why had I finally been ready to hear about her past? About her life with Brother and her siblings and her widowed mother in a remote hill-country community? Partly because I wanted to know her. Partly because I wanted to feed my newfound pride in her and who she was. Partly because the world had changed so much, was changing so much, and I wanted a record of what had been. I wanted her life story to dominate the narrative. I wanted to understand. Because I stood on her shoulders and wanted to know who I was.

In the end, what had she told me? That her first memories were of hurt. That she lived in "raggedy" houses. Toiled in the cotton fields from "can see" to "can't see." Feared and respected her hard-hearted mother, loved her too. Didn't even know what to do with a ball. Played on cotton bales and in piles of leaves. Got laughed at for loving to read books. Saw her pet chicken "hogged down" by her brothers and sisters. Raised a calf to pay for her class ring. Finished high school at twenty. Owned one pretty dress. Didn't trust Black people, or boys, but thought my father handsome. She'd feared boring me, having nothing interesting to say, maybe embarrassing me with what she said. She didn't know that she couldn't be more fascinating to me. I had more questions, many about her married life, but the rest would wait. It had to. Finally it was time to move Mama into the Green Houses.

Twenty

A Stroke of Bad Luck

On that November morning when the movers came for my mother's belongings, I stood in the doorway of her vacated room, with its bare China Doll walls, and thought how bereft it looked without her. The hanging sink was once again the room's most prominent feature. Lisa and Joel had driven up for moving day, and we waited with Mama in the TV lounge. How often during the past five months had I sat on these hard leather chairs, shielded from outside by these filmy Dacron curtains, watching TV with Mama, and years before that, with Vashti? Hard to believe this would be our last time inside the old building.

In the past month the ambiance in Martha Coker had shifted from TV-watching, chicken-salad-snacking languid to moving-an-entire-nursing-home edgy. Anticipation could also be felt in the town, as reported by the *Herald*. The Green Houses were a new concept in nursing-home care, based on the principles of Dr. Bill Thomas and his Eden Alternative, which promised private bedrooms and open-space living, creating a physical and emotional environment to counter loneliness, boredom, and helplessness in the elderly. The company's website bragged on Martha Coker as "America's first stand-alone Green House skilled nursing facility," and its construction represented a ten-million-dollar investment in this small Delta town. Yazoo City was proud—plus it meant more local jobs.

Around noon, several staff members came to the lounge to escort the residents to the van for the short drive to the Green Houses. We followed in our cars. By midafternoon we were reunited in Mama's new bedroom in Hilderbrand House, opposite the kitchen. From her room she would hear the banging of pots and pans, the opening and closing of refrigerator and oven doors, and the grinding of dishwashers and blenders, and I liked that. She had taken her double bed with her to the new room, and Gerry kicked off his shoes and climbed on top. Joel and Lisa began rehanging the family pictures. Mama took it all in from her Med-Lift chair, which just fit in the only available corner. There's a photograph of her from that moment, dressed in her sage corduroy overshirt, flashing her elfin smile. One day, while seated in her wheelchair near the old Martha Coker entrance, she had charmed an executive from the parent company and managed to get her new room painted China Doll, though she'd had to promise not to tell anybody she'd received preferential treatment.

A few glitches remained, which was only to be expected. Her telephone wasn't working, and neither was the cable, which was a disappointment for my TV-addicted mother. But that afternoon we delighted in the serenity and the freshness of the newly constructed house and in my mother's cozy bedroom and tiled bath. We delighted in the communal hearth with its overstuffed sofas and in the open kitchen with its sea of granite counters. Digs much finer and more spacious than those of our own childhood home. As for Mama, she would be less isolated in the open-plan layout, where there was no long hallway to defeat her. She had only to settle in and enjoy the amenities. She'd made it to the promised Green Houses.

A few nights later, on November 4, we watched the presidential election results from Mama's room. She was an instinctive Democrat, whose rationale for voting against the other party included

"I just don't like the way they talk." Though she'd favored Hillary Clinton in the primaries and badly wanted a woman president, once Clinton lost the nomination Mama threw her full-hearted support behind the nominee. She'd voted for him on a paper ballot, from her bed, confessing that his name confused her. She called him "Barack-O."

A few weeks after that, on November 23, a Sunday, Mama got up early, pulled on her fluffy pink robe, and started toward the hearth, where she planned to enjoy a cup of coffee. But on the way, she fell. She lay on the carpeted floor, stared up at the concerned faces of the shahbaz, and giggled. She'd hit her head, and their initial concern was that she might have a concussion. They rang for the nurse. It wasn't immediately obvious to the nurse what was happening, because of Mama's giggling and because she was able to climb back into bed under her own steam. But then she went from giggling to answering "I don't know" to the questions the nurse put to her to being able to say absolutely nothing.

An ambulance was called, and one of the shahbaz accompanied her to the hospital. Willie Belle joined them in the emergency room, and after six hours of testing Mama was admitted to Room 145. Early that afternoon Lisa arrived, driving from Picayune in record time. After the election Gerry and I had gone back to Mexico, and we didn't get to Yazoo City until the following day.

Mama smiled when we came into her hospital room. But she couldn't move her right side, and on her left she could only flutter her fingers. She couldn't turn her head or raise it off the pillow, though she blinked rapidly. The doctors had said the stroke should mainly affect right-side movement and speech, but she was nearly immobile and could utter only one sentence, "I love you." And those words she could only repeat, not initiate.

I took my familiar place on the room's mauve vinyl loveseat. We'd gone on so many medical journeys with Mama over the last six years, some that she'd survived at long odds. What would this one bring? As we sat with her in the old vigil, we worried that her Sunday-morning stroke would be, as Lisa feared, "the one that would finally take her." At least, I thought, I would be with her.

―

On Thanksgiving, three days later, the on-call doctor predicted the stroke would take her then and there. Lisa had returned to Picayune, and at noon Gerry and I left my mother alone, venturing out to eat a quick holiday meal with Willie Belle and her family. When we got back to the hospital Mama was lying on her back, the sheets tucked in tight around her legs. She seemed to be sleeping deeply with her eyes open. When I couldn't rouse her, I asked a stunned nurse to summon the doctor. He insisted that my mother's condition was due to the stroke, not to her blood sugar, which registered in the high three hundreds.

He asked, "You know the prognosis, don't you?"

I shook my head. "She's not dying."

And at that very moment, she snorted awake. She looked at me so intensely, with such dark, comprehending eyes, that she didn't need to speak. Then she looked at the doctor, an older man she'd known for most of her life.

"I am fine," she said to him, with pristine enunciation.

He seemed amazed. He lingered, probing me with questions about where I lived and what I did for a living, and where my mother lived. Finally he called for insulin. His parting comment: she should lose weight, so she would be easier to "manage" in the nursing home.

All this while Mama, breathing heavily, had kept her eyes on my face. After the doctor left I asked her if she felt hungry. She nodded. I opened the jar of baby food I'd bought at her speech therapist's suggestion and fed her small spoonfuls. The tiny jar, the silky texture, and the smell of vanilla brought back memories of my childhood, when Mama used to feed this same pudding to

Sol and Lisa. I'd loved the sugary taste and had begged her to let me eat their dessert. She hadn't.

———

She didn't die. A week and a day after her stroke she was released to the Green Houses, where she began speech, occupational, and physical therapy. Gerry and I made plans to stay in Mississippi through January. One wintry afternoon before Christmas a large package arrived on the duplex's front doorstep. Debbie had sent us some wild game. At first this seemed like an odd present, but as I searched for recipes for the exotic meats I realized my sister's choice was a wily one. I would forever remember this holiday not only as the Christmas of my mother's stroke, but also as the Christmas of antelope and boar. My mother, though not partaking, enjoyed hearing us rehash our culinary misadventures. We hadn't tweezed all the wiry hair from the boar leg, but the antelope roast proved tasty.

Mama did what she used to tell me to do: she got on with it. But would she have chosen to get on with this new, reduced life? Around me, around Gerry, she wasn't in bad humor (did she hide her true feelings?), though she seemed uncomfortable. That is probably a weak description of how she experienced life in her diminished body. Tormented? Humiliated? She was bedbound, in diapers. But she got on with it. Twice a week the shabhaz gave her a whirlpool bath. At least once a day she ate with the other elders at the dining table. Eating was an activity she still enjoyed. She didn't lose weight. The shahbaz managed.

I was visiting the morning that the therapist, Phoebe, decided to walk my mother. Phoebe was a large, effusive woman with blue-black hair, someone my mother adored. She pushed Mama to the in-house therapy room, positioned her wheelchair next to the parallel bars, and helped my mother stand up. Mama tried to walk the three-foot length between the bars, but she bore all her weight on her arms. The right arm couldn't take the weight because of the stroke; the left, because of the old failed arm surgery. Phoebe had to reposition my mother's feet with every step. The effort exhausted Mama. Phoebe tried another day, and another, but Mama's right side wouldn't come around. Walking was finished.

Yet, mysteriously, at times the shahbaz would discover her with her legs slung over the edge of the bed. Once, they said, she cried out, "I need to stand up. I'm through, I'm through with this." These anguished (and articulate) moments took place when I wasn't present, allowing me to doubt that her pain really existed. When they happened, what could anybody do? The shahbaz would change her position to take pressure off her dead leg and hip. They would pile pillows under and around her. The Green Houses bought her a wider-and-longer-than-normal hospital bed, with a memory-foam mattress. The Cadillac of hospital beds. They bought her a new wheelchair, the deluxe Tracer. The Cadillac of wheelchairs. But nothing helped. She was dealt the agony of living in a paralyzed body.

She learned to compensate for her physical disability—somewhat. She learned to look at things. She studied the birds at the feeder outside her windows. She smiled at their greedy antics, and when their seed ran out, she watched as they came and went from the telephone wires in the distance. Once I tried to throw away a deflated balloon shaped like a rabbit, which had been tied to her TV since Easter, but she stopped me with a shake of her head. Why? I asked. "Because I look at that," she replied. Another time I couldn't find my cell phone anywhere in her room. She managed to say, "In your shirt pocket." She was a prisoner in her own body, in her bed, in her room, in that ten-room house, and she had to develop ways of making up for the deprivation she endured. She became the observer.

She had achieved stasis, and she wouldn't make any more progress. Therapy was discontinued except for touch-up sessions to maintain the functioning she'd gotten back. Her left hand became her most expressive body part. By waving her fingers, together or separately, she signified likes and dislikes, frustration, uncertainty, affection. After months of therapy her speech remained sketchy. One of our last conversations before her stroke had been about the Yazoo Motor Company, where my father had worked after leaving the Nicholas Cash Grocery. It was for sale, I'd told her, and she'd replied, "There's nothing I can do about that." Six months post-stroke, she couldn't say anything as complicated even as that. Mama's most enduring sentence, uttered in defiance of disability, became "I love you."

No, she didn't die. But for the next two years she struggled with health problems. The body is not meant not to move. A blood clot formed in her lung. Heart arrhythmias came and went. She had a recurrence of C. diff, which was finally stanched with a six-week course of vancomycin, which compromised her liver. She had UTIs. More bouts of pneumonia. (The suspicious spot on her lung? It never amounted to anything.) There were loose teeth. Up and down she went, from stasis to sickness, sickness to stasis, in and out of the hospital a half-dozen times (or was it a dozen?), the same rooms with the same mauve settees. The same measures taken: the shahbaz would escort Mama to the emergency room; she would spend a week in the hospital. After one hospitalization, for pneumonia, when she got back to Hilderbrand House she managed to say, "Glad to be home." Her speaking ability varied with how she was feeling, but generally it trended toward deterioration.

After each hospitalization she would go back into speech therapy, and the therapist would try to regain ground lost to the blood clot or the pneumonia or whatever. They would try to train her not to say "yes" when she meant "no" and "skinny" when she meant "tall." But the lessons didn't stick. She said the opposite of what she meant to say, or she said something like what she meant to say. She called flowers "posies." To show excitement, she might say, "Yabba dabba doo." She described difficulties she might be having as "snatching and grabbing." If you phoned her at a bad time, she would just as likely say, "Don't call back." One Sunday we went to have dinner with her. She'd just gotten out of her bath. She seemed content. Loose, relaxed. We talked about Lisa. She told me enthusiastically, "Tell Lisa 'happy birthday.'" This was six months after my sister's birthday. I must have looked at her funny. She corrected herself. "I'd better not say 'happy birthday,'" she said. "Say 'I love you.'" Her most common coping mechanism: she repeated phrases we said to her. Another Sunday when I called her we had this conversation:

Me: "Hi, Mama. I love you, Mama!"

Mama: "Hi, Mama. I love you, Mama!"

(Long pause.)

Me: "Mama, are you still there?"

Mama: "There."

One of her clearest post-stroke sentences had to do with fleas. I was recalling with her how, when we were growing up, we would sometimes have an outbreak of fleas in the duplex. How she would sprinkle white flea powder all over the floorboards. How we would track it everywhere. Did she remember our flea infestations? Much nodding. "We laid it off on the cat," she replied. (But we hadn't had a cat. Not an indoor one anyway.)

Walking was finished. Talking was nearly finished. Not that she didn't try to talk. She tried. She laughed at the results—sometimes. But there wouldn't be another interview about her past. I wouldn't learn anything more about her long marriage with my father. I wouldn't learn about her pregnancies and childbirths. I wouldn't learn about the twins, if after Fred had died how they'd hoped Ed would live (had they dared to hope?), and if after he had died, she and my father had been able to comfort each other. I wouldn't learn how she felt about the move to the duplex, about the march of the years after I'd left home, about how she coped with Sol's sickness and death, and my father's.

There were so many things I wouldn't learn. Talking was finished, though communication was not.

—

Her desire to speak waxed and waned, as did her ability, but the two were not necessarily in sync. Never did she want to speak so much as when she learned Lisa had cancer. Never did she have such difficulty speaking as then. This frustrated and depressed her. Between her debilitating treatments and her occasional setbacks, Lisa didn't have many chances to visit. About a year later, after she phoned Mama to say she was in remission, my mother said to me, "I wish Lisa would call and tell me again." Weeks later she thought to say to Lisa, "I want to congratulate you," but couldn't explain for what. But I knew for what. Lisa's good news had stayed in Mama's mind. When Lisa told Mama she would be visiting her soon, Mama exclaimed, "A bunch of people!" and I figured what Mama really meant was, "You're the one person in the world I most want to see." When Mama finally got to visit with Lisa she said, "Your hair is beautiful." My sister did have the best hair of us all, long and golden as a child, thick and dark as an adult, but with the beginning of its regrowth I knew it was my sister's return to health that my mother was really celebrating.

But Lisa wasn't the only sick sister. Debbie suffered with a difficult-to-treat lung disease. I seemed immune from illness, though I had chronic neck pain and frequent nightmares. Since I was the daughter most able, I took over Mama's "care-planning meetings" with the nursing staff. Why were her teeth falling out? Could her nails be cut more often? Could anything, anything more be done to relieve her pain? Antidepressants were prescribed. Neurontin, for nerve pain, was prescribed. Other pain pills were prescribed.

Gerry and I were spending as much time as we could in Yazoo City. But despite our misgivings about Mexico, we were trying to qualify for permanent residency, which would allow us to come and go more freely. We weren't supposed to be out of the country longer than thirteen weeks a year, but that wasn't enough to care for Mama, not in her condition. We cheated the time, hoping to work things out later with the Mexican authorities. There was always the *mordita*, the bribe. Maybe we could find someone to accept the *mordita*.

And so for a while I carried the major burden of my mother, and the past, and memory. The role had fallen to me by circumstance and illness, and yet it was the role I would have chosen for myself. How marvelous that everything had worked out. "Just get on with it," Mama had often said. I became the one who most often spoke to her doctor and to her dentist. I was the one who spoke to her social worker. To the shahbaz. To the visiting priest. To the ladies from St. Mary's who came bearing Communion. I looked at old movies with her. At birds with her. At clouds with her. The shahbaz would settle her in the wheelchair, and I would roll her outside, onto the patio, and we would park under the covered porch with the overhead fan. Mama would wear her dark glasses (the ones they'd given her after her cataract surgery) over her regular glasses, and we would look at the sky. We called it the cloud parade. I might say, "I see the state of Mississippi. Do you see it?" And she would wave her left hand heartily. "I see an elephant. A bear. A fish. Do you see them?"

Walking was finished. She would not enjoy the amenities. Talking was finished, though she still had her hand. Like that, we took in the sky. Like that, we got on with it.

PART THREE

Twenty-One

More Than Two More Birthdays

January 1, 2011. At the Green Houses, we ring the doorbell and wait for Darleen, one of the shahbaz, to let us in. Last night's storms have left a dome of cold blue sky sitting over us like an overturned bowl. There were thirty-seven tornadoes in the outbreak, not all in Mississippi. But inside Hilderbrand House this morning there's no reminder of our holiday-eve weather watch, with its nonstop radio and TV alerts. The hearth is quiet, with the elders either still in their rooms or already out visiting their families. In the kitchen, Hattie moves unhurriedly, cooking the festive dinner. On the way to my mother's bedroom we walk past a counter loaded with plates of cookies, bright packages of snacks in wire baskets, and a cake on a high glass stand. There's the house telephone, a pad and pencil, a staffer's folded jacket.

I wave at Hattie, Hilderbrand's best cook. "What's for dinner?"

"Ham and black-eyed peas. Broccoli casserole and sweet potatoes. That carrot cake over yonder." Southern staples, including the requisite peas for luck. Hattie doesn't ask if we are eating. When we are visiting, we are eating. Every Sunday. Every holiday.

We pause in front of my mother's door, then knock and enter. She's in bed on her back, with her upper body elevated about thirty degrees. Near her left hand, there's the over-the-bed hospital table with her princess telephone. Also on the table is a low round vase filled with fresh-cut flowers. On the first of every month my sisters and I send Mama a small arrangement along with a handwritten card from the florist that reads, "Love from all your children." Years' worth of these little cards can be found throughout her room, tacked on the bulletin board, tucked in the drawers of the bedside table, heaped in the pottery bowl on top of the bookshelf. Yesterday morning, over the phone, I asked her if the much-anticipated "posies" had been delivered. Why yes, they had.

"And who are they from?"

"Medicaid," she replied. A good guess: Medicaid was paying all her other expenses.

But these aren't the only flowers in her room today. Before Christmas Lisa sent her an amaryllis bulb in a clay pot. When she saw it, Mama said plaintively, "Flower died." Actually the bulb only needed activating. Since I've been watering it a stalk has sprung up a foot, and at its top four blood-red trumpets are emerging. Without my realizing, Mama has been keeping a careful eye on the process. And apparently she's been looking forward to the bloom. Yesterday she offered this unsolicited remark: "Blessed be the flower."

There's no chance to ask anyone how my mother fared during last night's tornado warnings, because a scene is already playing out inside her room. Frances, another shahbaz, stands by Mama's left side, holding up a maroon-and-cream-striped T-shirt. Mama is still wearing yesterday's T-shirt, which she slept in, and her diaper. She's thrown the oxygen cannulas up onto her forehead in an effort to tell Frances something.

Frances shrugs when she sees me.

My mother has a fierce look in her dark-black eyes, somewhere between agitation and despair. Gerry strolls over to her right side and asks, "Mama, what's the matter?"

She's briefly distracted by his sweet entreaty (anything for Gerry) and awards him a tiny, pressed-lip smile. But she quickly turns back to Frances, who's still waiting to dress her.

"I think that old bad leg of hers is giving her fits again," Frances volunteers.

Though my mother is paralyzed on the whole right half of her body, it seems that only the leg causes pain. Neurontin helps, but not enough. Recently Dr. Thompson has prescribed a more potent pain pill, dispensed as needed.

Jayden, the nurse on duty, rushes in. Has Frances called him? My mother assumes he's come to stick her finger for her blood-sugar reading before she's released to eat. Dutifully, she raises her left hand and jabs her pointer toward him. I can't imagine what their daily give-and-take must be like: my mother, an old white woman, a dirt farmer from the hills and the Delta, and Jayden, a young Black man and former medic in Iraq with the state of Mississippi tattooed on his neck.

She pulls the sheet up to her chin and exclaims, "The red pill!"

Jayden explains that the red pill is the strong pain "med" the "doc" has ordered. He looks expectantly from me to Gerry. Yes, yes, we say, anything! He runs to retrieve it from the locked medicine cabinet in the nurse's office off the hearth, where all meds are kept.

My mother shoots the room a wan smile. I pry the sheet from her left hand and take her fingers. She pulls my hand toward her, holds it under her chin. She's become a hand hugger. Frances coos at her to get dressed and get up. Not to miss a special dinner. Jayden hurries in with the pill, which she frowns at for a moment but swallows uncomplainingly.

After dinner, still at the table, I ask Mama if she wants to play "Deal or No Deal" on the public computer in the hearth. She's uncannily lucky at the silly game—a few days ago she made off with half a million in winnings. Usually the competition thrills her. But she only stares straight ahead, out the wall of windows, dark eyes narrowed. Last week when the nurse practitioner stepped away I took the opportunity to sneak-read the first pages of my mother's medical chart. According to this inches-thick sheaf, she has dementia. It's a way she's not seen, I think, and not understood:

the invisible elder. I wonder if the comment is a pile-on diagnosis, another means to obtain government reimbursement. As my mother stares with narrowed eyes toward the blue bowl of a sky, I decide that nobody with dementia could have such a look on her face. Such a faraway, complicated look, full of comprehension, acceptance, sadness, even appreciation of the absurdity of her condition. I resist the hateful diagnosis, one more piece of my mother to lose, but on the other hand, it's true that by suppertime she usually can't recall what she ate for breakfast that morning.

She begins to look sleepy. Is it the red pill? I wheel her to the hearth, where we wait in its imitation cheer. We watch as Darleen and Frances help elders to their rooms. My mother seems content, and since she's with us, they save her for last. But she begins fidgeting. She shakes her head. The emotion in her body must go somewhere, and I'm afraid she will start crying. I've never seen her cry. In the sixties, when her brother Wilmer died, the first of her siblings to go, she sat for a long time in an old rocking chair whose springs were spilling out. Wilmer, her oldest brother, who toted her shoeless to school. When Wilmer died, when my father died, when Sol died, maybe even when her own mother died, she didn't cry. She knows sadness. But cry in public? She doesn't.

"What's the matter?" I lean over her to ask. I'm used to studying her every effort, but she's moved into a space I don't understand. A space I can't interpret. A space I fear.

Hattie dries her hands on a dishcloth and comes over. I ask her please to take my mother to her room. She pats my mother on the shoulder. But Hattie can't leave her post in the kitchen. Anyway, it takes two shahbaz to get my mother into bed, even with the automatic lift. My mother must wait. It will only be a few minutes, Hattie tells us.

"They're coming. They're helping someone else," I say.

Nothing helps, not even the red pill. How much longer can she go on? She's so fragile that a draft of cold air, a wet head, a skipped breathing treatment brings her down. Darleen and Frances emerge from a room and rush her to bed. Let sleep take her.

I bend over the side railing to whisper that we're leaving.

"Leaving?" she asks, sounding alarmed.

"Not leaving for good. We'll be by to check on you at supper." She awards me the wan smile.

"Though we're really leaving in three days," I blurt, and immediately regret it.

She nods. Blinks rapidly. Draws a deep breath.

"But we'll be back soon, early March," I promise.

She nods again. The wan smile again. "Thirteen hops," she says.

Was it because of Easter? The hops? Had we been speaking of Easter, the next holiday we would have together? The next special meal we would eat together?

"Thirteen hops," I answer, kissing her forehead.

—

She has outlived her bones. All that January her pain increases, settles into her low back. X-rays are taken and vertebrae found to be fractured. Dr. Thompson mentions a procedure, vertebroplasty, to glue the spinal bones in place, but Mama would have to undergo the operation in a Jackson hospital. We worry about the distance, and about her having another stroke under the anesthesia. He recommends bed rest instead.

One Saturday morning I call from Mexico and, making idle conversation, ask if she's ready for lunch. She replies, "I don't go to lunch." (I hear the voice of deprivation: *We was powerfully poor. We didn't have what other people had.*) I explain she's having bed rest to help her back heal. I ask if she wants to get up. "I was tempted," she answers. I feel guilty she's dealing with this by herself. I feel sad her already reduced world has been further reduced. I can't stop thinking about her. I can't stop feeling guilty. She has outlived her bones.

She spends the first six weeks of the year bedbound. Slowly she gets better. Toward the end of February she's cleared to get up. At first she seems not to tolerate sitting in the Tracer. Slowly she learns to tolerate it. Then Lisa plans a visit. When I ask my mother who will be with her for the weekend she screams into the phone, "Santy Claus!"

—

We all get together for her birthday in March. Her eighty-seventh. Coincidentally, my memoir, *Buryin' Daddy*, comes out that month from the University Press of Mississippi. It's been a long time, over five years since I sent a draft to the agent. I show my mother the book, a hefty volume with a handsome blue jacket. She smiles, nods vigorously, but she can't read it. I suspect she's relieved she can't. Later Debbie reads her the first chapter—enough, apparently, because she shows no curiosity to hear more. I think back to my interviews about her life, her refrain: *Don't nobody want to hear nothing about that mess.*

Her birthday is on Monday, but we hold her party Sunday afternoon. In addition to Debbie and Lisa, there's Willie Belle, my mother's sister, Ada, and her husband, Lou, and all the elders of Hilderbrand House. Hattie makes chicken salad, a favorite of my mother's, and we linger at the dining table, polishing it off with saltines. Willie Belle has baked a birthday cake, vanilla with vanilla icing, and Lisa has brought pink sugar-free cupcakes. The party lasts until four, and my mother and Ada hold hands for much of it. Lisa gives Mama a framed photo of her trip to the Grand Canyon, while we give her the duplex's street numbers fabricated from Mexican tile. Doubtful that this gesture means anything to her, but I'm still unable not to remember, unable not to associate her long life with the duplex, even if she no longer does, even if she can't recall what she's eaten for breakfast that morning.

Gerry and I stay in Mississippi for another month. One day my mother says, "I feel fit as a bowling ball." Another day, in response to my question "Are you poky?" she replies, "Poky is as poky does." Despite the occasional humor, she seems sad, remote, washed out. There's no light in her eyes. Some days she eats, other days she doesn't. Sometimes after her whirlpool bath she sleeps all day. That's normal, now and again (isn't it?). What does she have to get up for? Sometimes she might look at me and smile, but sadly. There might be some gladness in her smile, but it's embedded in sadness, in tiredness, in remoteness.

She bears up, or tries to. One day her voice might be clear—"Poky is as poky does"—and another she might produce whole paragraphs that are only sounds joined together like strings of lights. The sounds go up and down, start and end, but there's no meaning. One night the shahbaz leave her alone to brush her teeth. Don't they realize how hard that is for her, with only one hand? And with no language to ask for help? She bears up, or tries to. Perhaps her life is not so bad because she doesn't remember? Because she can't think at supper what she ate for breakfast? Does she also forget her pain? Is there something about old-age forgetfulness that aids the spirit of the elderly? In forgetting, is there forbearance?

One late afternoon we sit, she and I, in the half-dark of her bedroom. She is alternately watching *Gunsmoke* reruns and the greedy sparrows that come to the bird feeder outside her double windows. All of a sudden she extends her left hand toward me.

I look up from the book in my lap.

"My fingers are swelling up," she says, dropping the hand and letting her wedding ring slip off onto the bedsheets.

"Do you mean your fingers are getting slender?"

"Swelling up," she answers. Her meaning is a muddle, but her speech is clear.

I pick up the wide gold band, which is actually her second wedding ring, a replacement for the original that had grown dime-thin over the many years she'd worn it.

She waves her hand high in the air, an arc of loveliness originating at the elbow. "Mail it to Debbie," she says. Three years ago, when Mama was about to be admitted to the nursing home, Lisa asked to keep her diamond engagement ring. Mama decided that someday she wanted Debbie to have this replacement band. Now that day had come.

"And tell her to pick up the dishes," she added. She meant the Syracuse china, a wedding gift that we used only at Christmastime. Debbie had been bequeathed the china, Lisa the Reed & Barton silver, me the Imperial Candlewick crystal.

Easter dawns bright and quiet across the town. At the Green Houses, there's the traditional dinner of ham and broccoli casserole. On Easter Monday we enter Mama's room early. She is sound asleep, slid down in the bed, toes jammed against the footboard. We turn on the lights and pull her up. The shahbaz bring in breakfast. We wait while she chips away at the bacon, eggs, grits, and biscuit. Later, I know, she won't remember. We say our goodbyes. I try to be casual, cheerful. She does too. We both must wonder at moments like these if we'll see each other again. We both know the end could come quickly. But will it? And will I be with her?

I parcel out the year by the seasons. By the holidays. It's July, right after the Fourth, and once again I'm with Mama. As she used to say, when she could still talk, it's hot, hot. She is watching TV in her room. Earlier, she got up to have Kathy fix her hair in the house salon. She looks sleepy, but she holds on for *Bonanza*. Willella, a shahbaz, comes by to ask if my mother would like a snow cone—sugar free, she mouths. Mama smiles at Willella and wiggles her fingers. Willella drapes a white cloth on Mama's striped shirtfront.

When I'm with my mother, everything pales in comparison to how she is. Even with her few demands, made mostly by moving her left hand, she occupies a huge place in my consciousness. I'm used to studying her every effort. We have our secret way of communicating; I know what each gesture means. When it's a wave of dismissal, when it's a negation of what she's just said. When she wants attention. I know how she feels by whether there is light in her eyes, or dullness; it's then that she stares out the windows at her birds. Usually, even then, she awards me the wan smile, as if to say, "I can stand it."

But today, a few days after the Fourth, my mother slurps a grape snow cone, and another episode of *Bonanza* finishes. Another begins. She seems to be enjoying herself. Is her life so terrible? The answer is probably yes. But I don't know. Her hand can't tell me.

—

Fall brings a new affliction. In September, around Labor Day, she loses her voice.

Why does it disappear? Dr. Thompson and the nurses can't say. Before, she made simple sentences ("Blessed be the flower," "My fingers are swelling up," "I feel fit as a bowling ball") or repeated phrases in a normal tone, but now she only whispers. This new voice is rasping, like breath itself. But over the phone from Mexico I'm able to understand her as well as before. When I say, "I wish I was there with you," she replies, "I wish you was too." Weeks pass, and still her voice doesn't return to normal.

In Mississippi again, on a blustery October day. Mama seems content as I sit with her in her room, though we're watching an Elvis movie, not one of her favorites. In the late afternoon Jayden blows in to dispense pills and set up a breathing treatment. She takes the treatment from him halfheartedly, since she hates to cough, which is what it makes her do. She's polite, though. Hand-waving is at a minimum. She will eat supper in bed. Preparing to go, I start my rituals—adjust blinds and air, position the stuffed animals, switch on the bedside lamp. As I'm leaving she grabs my hand, pulls it under her chin and squeezes. She kisses it. As a child, I may not have felt mothered, but now it occurs to me, maybe the mother-ing she did was the best kind, hands off but present, letting me go my way without drama. Anchored but not tied down. Not all that different from the way we are now. Another plus: she was as good as her word. She never made her children eat last.

—

By Christmas my grandmother's bungalow is lived in again. The new owners have strung blinking colored lights around the front porch and put up an inflatable Santa and reindeer in the yard, while on the duplex's screen door we've hung a plastic wreath from Family Dollar. On Christmas Eve I take out my mother's Syracuse china (Debbie has yet to pick it up), only two place settings. I run warm water in the sink and add green dish soap. I see my mother standing before this sink, her reflection in the picture window that looks out on the hackberry. Then, I think, she could wash the dishes. Then she could drive a car. Then she could buy groceries and carry them into the house. Then she could cook dinner. Bathe herself, wash her clothes. When she washed the dishes, she would leave warm, soapy water in the sink. When Gerry and I lived in New York I bought six place settings of Mayview, her pattern, but found it lacking—because it hadn't been taken out and washed once a year, handled gingerly and lovingly; because it didn't have the right history, the right memories imbued in it. This was mere china, imposter china. Though it looked the same, it was wrong.

On Christmas Day we get to my mother's room early to unwrap her presents, most from Lisa. She sits in bed, scraping off foil paper with her left fingernails. This is another day full of memories of how things used to be. During the big unwrapping, both sisters call. Debbie says, "I hate it. What has happened to Mama." Later Gerry and I keep company with my mother at the dining table while she finishes her Christmas meal with the other elders. Today we're not eating at the Green Houses. Today we're eating with Willie Belle.

But we return and spend the afternoon with my mother. Watching old movies, we make it through. This Christmas Mama can't say, "Flower died." She says nothing. There's only her hand.

We celebrate New Year's Eve in the nursing home too, around the dining table with the elders. Mama puts on a silver paper hat with a gold brim and tries to blow a purple noisemaker. (She inhales.) Her cheeks are plumped and colored like apples. She drinks fruit juice from a stemmed plastic glass. "Happy New Year," I say. She chuckles. What is the meaning behind her chuckle? That she doubts having a happy new year? Nobody wants to leave the table, not the elders, not their visitors, as if leaving means leaving for good. As if they know they have to savor this moment in which they are alive, cognizant. After all, who knows what will come next? At least this New Year's Eve, unlike the last, is tornado-free.

"I am tired of life," Mama told me yesterday. When we are with her, does she feel more alive? Does she look forward to our visits? To maybe three hours of cheer each day? Is that enough to keep her alive? Have I kept her alive thus far? Have I done her a disservice? If I hadn't spoon-fed her baby food after her stroke, if I hadn't encouraged her to go on, would that have been better? Better for whom? And if I am the one responsible, a big if, am I also the one responsible when she doesn't do well? When I'm not here and she languishes, sleeps sixteen hours a day, doesn't smile the wan smile, doesn't get up? Is that my fault too?

When the time comes, will I be able to sell my mother's house, the duplex? (I still think of it as hers, even though my name is now on the deed.) Can I part with her things? Even throwing out her old white tennis shoes is hard. Once they were her symbol of normalcy. Now the rubber has flaked off the bottoms and fallen onto the floor of her closet. Little pink rubber crumbs. I vacuum them up; they don't want to go. I pick up the shoes to put them into a garbage bag. My hand hesitates. Can I bear to throw them away? Into the bag they go, but not without memory. When did I last see her wear these shoes? Stand in them? Walk in them? After her last stay in rehab? They have sat for years on the closet floor, next to a pair of Peds. If I throw these away, do I throw her away, her life? Is this what a life comes down to? When it comes time, will I be able to part with her things? To sell this house? To care for someone in my mother's condition is to question, everything.

New Year's Day. We're leaving in two weeks. Lately Mama has been brighter. Not bright, but brighter. She giggles when she makes mistakes talking. (I wonder if the giggling is due to neurological impairment, some quirky manifestation of dementia.) When I'm here, am I training her to be brighter? When I go, will she slip into glumness? I dread going, but I can't stay. Bit by bit I'm watching my mother die. Yesterday before Dr. Thompson checked on her, I asked her to tell me her biggest concern. She replied, "I want to know what he is going to do with me." As if he could do anything more with her.

We're leaving in two days. We buy her some cut flowers along with a new sock monkey from Gilbert's Gifts. A green sock monkey with polka dots. Darla the shahbaz names him Darla. My mother seems to cheer up, but it lasts only a few minutes. Then the anguished look returns, the furrowed forehead, the "ouch" and "oh" of the leg pain.

We're leaving today. We arrive early to her room. She attacks her cereal with gusto. We hover, Gerry and I, for a few minutes. "Take care." "Be good." "See you for your birthday in two months." Words uttered in habit and haste. On the plane, I stare down into the rising clouds and see the sketchy earth and wonder what she's doing. Eating? Sleeping? Watching an old movie? A western? Her life so small, so circumscribed, and I have been with her in that small life, out of the world for these last months. My life too has diminished. But this world of airplanes and movement and luggage seems as false as hers seems real. Will this change in time? Will the days in San Miguel chip away at my small reality?

One day in late January I call my mother and she says, "Hello, darling daughter." Just that clear. When will I hear these words again? When will I have such an open path into her mind? And she has been clearer of late, her voice stronger, her speaking almost normal. She says her leg hurts "on and off." That she will "think about getting up for supper." That she misses me. She has been giggling a lot lately too.

I tell friends in San Miguel that I feel guilty. They seem surprised. The situation is nobody's fault, they say. You are doing your best, they say. At fifty-seven, I have my own life—isn't that what we always say? But what about her life, easing her from this pain-filled existence—where is my responsibility? I know she would not wish me not to live my life. Yet I know she wants me with her. So what do I do? My best is not good enough. Not for her, not for me. Where do these feelings of inadequacy go? To care for someone in my mother's condition is to question, everything.

—

We visit for her birthday in March. Her eighty-eighth. The celebration around the table has a sameness to it, though this year the party is smaller. Debbie, Ada, and Lou can't make it, so it's just us, Lisa, Willie Belle, and the elders of Hilderbrand. A second cousin arrives unexpectedly, bearing a bar of soap. Soap and lotion, the two standard elder gifts. Hattie prepares the chicken salad. Lisa brings a sheet cake decorated with magnolias. We supply sugar-free ice cream. My mother seems to have a good time. But after two hours she breaks into tears. Broken, she breaks. The shahbaz rush her to bed.

Willie Belle tells me that lately my mother cries often. On and off during the next two weeks, several times, she tears up in front of me. Where is the pain? Leg? Arm? Heart? Everywhere? An X-ray reveals no fractures. Or is it psychic pain? Dr. Thompson triples the dose of Neurontin. It may make her sleepy, he advises. But sleep is good. When life as it used to be can no longer be lived, to sleep toward death is good. Let sleep take her.

This Easter is another quiet holiday at the Green Houses, with fewer elders than usual at the dining table. We have the dinner of ham and broccoli casserole. On Easter Monday a workman comes to the duplex to install heavy security doors. When the house sits vacant, waiting for us to return, will these iron doors let me worry less? Still, it's hard to see the old screen doors come off. The old entrances to this life. Yet more evidence that I don't want anything to change. But everything changes all the time. Will she be here in June? Will she?

Twenty-Two

Scribble It on the Sky

The presentiments you have. The way you can know something before knowing it. Her increasing pain, the bouts of crying—these signs, which I want to disregard, which I do disregard, I take note of someplace. In that veiled someplace within, I note the shift in Mama's health, though that Tuesday, when we leave for Mexico, she looks the same as always: her face still full, her body still thick with bone and muscle. Her body still in stasis. From Mexico over the phone on Tuesday night her voice still sounds strong.

The state of her health shifts again when she begins another phase of low talking, her voice raspy and shrunken. Barely a month after we get back to Mexico the new nursing director calls and says, "Miz Florence has an infection." No cause for alarm, she says: it's the old story, the recalcitrant bladder. But ten days later Mama is diagnosed with pneumonia. Not with a bad case, the nurse says. They will treat her at the Green Houses.

It's May, the hottest month in the mountains of central Mexico, and the town waits on the rains. One evening I venture out to visit a young Mexican friend who lives on our street. Around eight o'clock Gerry meets me at the door, looking worried. My mother has gotten the shahbaz, Darla, to dial our Vonage number, saying, "Call Teresa, just one time."

I run upstairs to our office and call Mama back. Darla is still in her room. She hands my mother the phone. Mama fumbles the receiver. I hear her ragged breathing.

"What is it, Mama?"

She replies, "You've been good to me."

Once she's delivered her message she unceremoniously hands the phone back to Darla. *Click.* But I recognize the words, subject, verb, and object, for how she intends them. I run downstairs to tell Gerry about the unprecedented phone call. About the motherly effort she has made to release me from any burden, about the sweet concern that lies behind the effort. That night we move our plane reservations forward to Memorial Day.

We arrive in Mississippi late on the holiday afternoon and drive straight to the Green Houses. My mother is in her room behind a closed door that can't be opened, receiving an echocardiogram in bed. An hour passes while I wait in the hearth, half-watching Judge Judy on the giant TV. Finally the tech emerges and says, "It was difficult, but I got something."

Mama's hair is neatly brushed and her eyes focused and merry. She looks only slightly changed by her illnesses of the last seven weeks: her skin grayer, her face thinner, her wrinkles deeper. A littler, more furrowed version of Mama. Relieved, on Tuesday I make the mistake of assuming things are the same as before, and I don't get to her room until after lunch. She's sunk down in the bed, her blood pressure low, her mouth drooping. I worry to the nurse: has she had another stroke? The question is left hanging. Later the nurse practitioner comes by to give me the echo results. The test indicates that her heart is "pretty good," but my mother has COPD. The NP recommends starting her on the drug Advair.

On Wednesday she's better, on Thursday worse. I email Debbie, who's due for a visit on the weekend, to let her know about Mama's condition. On Saturday, in Mama's room, Debbie and the NP review her medical file. With the UTI and pneumonia, her Coumadin level has become hard to control. Her heart seems to be in atrial fib; might she be having TIA's, or small strokes? A plan comes together. The NP will order an EKG. My mother will get a short course of steroids. Everything is set to begin on Monday. The new medications will be in the house by then. Mama will get better. Mama is still fixable.

At what point does she become unfixable?

She is still fixable Saturday afternoon, when we make a game of swatting flies. For some reason there are a lot of houseflies buzzing around her bedroom. Debbie and I whack at them with plastic swatters.

"Mama, can you say 'fly'?" I ask, swatter poised for another strike.

"Fly." It's her voice, tiny but sharp. She seems amused by her team of flyswatters.

She is still fixable Sunday, when Debbie and I shop for a neck pillow for her in the drugstore. When Debbie pulls up a chair and gives her a manicure in bed.

She is still fixable Monday morning, when I get to her room early, without Debbie, and she asks, "Debbie how?"

"She's coming at ten," I answer.

She is still fixable at noon, when she says goodbye to Debbie, who leaves with Gerry for the drive back to the Jackson airport.

That, maybe, is the last moment she seems fixable.

I do not want to draw the scene, to fill in the description, the dialogue, the pauses, the gestures. To sketch the profound and the mundane of her dying, the days of it. For months there was the knowing but not knowing, watching her die bit by bit. The end is no different. Just as a mother's body prepares her baby for birth, to take a first breath, so the body at death prepares, gradually ending until it takes a last breath. I know but do not know. I expected dying might be like an on-off switch. Maybe that is all there is to know about my mother's death. But there are surprises. She is not without surprises at the end.

After Debbie leaves on Monday, the shahbaz position Mama on her right side, facing the windows. "Go on and get you a good nap," I say. She has hardly eaten any lunch, just a few bites of cantaloupe and cheese I brought from home. But she seems content. She reaches her left index finger toward me, and from my chair next to her bed, I reach mine toward her. It's the last time we really look at each other. The last time we connect. She sleeps all afternoon. I read next to her, a foot away. Midway through her nap, her breathing changes from light and quiet to hard and labored. When I leave after supper she's still asleep.

The next morning during breakfast my cell phone rings. They can't rouse her. Gerry and I throw on clothes and rush to the Green Houses. Father Lincoln, the priest from St. Mary's, arrives to perform extreme unction, the last rites. He is a kind and solemn man with a healing presence, but he is also practical with a sense of humor. We stand around the hospital bed, looking down on my mother. Gerry, me, this priest, her doctor. The priest recites the holy words over her inert body, asking for forgiveness. Dr. Thompson excuses himself.

Mama wakes up, lifts her head off the pillow, and looks around the room.

Father Lincoln, overcome, says, "It's the Holy Spirit."

The Holy Spirit here? What to do? I ring the buzzer for the shahbaz. She rushes to summon Dr. Thompson, who's just down the hall. We gather around Mama's bed again. She relaxes her head back on the pillow with her eyes wide, staring at the ceiling.

Dr. Thompson cradles her head, turns it gently left and right while examining her pupils. "Doll's eyes," he pronounces.

Doll's eyes. Fixed eyes. Meaning stroke. Meaning brain dysfunction.

But she's awake. Staring at the ceiling.

A short while later she falls back into a deep sleep. Or to wherever she's been.

———

Mama summoned the Holy Spirit? The priest thinks so. He believes the Holy Spirit brought her back. I wait at her bedside all day, but Mama doesn't come again.

Wednesday morning, very early, I'm gulping down coffee while standing over the stove, about to leave for the Green Houses. There's an air of urgency about every action. My cell phone rings. It's the nurse at Hilderbrand House, calling to tell me that my mother is awake again. Calling to tell me to rush and see her one more time.

I enter her closed room, which is heavy with the smell of sleep. Gerry is with me. The overheads are off; her little lamp casts its calm, yellow light. Mama is awake, but she doesn't seem happy about it. In a photograph of us taken later that day, my arm is draped around her shoulders in bed. She's dressed in a dark pink T-shirt, her head thrown back, her eyes staring vacantly off camera. There's her slight frown, one raised eyebrow. An aura, perhaps, of sadness. Otherwise, her face is a mask. What kind of wakefulness is this? I'm not used to seeing her looking so disengaged. But she doesn't appear to be in any pain.

She's awake through Wednesday, Thursday, Friday.

Through Wednesday, when Lisa visits and Dr. Thompson rounds and recommends that we sign Mama up for hospice. Wednesday evening, while sitting on the floor of Willie Belle's den, I email Dr. Thompson to ask if we have made a mistake. I'm afraid hospice means we're giving up on her. He assures me we aren't.

She's awake through Thursday when Dr. Thompson comes to examine her and when Lisa leaves. Lisa cries while saying goodbye, while Mama stares up at her. But are Mama's eyes seeing or unseeing? Later the hospice nurse arrives and sponge-bathes my mother and dresses her in the maroon-and-cream-striped T-shirt. In a photograph taken after her bath, Mama puts her head back against the pink pillowcase and stares at the ceiling.

She's awake through Friday, when she passes a swallow test and takes sips of water, dollops of applesauce, spoons of sherbet. The nurse, Jayden, the former army medic, asks the shahbaz to scramble an egg for my mother, declaring in a loud voice, "I'm going to feed her this egg and get her back to eating, and then I'll tell everybody, 'I told you so!'" But my mother spits out the egg and waves off Jayden, and then we all know she has accepted what we haven't yet accepted. That evening she falls deeply asleep but moves her left arm ceaselessly, and we give her the first morphine.

Moving the arm ceaselessly is a new gesture to interpret, and I do not want her to die agitated, so on Saturday I ask for her to have more morphine. All that day she sleeps while Lisa visits, holding Mama's restless arm. Mama hasn't eaten since Monday, when she ate some cantaloupe and cheese, and she hasn't drunk much water. The staff can't hang a proper IV, because they don't have the equipment, but they rig one up with a wire coat hanger.

On Sunday Gerry and I arrive early to my mother's room. Her breaths are coming fast, over forty per minute, and I ask the nurse to administer the morphine. I do not want her to die agitated. This has become my new fixation. I know, without knowing, this will be her last day. She hasn't been conscious since Friday afternoon.

We sit with her all that morning. We keep the door to her room closed, the first day we have done that. Before noon Willie Belle knocks. We ask the shahbaz for another chair and my aunt waits with us for a time. She asks, "Is she cold yet?"

Throughout the day she gets colder.

At dinnertime, the shahbaz knock and, without our asking, bring us plates of pork chops. My mother might be dying, is dying, but we eat the meat and three. For the rest of the afternoon Gerry and I are alone with her. We hold her hands. She becomes a body breathing: at times breathing fast, then sighing, then breathing slowly. Gerry says it's like watching the worst thing you can imagine but hoping it won't ever end. At the end her breaths get shallower, coming softly from her throat, until they stop. Gerry says, "Go, Mama." Her tongue moves twice, curls toward the roof of her mouth, and she is still.

"Is she gone? Is she?"

Gerry nods. At 3:50 he stops the clock on her wall. We hold her hands.

After a while he calls Rebecca, the nurse on duty in the house. Through the phone I can hear her ask, surprised, "She's not breathing?" She comes right away and listens to Mama's heart. She pronounces the death. Somehow, the death certificate will incorrectly state 3:25 as the time. But then she would still have twenty-five minutes to live.

Mama's mouth has remained slightly open in death, as it was all day. I tell Rebecca I'm upset her mouth is open. I take the scarf off Tempe, her teddy bear—a white and green and blue scarf—and tie it around Mama's head and neck. When I can't press her mouth closed, Rebecca tries. I like that she tries. Finally I ask her to give up.

"Don't worry," Gerry says, "Mr. Haymer won't let her go to eternity with her mouth open."

Rebecca tells us we can stay as long as we like. That we don't have to clean out the room right away. "But maybe you want to take a few things with you tonight," she advises. "Like those monkeys." She points to the big sock monkey and the two magnet monkeys stuck to Mama's bed rail. I like that Rebecca gives everything equal seriousness. The pronouncing of the death. The tying of the scarf. The taking of the monkeys.

Then she leaves. We make phone calls. Lisa, Debbie, Willie Belle, Father Lincoln. Lisa and Debbie have been calling throughout the day. Dr. Thompson stops by, just back from his weekend trip. Stethoscope slung around his neck. He sits on the bed on Mama's right side and hugs her neck and cries. "Death," he says, "the great enemy." He leaves.

We sit with Mama until six o'clock, when the coroner, Ricky Shivers, comes.

"Mr. Shivers," I say to him, "at the funeral home, tell Mr. Haymer not to put too much makeup on her. But do close her mouth."

—

Monday is a blur of arrangements. We go to St. Mary's rectory to plan her service with the priest. To the funeral home to drop off her burying clothes. To Black's to pick out her underwear. She can't be buried without underwear, in my opinion, but Mr. Haymer says shoes are optional. While we do this, Lisa and Joel clean out Mama's room.

Later that afternoon a strange storm comes from the west, a *derecho*, or straight-line winds, bearing tornado warnings. From Willie Belle's sliding glass door I see tree branches and garbage-can tops blowing down the block. In this *Wizard of Oz* atmosphere, Debbie is supposed to drive from the Jackson airport. At eight o'clock the lights flicker and stay out; we wait for her in the dark of Willie Belle's den. Who doesn't fear a tornado? My mother. I worry about Debbie in the storm, driving alone. She doesn't answer her cell. My anxiety, about everything, focuses on this wind. I keep thinking, *Mama is leaving the earth.* As if it were a process, as if it hadn't already happened. Finally Debbie turns up. There's no power from Jackson to Yazoo City, she tells us, and a train is stuck on the tracks nearby. She's had to circle the entire town searching for a free crossing. After she eats some barbecue, we tramp through the soggy yard to the duplex. The lightning is close by. It thunders all night.

The day of the funeral starts wet but then clears. There is the visitation at the funeral parlor, but only for us and Willie Belle. Mama never wanted anybody to see her "laid out" in her coffin. She would not have liked hearing it, but she is beautiful in her white jacket and pleated lavender skirt. I hope she forgives me for not buying the navy jacket and pleated white skirt she asked for. As we look on her body for the last time, Mr. Haymer whispers to me, "Embalming works wonders." I can tell he thinks it's a shame that there's no one else coming to admire how well she turned out. Then he wants to know, "Is it too much lipstick?" I nod, and he gently swipes her lips with a tissue from his breast pocket.

We get in the cars for the ride to St. Mary's. The flowers are laid on the casket. White gladioli and calla lilies, purple orchids and irises. The visitation in the church is brief. Father Lincoln segues to the Mass, and we stand and kneel, kneel and stand. We hear W. H. Auden's poem "Funeral Blues" and the hymn "Ave Maria." There were white gladioli at the altar for her wedding and "Ave Maria" sung then too. Then the short ride to the cemetery: the crawl along the empty downtown streets. The damp walk to the graveside. The coffin in its place. The flowers in their place. The last words of the priest. Back at Willie Belle's, funeral food is laid out on the dining table. A cousin has sent a sandwich platter from Subway; an aunt has baked a chocolate cake. The talk. The food. The mourners. My childhood friend Georgette has brought our kindergarten photo. Later Gerry and I return to the cemetery. Circle back to our pain. The heaped earth. The wilting flowers. There we remain. My mother is dead. Scribble it on the sky for all to read. So the poet wrote in "Funeral Blues."

Twenty-Three

Two Visitors During a
Year of Mourning

For the four years after Mama's big stroke, I worried how I might manage to be with her when she died. I'd never wanted her to be alone on her birthday, and I sure didn't want her to be alone at her death. My worry bordered on obsession. To die alone in a nursing home—even a good one like the Green Houses—would be a lonely exit; to die alone would equal dying unloved. Equal another hard knock. There was an old Mexican song whose lyrics went: "Life always begins with crying, and with crying it always ends." To be present when Mama died became something I could do for her, maybe something that would compensate a little for her tough life. And then the timing had worked out, despite all the back and forth, as if the magic of Mexico had been transported to the state of Mississippi.

But I hadn't gotten my wish about what her last moments would be like. I'd pictured our final goodbye like a scene from one of her westerns, where Little Joe or Matt Dillon cradles the cowpoke's head and exchanges meaningful words. She'd died unconscious, but at least I'd been with her, and that had been momentous enough. Really, this was something I needed to do not for her but for myself. She'd been with me at my beginning; I'd been with her at her end. And so, following the funeral service, a kind of relief took over.

The relief didn't last. Mama was still new in the ground when Lisa asked if maybe we shouldn't clean out her closet. Clothes-cleaning-out was what you did to move on. I wasn't sure if she was ready to give away Mama's clothes either, but on the chosen day she and Gerry and I met in Mama's bedroom with a box of black leaf bags. When we opened her closet door, the hanging shoe bag, stuffed with her pumps and loafers, flapped to greet us. I mostly stood by, idly reminiscing over articles of her clothing, while Lisa and Gerry emptied hangers. Out went the pink formal she'd worn to my wedding. Out went the fifties-style car coat with the white "fur" collar. Out went the blazers, the red and the camelhair that she'd struggled so hard to afford. The only pause came when Lisa asked, a little sheepishly I thought, "Do you want to smell Mama?" and we sniffed her sage corduroy jacket. The intimacy of that act, of sharing Mama's bodily scent with my sister, felt overwhelming. Later Gerry carried the black leaf bags out to the Crown Vic's trunk; those that wouldn't fit, he left in the Toy Room. Then we went back to Mexico. Without donating her things.

In San Miguel my friend Kate gave me a small bouquet of roses and lavender from her garden, tied with a simple ribbon—"for remembrance," she said. We learned from our fellow expats that while we were away Mexico's immigration laws had changed again. With the nine years we'd lived in the country, we would qualify for permanent residency visas. Finally we could come and go freely from Mexico; ironically, there was no longer any need.

But in Mexico life had become all about problems. There were legal disputes with neighbors over the condo's boundaries, and landscaping disputes with fellow owners over putting in a native garden, with an older woman opining we couldn't plant órgano cacti because they reminded her of another type of organ. Owners broke into camps. One filed a complaint with a government agency when the landscapers cut down a lopsided evergreen, her discarded Christmas tree. Bitter quarrels erupted over an application of Roundup and even the use of fertilizer. There was no resolution in sight, magical or otherwise, and everyday life in the old hacienda felt foreign and hard. Felt like an angry distraction.

So in early September, before the chaotic *fiestas patrias*, we left for Mississippi. It was the first time I'd made plans to visit my home state with no reason other than to be there for myself. That is, with no living parent drawing me back.

—

I'd grieved for a brother, a father, and three grandparents. I'd grieved for a best childhood friend who'd been killed during a robbery in her antique shop in Yazoo City. I'd grieved for a best adult friend who'd died from liver cancer in Palm Springs. Even so, I was unprepared—because of our inchoate early bond?—for how to grieve for my mother. But in her house, I kept her near me. In her house, I could feel her presence. Conjure her back to life. Every day for a month I cried, and then one day when I didn't, I cried because I hadn't cried.

By mid-September we'd been in Mississippi for two weeks. One night we drove to a restaurant on the Ross Barnett Reservoir, outside Jackson, to attend my fortieth high school reunion. Georgette was there, and she'd brought along old photographs of my parents in her parents' wedding party. Taken in front of the altar at St. Mary's, the photos showcased their large, formal wedding, with six smiling bridesmaids in full-skirted gowns and groomsmen in crisp white dinner jackets. My father was thin-waisted and curly-haired, my mother swan-necked and slender-armed. They would have been in their late twenties. Later I would know my mother's arms, the right one still as glass, the left a frantic communicator, but in the moment of these photos they were beautifully proportioned, strongly muscled, elegantly gloved. She'd been lovely, with short dark hair, wearing a lacey Juliette cap; she'd been smiling, youthful, public in her expression. I'd believed that I hadn't known my mother when I was growing up, that she'd been mean and remote.

I certainly hadn't known her in any of her complexity, in any of her public-ness. Why had I judged her so? Why hadn't I left room for doubt?

—

One painfully bright day in late September, Arcell paid us a visit in the duplex. Arcell, my mother's plumber. He came to the front door looking a little embarrassed, I thought. "AR-cell," I greeted him, emphasizing the first syllable of his name, as my mother had. "Come in and sit down." I unlocked the security door. I was glad to see him.

"I tell y'all, it's about time to clean those roots out again," he began. He meant time to ream the sewage line, which had a tendency to clog with roots from the sycamore trees. Arcell took a seat opposite me, his mahogany skin a rich contrast to the loveseat's blue-and-gray upholstery. Nowadays there was more salt than pepper in his close-cut hair.

Arcell talked about how his plumbing business was going and about his recent visit to the doctor and about his daughter's purchase of a car. His sister was feeling poorly, his mama fine. In the last few years, Arcell and his mother had moved from that stretch of rundown houses known as Brickyard Hill to respectable Country Club Drive. They were among the first Black families to live in the Bella Vista subdivision, where big houses farther up the hill enjoyed sweeping westward views of the Delta. Did he and his mama like their new place? She had been having some trouble adjusting, Arcell admitted. Their modest ranch sat one long block from Highway 49 and another long block from the railroad tracks, but still his mother was bothered by noise. Gradually she was acclimating to the trains.

As Arcell talked, I realized his visit had nothing much to do with plumbing. He visited because of the bond he had forged with my mother. All the occasions he'd come to her house—fixing her plumbing through ordinary times (tree roots) and extraordinary times (mold)—he'd never mentioned he'd been a year ahead of me in high school when the schools integrated. He'd never mentioned he'd been a running back on the football team, one of the most successful teams ever, along with defensive lineman "Gentle Ben" Williams, who became an All-American at the University of Mississippi and went on to play for the Buffalo Bills. Never mentioned he'd gotten a college football scholarship but had declined it to get married. He spoke with a touch of sadness, with a pinch of philosophy. "If you stay in it long enough, life will show you what it's about," he said. He reminded me of how older people here used to talk, holding forth with homespun wisdom and knee-slapping humor. He reminded me of how my mother's family had talked at their reunions. Now Arcell and I were those older people, and he'd absorbed the old-fashioned, roundabout way of expression.

He was going on about our cutting down the hackberry last winter. "I was proud of y'all for doing that," he said, as if we'd chopped it ourselves, but all we'd done was find a company in Jackson who would tackle the multi-story tree. Once this tree, along with the privet hedge beneath it, had provided a hiding place for us children, but in the last few years it had started dropping heavy branches. My mother's elderly yardman, Johnny, was afraid to mow under it. Even the tree's resident screech owl seemed to have moved off. One day last January, Arcell had watched the tree come down. From where? I wondered. Willie Belle had watched too, from the bench on her front porch, but she hadn't mentioned seeing Arcell. I wondered something else. How had Arcell known that he would find us in town? He was probably keeping an eye on the duplex, as its unpaid steward. It was that bond again, forged with a kind old white lady with a shock of gray-white hair and a soft little laugh. She was still reaching out to Arcell, and he was reaching out to her too.

A few days later, on a warm evening at about six o'clock, Gerry and I were settling down to a beer and a turkey sandwich in front of the TV newscast when out the open front door I noticed a car pull up. Another workman of my mother's, Leon, hopped out and came trotting up the sidewalk. He was dressed in athletic shorts and a T-shirt. "Oh, no," I said to Gerry as I scrambled to hide my half-eaten supper in the kitchen.

My "Oh, no" had to do with two things. One, Leon took ruminating to impressive new lengths; he was the kind of talker who couldn't be hurried or interrupted. But mostly my reluctance had to do with the fact that I'd forgotten to tell him my mother had died.

Leon and my mother, even more so than Arcell and my mother, had an unlikely attachment. Everybody needed a plumber, and you were lucky if you got one who liked to sit and chat after he finished reaming your pipes. But the role Leon played in Mama's life wasn't so clear-cut. Leon occasionally washed and waxed my mother's car and did other little jobs around her house. He also served, unbidden, as her freelance spiritual advisor.

I didn't know if Leon had any formal training as a preacher, but he sure could preach. One Sunday morning, when Lisa and I were enjoying a leisurely visit with Mama at the nursing home, he'd dropped by on his way to church and stayed so long—telling inspirational stories and stirring us up to a fever pitch—that by the time he left he'd missed the start of his church's service and Lisa and I were overcome. From where she lay in bed, Mama had looked from me to Lisa, from Lisa to me, trying to fathom what in heaven's name might be wrong with her grown daughters. Why, this was just Leon preaching.

When Leon plopped down in my mother's recliner, the springy chair bounced back and forth before he got control. "Leon, I'm so sorry I didn't call you," I said preemptively.

"Let me tell you what happened," he began. "I went by the nursing home one Sunday to see your mama, and she was fine.

That must have been several weeks before. We had us a good visit. I couldn't go the next week. But then I went again. I knocked on her door. I said, 'Where's Mrs. Nicholas?' and that's when they told me that she'd done passed."

"Leon," I repeated, "I'm so sorry."

"I was so shocked," he said. "I just couldn't believe it. Done passed!"

I proceeded to tell him how she died. Leon sat quietly for a few seconds before telling us the story of one elderly lady, and then another, who had been in the nursing home one Sunday and then had not been there the next. "They teach me so much," he said. "They teach me wisdom. That's why I like to visit the old people. And they're so lonely."

I was relieved Leon didn't preach over us right there in the living room. Then I asked him if he would wash and wax Mama's car once more for old times' sake. When he seemed to hesitate I suggested we walk outside and take a look at the finish on it.

"You know, I always used to tell her I wanted to buy that car from her," he said.

"Leon, I bought it," I told him.

We sat talking awhile longer, speculating about what the car might be worth. Since the odometer didn't function it was hard to know, but Leon thought I might have underpaid. The subject of the car seemed to make him more reflective. "That's how I met your daddy," he said. "Your mama and your daddy." He told me that his wife, who was pregnant with their first child, had been driving on Calhoun Avenue when somebody ran the stop sign across from my parents' house. As his wife swerved to miss the car she ran up in our yard and hit my father's "new" gold Pontiac, which had been parked in the driveway.

"Your mama stayed with her and comforted her until the police came," Leon said. "I told your daddy I would pay for the damage to his car, but he told me to forget about it. That's how I met them."

Under the carport, Leon bent over to inspect the hood on the Crown Vic. He rubbed his dark fingers across the white paint. It was finely pocked with tree sap.

"It does need a good waxing," I said.

"I'll make her a good price," Leon said. "Come tomorrow and take care of it."

I thought of how all those years ago my mother had stood on this same spot and comforted Leon's pregnant wife. It still meant a lot to Leon, I could tell. And I thought of the people he told me about, my parents. How my father had loved that gold Pontiac, but how he'd done the right thing. How life could still teach me something about him.

—

By October it felt right to give away my mother's clothes, which had remained in the black leaf bags long enough. But I would keep some of her "important" things. I bought a large plastic bin to make up a keepsake box and put inside her black handbag, her word puzzle books, two pink shawls, and her devil horns. (We'd bought her this black-and-red-velvet headband last Halloween and slipped it on her right as Father Lincoln strolled into her room.) In June as we'd stuffed her clothes into the leaf bags Lisa had lamented, "No more smell of mother," but with this keepsake box we could take out her shawls and revive her sweet, sharp smell whenever we liked. Gerry called it "Mama's time capsule." The clock he'd stopped at 3:50, to record when she died, wouldn't fit in, so he hung it in the Junk Room.

Later we drove downtown to Manna House to donate her clothes. The next day we cleaned out Mama's kitchen cabinets and took some of her old pots and pans to the charity. While Gerry chatted with the custodian about the new donation, I waited in the car. A middle-aged woman ambled out to ask if she might help ferry things inside. As she walked away, I noticed she had on Mama's T-shirt, the maroon one with the cream stripes. The shirt she'd worn her first day of hospice care, when we'd taken her photo, when she'd stared at the ceiling. It struck me then that I did not want to give away my mother's things. I had given them away, and I wanted them back. The way I wanted her back.

I was afraid that, without her things, I might not see her anymore. See her in the stretchy gloves with the leather palms and in the single dangly earring I'd found in the black plastic tray in her car. See her sitting on the edge of her four-poster, her back hunched, wearing her camel blazer. I tucked a snapshot of her in the corner of her dresser mirror, where she'd kept photos of us. She was wearing a pink shawl and the black-and-red devil horns. I would keep the rest of her things. The birthday cards from us. The check stub from her first Social Security payment. The manila file folder with the doctors' name cards stapled to it, reminding us of her medical appointments. The yellow Post-It Notes Debbie had written about her medicines. I would keep the box of Sol's things that she'd saved. With his fourth-grade report cards. His high school athletic letters. His college application and transcript. His college commencement announcement. I would not throw away more of her things. I used to call her that, Old Thing. I would see her in her things.

I wasn't able to stop thinking about my mother. They said this was normal—Gerry, the TV, the literature about grief. "It's only been two months." "It's only been four months." And so on until a year of months, a year of seasons, a season of years, would have accumulated. But I doubted it was normal. And I doubted I would ever stop. I sat in her recliner chair. I looked out the front door she looked out of. I slept in her bed. Was it normal to dream my death? Wind, water, earth, clouds, a bright light: I woke before I flew into the light. I'd made myself look behind me, for Gerry, because I hadn't wanted to leave him. When I woke up, I experienced an auditory hallucination: someone whispered, "Psst." Was someone making a joke? Was I? But I couldn't laugh, because I was shaking so hard.

One place I didn't see her was in the town cemetery. She'd told me, "Visit my grave," and I had, but not often. Not every day. I didn't see her there. There I felt her absence, as if her grave were vacant, even though I knew full well she was six feet down, still looking young. ("Embalming works wonders," Mr. Haymer had said.)

On an unnaturally warm October day, Gerry and I went to the cemetery with Willie Belle and Lisa. Nearly a year had passed since we'd bought her the devil horns. We placed a tiny pumpkin on Mama's tombstone. We wriggled silk flowers in fall colors into her narrow vase. On her grave, the grass had not yet grown to meet in the middle. We planted azaleas, which Lisa had bought, small ones that would bloom twice a year, with blooms that looked like tiny magenta dresses. "Mama, we are planting Red Ruffles," I said to the clods of earth.

"She knows," Willie Belle replied. The young plants looked perky next to her stone, but within the year they would die. We posed for a photograph, stiff from bending. Later on when I studied that photo I would see that our smiles were like stones.

I had meant to take her some spider lilies. Plant the bulbs at her grave. But I didn't know where, the head or the foot. It seemed too important a decision, so I avoided it.

—

We thought more and more about buying our own house in Mississippi, maybe in Jackson, of selling the duplex and the condo. We stayed in Yazoo City all that October, through the last season of heat that sputtered and fell before the promise of the cool. The spider lilies in the backyard dried on their spindly stalks, and Johnny cut them down with the grass. We were there for the season of leaves, the tumbled sycamore leaves that swept the yard in great circular motions. We were there through the holidays, when the iris, heavy with hoary frost, heavy with January, stooped and sank with the weight of my mother's absence. Because now she felt gone. I didn't see her standing in the corners of the rooms. Didn't see her sitting on the side of her four-poster, stocking feet dangling, slump-shouldered in her camel blazer, about to slip on a pair of crumbling loafers. I didn't see her in the green rocker on the front porch, silhouetted against the cream clapboards, a shy smile on her aging face. Each season she felt further away, and I could imagine the time when we would sell her house and her four-poster and her green rocker. She would become memory, and the only evidence of her would be the stone that gave her birth and death dates. No more smell of mother.

The spring after the spring my mother died, her irises bloomed in great profusion. Over the fall they had proliferated in their bed, and by April they stood tall and strong. And an odd thing happened. The buds showed yellow, though the full flowers blossomed purple. Were they two-toned because of what we'd done to the hackberry? Had its demise provided the soil with extra nourishment? Yet more yellow buds followed, and hundreds of majestic yellow-purple irises broke out. I took a photo, or tried to. I pushed the wrong button and made a video instead. In the video the heavy-topped irises swayed in the breeze, as if they were breathing. But it lasted for only a few seconds, before the irises went still again.

Twenty-Four

Letters from the Past

The next September, fifteen months after Mama died, we bought an old house in Jackson, in a leafy neighborhood not far from the state capitol. While researching a biography of Willie Morris I had come across this quotation about his own delayed Mississippi homecoming: "A man had best be coming back to where his strongest feelings lay." New York and Mexico had meant anonymity, reinvention, and freedom from the past, but like Willie's, my strongest feelings lay in Mississippi. It was Mississippi I always came back to, Mississippi that thrilled me. "My nerve ends come alive," Willie had written, "when I cross the state line." But once in the state I often felt impatient to leave again. Mississippi, unlike New York or Mexico, was my place of memory. And as a place of memory, it could be a difficult place in which to dwell.

Mississippi meant family, past and present, and it meant my Nicholas grandparents' bungalow. The old homeplace. As a girl, my mother hadn't felt the rootedness of ever having a home. "We was nomads"—that was how she'd characterized the Hoods' peripatetic farming life in the Delta. Even the houses they'd rented in Midway she'd described as shacks. Her family didn't have a true home until they pooled resources and bought their house on Dunn Avenue. But about my grandparents' bungalow there had been a sense of permanence, of its being our homeplace, because it had been in the family, and in our imaginations, for so long. After my grandmother Vashti was admitted to the nursing home, my father couldn't bear selling the house he'd grown up in. During the winter months he would walk the dark, silent rooms, lighting the gas space heaters against the cold.

But our homeplace had been sold more than a decade ago, and several new owners had already come and gone. The last proprietors had painted its broad clapboards muddy brown, and now whenever I rode by I had to strain to see our spirits there—my grandmother in the backyard, tending her purple larkspur, my grandfather on the front porch, reading the Sunday paper and smoking his cigar. With my mother gone, my nostalgia for the Nicholas homeplace had been, oddly enough, supplanted by the duplex. And so, despite having my own bungalow in Jackson, I, like my father, couldn't bring myself to sell the house I'd grown up in. Instead, tired of its thorny problems, we sold the condo in Mexico, though we made plans to rent a friend's casita for regular visits. All this begged the well-worn question: Could I live full-time in Mississippi? Or was I still too conflicted about home and place?

That September, when the moving van pulled up to our house in Jackson—also originally built as a duplex—it held possessions that had been in storage in New York for eleven years. The movers put our few pieces of furniture into position and deposited fifty or so cardboard boxes in the studio building (our Little House). Every afternoon Gerry and I would unpack more boxes, rediscovering stuffed animals from our childhoods along with clothing and household items we must have bought right before leaving New York, because we couldn't recall ever seeing them before. Deep memory had survived the eleven-year deep freeze, recent memory had not. After a week, a debris pile remained on the studio floor: dried-out scuba wet suits, a combo TV/VCR, and scratched-up pots and pans, along with the army surplus footlocker I'd carried to Pennsylvania when I'd left for college.

This blue metal trunk had been packed with my few books and clothes, including the black-and-red-checked skirt my mother had sewn for me to wear to the opera. During college, I'd used the trunk as storage for every letter I received. I'd had a hard time adjusting to college life, from the slushy mid-Atlantic winters to freewheeling co-ed dorms to classes with quirky professors and privileged, prep-schooled students. My mother understood this from our weekly telephone calls, and so she wrote me. Long-distance calls were expensive, but postage stamps cost eight cents. In that trunk, I knew I would find her letters.

The bright fall day we dragged the trunk into my home office was, as my father might have written in one of his letters, "a beautiful sunshine day." The trunk, still with the name of my sophomore dorm scrawled on top in blue magic marker, held a mishmash of epistolary memorabilia, from hasty notes passed in classrooms to newsy dispatches from family members. It took days to sift everything and gather up the cards and letters from my mother; then I sorted them, so I could relive the story they told chronologically. There were about eighty letters from her during my college years—some handwritten in red ballpoint, her loopy script filling the lined pages; others typed on the stationery of the farm-implement company AMCO, where in her early fifties she'd gone to work as a secretary. Others were penned on notepads with suppliers' logos, such as "Capitol Bolt and Screw Company" and "Keystone Tubular Service, World's Largest Inventory of Pipes and Tubing."

It was yet another beautiful sunshine day when I sat down at my desk to begin reading and felt the thrill of her written voice in my ear, a voice I hardly recognized: young, playful, active, optimistic, and loving. Her job at AMCO, she wrote, was in whole goods. She explained, "That's diskers and harrowers—isn't that exciting?" But I wasn't sure whether she was expressing genuine enthusiasm or uncharacteristic irony. To her dismay, because she liked keeping busy, the job often left her with nothing to do by noon, so after typing the day's orders she wrote me from the office when her boss wasn't looking. She also wrote from home on Sunday mornings, after putting a ham on to bake for dinner, while my father and siblings slept. And she wrote from under the hooded dryer at the beauty salon on Saturday afternoons, timing her letters to end when the dryer clicked off.

She wasn't a letter writer by habit. There had never been any need: her family lived within a day's drive. Besides, at forty-eight, my mother's age when we started corresponding, she was ashamed of her imperfect literacy. She sometimes wrote that she imagined me laughing at her as I read her letters. Whenever she made cross-outs, searching for the correct spellings, in the next sentence she would call herself "dumb." But she kept on writing.

Her letters were a history of many small things. They contained her modest hopes: to take a rare vacation with my father, to the Gulf Coast or New Orleans; to fix up the duplex (always); to improve herself. She asked that I send her word-power books. She took shorthand and bookkeeping but failed the shorthand. She tried to learn to ride a bicycle but fell off. Despite working at the farm implement company, at home she kept up a manic schedule, cooking, cleaning, and sewing. In one envelope, she folded swatches from a dress she was making for me. She preserved figs and pears and put up fresh peas and beans in the freezer. Aside from the weather, there was little in her letters about the external world. They were about her world, the circumscribed, task-filled, family-filled world she'd always known.

She visited her mother, Grandma Hood, often and phoned her on the days she didn't. During these years, Debbie was studying in medical school in Jackson. Sol was playing high school football. On winter weekends he went to the woods to deer hunt; in the summers he worked on a highway crew, so she got up at five o'clock to wake him. Lisa was playing saxophone in the stage band, taking humanities courses, babysitting, and painting the baseboards in the duplex's living room. As I sat at my desk reading my mother's letters from my vantage point of forty years further on, hindsight was poignant: I knew what life was holding in store for us. As my college years drew to a close, Grandma Hood would die of a stroke. My grandfather would also die, of a heart attack. About a decade later Sol would die of leukemia, at thirty-one. My father would suffer from colon cancer and die in his sleep of a ruptured aorta. And Vashti's health would slowly deteriorate with Parkinson's. "My hand doesn't want to act right," she wrote in one of her last letters to me, a harbinger of the disease.

But Mama's letters were more than a history of time, family, and place. They were a testament to my relationship with my mother, free from the impurities of memory. One letter stood out, four fat, folded pages in which she laid out answers to my questions about her past. These were the same questions I'd posed when I was young and she'd snapped that I asked too many questions, and anyway, that she couldn't remember. They were the same questions I'd posed in the nursing home before her big stroke, when she'd tried so hard to tell me what she could still remember. I'd forgotten asking these questions when I was in college and forgotten about this lengthy letter she'd written in response.

"It would be kinda hard for me to tell you all the things we did when we were growing up," she began. "First I will say that we were so poor and backwards it is pitiful." She couldn't ever remember not having to work: "We were just six or about when we went to the field with Mama." But to my surprise, she also described some happy childhood moments. In the cotton fields she often spotted "some of the biggest and prettiest butterflies you will ever see." She recalled enjoyable chores, such as picking wild blackberries and hunting the nests that the hens would hide in the weeds. After they moved back to Midway from the Delta, her family lived near some cousins who had a mule named Yip. "They would come by and get us and we would all get up on that old mule, sometimes as many as five kids, and go to the woods to get some wild grapes. We did have fun with that old mule."

She described in detail the schools she'd gone to in the Delta. "I was up at Grandma Hood's looking at her old pictures and found this one," she wrote. The snapshot had a vintage Art Deco border and was stamped with the company's name, the Sauer Studio, from Greenville, Mississippi. "Believe it or not, this is the very first school I attended. When your dad saw it his remark was 'the first and only six foot first grader,' but actually I was in the third grade." This was the Shell Lake School, in Washington County, Mississippi, where her teacher had been Miss Johnnie Couch, who had taught twenty-five students through eighth grade. My mother walked two miles to get to the school, and she said, "When it was cold we nearly froze and when it rained we would take our shoes off and put them under the big old potbelly stove." She couldn't remember any desks in the school, only benches.

Two memories stood out in her mind. One, Miss Couch rode a horse to school, and "all the kids would hang on to the horse's tail then on to each other like an elephant caravan." Two, the school-house was "set back in the woods and once a forest fire raged all around and all of us that were big enough were out beating the fire out." As for the snapshot, she'd mentioned it before, at the nursing home, but I hadn't been able to find it in the duplex. Now I knew why: the photograph had been in an envelope in my trunk for forty years.

On the photo's right side stood the schoolhouse, a simple wooden building with two eight-pane windows. On the left side was a thicket of winter-bare trees, though the students playing in the schoolyard were dressed in shirtsleeves. In the center stood my tall, smiling mother. She had drawn an arrow to her face in red ink and written, "Me." In her letter, she explained. "The game we were playing was called Squirrel. We had some silly games." But why had a photographer wanted to capture this modest school and its students?

"I guess the next school I went to was Indianola and that was the biggest place you ever saw," she continued. "I could not keep

my mind on anything but where the school bus let us off. I just knew that I would lose that old school bus and have to stay at school all nite." In the 1930s, Indianola, in the upper Delta, "the biggest place you ever saw," had a population of three thousand.

The surprising thing wasn't my mother's skewed perception of Indianola's size, but that she'd gone to fourth grade there. I'd assumed that after her father died in 1929, when she was five, Mama and her family retreated to Midway, where they helped Uncle Will farm. But Mama's letter implied that they remained in the Delta five more years. For as hard a life as they must have had in the Midway hills, it would have been even harder in the Delta, where they had no relatives. What circumstances would have delayed Grandma Hood's return to the place where her family lived and which she thought of as home? Surely after John Wesley's death, she'd been overcome by shock and grief. No doubt she'd had to get that year's crop in. Probably she wanted to give birth to her eighth child before moving. Perhaps she owed money to the landowner, and this held them in the Delta for a time. Whatever the reasons, Mama's letter upended the timeline I'd drawn of her life.

There were other revelations, some about my father. I'd wondered about the happiness of my parents' marriage. I must have asked outright in a letter whether she loved my father because here was her reply: "I do not mind telling you that I have always loved him and always will. Even if he is the stubbornest man alive." This was as unbridled a declaration of love for the man as she could make. A declaration that acknowledged not only that love, but also its struggles. That captured, with its understated (and grammatically suspect) adjective, his foibles. In another letter to me, she mentioned she was writing on her twenty-fifth wedding anniversary, adding, "I thought you should know."

More than these declarations of love for my father, her letters offered a portrait of my parents' shared life, a life I had never considered that they much shared. Daddy, seemingly disapproving of Mama's family, almost never came on our weekly visits to Grandma Hood, but here Mama told of the family get-togethers and fish fries they went to, of the school programs for my younger siblings they attended, of the trips to Jackson they took to shop or to visit Debbie. In one letter, Mama even went on tongue-in-cheek about the UFOs she and my father had hunted, during a bizarre week when the whole town got itself in an uproar about purported extraterrestrial sightings.

My mother wasn't a letter writer by habit, but I was. The blue trunk, which I was fast discovering to be my own time capsule, contained the note I'd written to her in third grade, imploring her to "be nice to me." The note reminded me how she'd seemed distant then, and mean. But now I knew that this presumed meanness wasn't hers alone. Others in her family shared the trait, a kind of toughness I supposed was necessary to eke out a living dirt farming in Mississippi during the Great Depression. Its hallmarks: nonstop hard work and no complaining. In that harsh world, there hadn't been room for sentiment.

We were never close—from as far back as my note to her in third grade, this was the story I had told myself. More than revealing a revised timeline of my mother's past, more than revealing her love for my father, more than anything, the letters told of our forgotten intimacy. She wrote me through college depressions, boyfriend breakups, a bout of mono, bad grades. Only once did her support and positivity waver. During my sophomore year, I felt downhearted and struggled through a period of insomnia: my choice of dorm room and roommate wasn't working out. "You might be in over your head, trying to keep up with all those rich people," she wrote. Then she apologized for sounding "harsh."

In her letters she was a gentle mother, a best girlfriend. "I promised you a first spring flower," she wrote, and pressed a daffodil between the pages. She counted the days until my vacations, when she planned long talks about "everything." She called me her "honey" and her "darling." She told me how glad she was to have me for her daughter: I was her "darling daughter" and her "dear little daughter." She told me she loved me. On one page, she typed "I LOVE YOU" over and over. Almost always, she signed her letters, "Love, Mother," not "Mama." She may have signed off formally, but she reminded me of the confidantes we used to be. "It is a lot of nonsense that you believe we cannot be or never were very close."

Why had I thought we weren't? Rereading her letters, I could again recall feeling ashamed of her hardscrabble past. Ashamed of her, and ashamed of having a sharecropper—or dirt farmer, as she'd called herself—for my mother. True, she'd been distant, held back perhaps by the tragedies of childbearing and the grind of taking care of four young kids, and by her own hard upbringing and lingering sense of shame. But I came to admit this: I had also kept my distance from her.

Ultimately the letters bore out the faultiness of memory. They were filled with words I hadn't remembered, about an early bond with my mother I'd forgotten. They were proof of a mother's love, and they spoke of its mettle and kind. Maybe she couldn't have told me these things, even before her watershed stroke. She'd never been much of a talker, even then. But in the intimacy of the letters, in the exigencies of my college absence, she found her voice. Through her letters, discovered in an army surplus trunk four decades later, I heard that voice again, and it was like knowing her for the first time. It was an antidote to mourning.

Twenty-Five

The End of All Things

On an August day three years later, we bought a house in San Miguel. It was a simple but pretty concrete house, with a hallway running along its length and rooms opening off to one side. Why did we do it, since not that long ago we'd been relieved to divest ourselves of our property there? Much about life in Mississippi invoked the past: its slow-to-change and contentious politics, its necessary but exhausting atonement for its racial history, even its stretched-out seasons. "That's the one trouble with this country," Faulkner wrote in *As I Lay Dying.* "Everything, weather, all, hangs on too long." I missed what Mexico had to offer—the possibility of anonymity, reinvention of self, and freedom from memory. And so began new years of back and forth, but with more months in Mississippi than in Mexico.

Four-plus years after my mother's death, we still owned the duplex, but now whenever we spent the night there any feeling of her was difficult to summon. My family seemed but ghosts in rooms that felt no longer familiar, but devoid of all spirit. If you live long enough, Arcell had said, life will show you what it's about. We made the decision to sell.

We chose a real estate agent, an older man everyone called Bee, whose family had helped settle the town. He had dark eyes and a salesman's open face, and he loved to tell stories. As the younger

brother of Willie Morris's best friend, he had grown up shadowing
his brother and Willie, whose biography I'd just finished writing,
and when we met to sign a contract in the duplex's living room,
he reminisced about the pair. About their childhood hijinks in
this small town during the Second World War. About their high
school days in the languid fifties. About meeting up once unexpectedly in Paris. Then, as he was leaving, he turned his attention
back to real estate. "It's not like a stock, you know. Just because
you're selling, doesn't mean anybody's buying." Selling the duplex
would likely be a long, even a years-long prospect, because houses
tended to move slowly in these Delta towns. As he got up to go,
he asked for a paragraph about the duplex's history. Later I sat
down and wrote:

> The house was originally built in 1938 as a duplex and located across
> from Main Street School. It was moved to its present corner lot in
> 1959 and converted for one-family living. It has been in the same
> family since then. The kitchen was totally renovated in 1996. The
> bathrooms were renovated in 2006 and the plumbing was updated;
> the interior was also painted, and new carpeting put down. In 2013
> the roof was replaced, and new flooring laid in the dining room,
> kitchen, laundry room, and bonus room; insulation was added
> to the attic, and the exterior painted. The living room and dining
> rooms were recently repainted. The house has high ceilings, three
> bedrooms and two full baths, plus a bonus room (could be used as
> an office or additional bedroom), along with a dining room, living
> room, kitchen, and laundry room. There's a modern storage shed in
> the backyard and a two-car carport. Mature trees, azaleas, attractive
> corner lot and spacious front porch.

Not the best sell copy, and for his ad in the local paper Bee amended
it to read: "Corner property, well-maintained 3 BR, 2 full baths, LR,
DR, Kit and Bonus Room." It was good editing: if only I'd been
able to excise the duplex so easily from my memory.

Before the ad ran in the newspaper, we wanted to clean out the house's contents. And so on a warm, blue-skied Saturday in early October, Gerry and I drove the hour to Yazoo City and parked under the duplex's carport. The spider lilies bordering my aunt's yard stood proud and erect, their waxy red crowns glowing in the sharp fall light. We paused, gathering steam for this task that we'd put off for years. I said to Gerry, let's start with the tall bureau in the Toy Room—the least memory-laden of the rooms. Cleaning out the duplex would be a simple matter: we would fill up giant leaf bags with things to throw away. But as we stood before the thirties-vintage bureau, its damp wood smelling of something slightly sour, I encountered resistance, and not only from the heavy, warped drawers. What to do with the legions of things belonging to Lisa and Debbie? We would also need to fill bags with their childhood mementos. Soon these "Debbie" and "Lisa" bags multiplied to include bags for our young great-nephew (the "Nick" bag) and for my aunt (the "Willie Belle" bag).

Into the Nick bag we tossed an ancient calculator and a six-inch baseball bat, from Daddy's miscellanea. Our family had lived besieged by his collections. Many of his things had no monetary value, and even their sentimental value could be questioned. Since my parents had been children of the Depression, they'd become habitual savers, but he'd taken it to the hoarding extreme. Most of his things, those he'd squirreled away in his bureau drawers and under his bed, had been cleared out soon after his death, but in the Toy Room we unearthed more of his stuff, including his keepsake box of the family hair. Inside this blond wooden box he'd stacked business envelopes full of our coils and curls, which he'd carefully labeled in ballpoint: "Debbie, first haircut, 4/15/52"; "Sol, haircut 7/2/59"; "Lisa Maria, first grade hair"; and so on. He'd even added his own middle-aged locks, a limp mix of inch-long black and gray strands. The first hard decision was what to do with all the hair he'd painstakingly kept. I couldn't bring myself to trash it but couldn't see keeping it either.

Next up, musty linens: lace doilies, cotton napkins, crocheted runners, and the Christmas tablecloth. Parting with this rectangle of bright-red polyester meant abandoning our holiday tradition and admitting that the times we'd shared around it wouldn't come again. Of course those times wouldn't come again, but by keeping the tablecloth I could recreate something of them on my own holiday table, if I chose to. If I put it in the giveaway bag, I was relegating the tablecloth to memory, relegating the past to the past. We started a new pile, the undecided, to address the conundrum of the hair and the tablecloth.

Before returning to Jackson, we stopped next door to catch Willie Belle up on the day's progress. We flopped down in her orderly den, and I told her about the family hair.

"Anything y'all don't want, bring it over here," she said. I knew it wasn't because she really wanted more things, but because she, also a child of the Depression, also couldn't bear to part with anything, especially anything sentimental. But she drew the line at our hair.

By the next Saturday the spider lilies drooped on tippy stalks. We'd hired an affable fellow—someone else I'd gone to high school with, as it turned out—to meet us at the duplex with his pickup, which he drove over the curb and parked right next to the shed. "This will come in handy someday" had been my father's frequent refrain, followed by "when I fix up the house," but the baling wire, faucets, rusty nails, screws, hoses, gaskets, funnels, and lengths of pipe that he'd stored in the Little House never had proved handy. My former classmate knew the value of scrap metal, and within two hours Daddy's lifetime accumulation of building supplies and vehicle parts lay neatly stacked in his pickup bed.

There was one last emotional frontier: Mama's bedroom, with the four-poster, bedside table, dresser, and bureau she'd bought from her salary at AMCO. Though we'd given away her hanging garments, Mama's folding clothes remained: beige nylon underwear; silky slips in pastel blues and pinks; church-going scarves in military colors, hard blues and sharp reds and golds; the filmy oatmeal-colored nightgown and coverup she'd worn on her honeymoon. I'd only been allowed to view this negligee, never to try it on. With these freighted garments spread before me at this crucial juncture, would I keep them? I could hear my aunt's voice chastising me. I could hear my own future voice chastising me. And worse, hidden among the intimate apparel: my mother's jewelry, in two small wooden boxes and a large leather case. These boxes, holding our beaded baby bracelets and the double-heart pin my father had bought for Mama at the Yazoo County Fair, evoked the private life of my parents. As a girl, I'd secretly fingered these trinkets. The undecided pile grew.

During the Saturdays to come, as we sorted these family things and others, I would look out my mother's curtained windows toward my aunt's house, beyond the row of drying spider lilies. How could I not save all the things that she'd saved? Without the linens, the negligee, the baby bracelets, and the hair, all I had was memory. But I couldn't save them. Anyway, who was there to keep the linens after me? The negligee? Who was there to love the jewelry box with the baby beads? And what about the hair? There comes a time, Arcell had said, when life shows you what it's about. What about this dismantling of a life? After the ephemera, it all comes down to memory. To straining to hear the voices, the footsteps, to see the smiles, the gestures, to remember the holidays, the everydays.

To clean out the duplex was to face not only my mother's mortality but my own. While in San Miguel the previous summer, and later in Mississippi, I had an unmistakable feeling that something strange was happening to me. I'd always been dependably healthy, but now my left foot dragged when I walked, and I could detect a slowly widening discrepancy between the strength and coordination of my left and right sides. I had trouble making up a bed, especially pulling on the pillowcases. I'd grown clumsy. What did these odd symptoms add up to? During the fall of 2016, in that veiled someplace, I knew I must be in the beginning stages of the same disease that Vashti had lived with for so long at the end of her life. It would take nearly two years to receive a firm diagnosis, but Parkinson's would begin to give a fresh perspective to my years-long experience with my mother, as I transitioned from caregiver to patient, and as I grappled with my own diminishing well-being.

But that fall, through the long succession of Saturdays, Willie Belle's bags grew in number, filled with photos, miniature Japanese vases, and milk-glass, black-glass, and rainbow-glass candy dishes. Soon the bookshelves in her den overflowed with knickknacks from the duplex, until she said she couldn't take any more. Redisplayed, the ephemera would live on, for a time.

—

And then it was done. The cleaning out of family things. Some remained behind, to show the house with furniture, but almost every keepsake and memento had been assigned to a new owner or to a trash pail. We moved on to the next phase of selling. Washing blinds and curtains and cabinets. Vacuuming carpets and scrubbing baseboards and mopping floors. We wiped and oiled the duplex until it seemed anointed. On the last weekend of this vast, sacred effort, late on a Sunday morning, we broke to take our great-nephew Nick on a picnic. We sat on an old army blanket under a stand of cedar trees near the cemetery entrance and ate tuna sandwiches. We walked past Willie Morris's tombstone and the plot of the woman said to be "the Witch of Yazoo," then past potter's field, toward Nick's grandparents—my brother, Sol, and his wife, Cindy. When we came to a section of African American graves, Nick, at age ten, wanted to know why they had been buried off by themselves. "That's crazy," he said after our explanation of slavery and segregation. On some of their graves he placed little stones and on others faded plastic flowers that had tumbled in the breeze.

And before much time had passed, before the ad had run for even a month in the newspaper, we had a buyer. A quiet man, a

family man with a young wife and baby daughter. He would sit at
our dining room table, where my father used to sit. He wouldn't
feel the presence of the heavy-footed ghost. For him and his new
family, the furniture we'd left behind would be devoid of memory.
My mother's bedroom set, purchased after years of hope. The
flowered loveseats and the TV table from Unclaimed Freight. The
bed that had been Sol's, the bed where Daddy had died. This new
family would create their own memories, of how the baby grew and
learned to crawl and walk. Of Christmases and New Years, and how
to prune the spring azaleas and gather the sycamore leaves each
fall. They would never know anything of the family who'd lived
there before them. Or of the grandparents down the block, of how
they'd given their son and daughter-in-law this plot of land, given it
with "natural love and affection," on which to put their homeplace.

—

There is a place in the imagination, a vast place that encompasses
all of us, even our soul, and when we think hard on it, produces a
tightness in the throat and eyes that exposes emotions long buried. It is a place we come back to often in our thoughts, reaching
backward and even forward in time, for we know we will rest there
one day too. If someone were to ask us, Where is your heart? we
would say that place's name, for it is where memory originates,
and where those we love most continue on. Home is the place of
our most indwelling self, the place we feel most obsessed about,
the place where even the air smells familiar, the place that somehow dictates all else about us even as we reject portions of those
compulsions.

Why did I want to come back to Mississippi? Why didn't I stay
in New York or Mexico, where I'd achieved stasis—not able to
live in my home state but not able to live without it? In the end I
just wanted to come home. To stop living in the foreignness. To
be around things and places known. To live, as the Mississippi

artist Andrew Bucci once told me, closer to the graveyard. To hear the sounds and to be with the people I knew, including most of my remaining family. This provided a kind of antidote to the ever-dawning reality of one's own mortality. I didn't have children to pass a genetic legacy on to, but like my five generations of Hood and Gilmore forebears I would lie in the Mississippi earth. My desire to write about family and home sprang not from an urge to create any literary legacy but out of a compulsion to dwell in the past, to see my people come alive again, even if only on paper, and maybe to figure something out. In the end it also came down to my mother. Home as mother. I'd come back home for my mother, the smallest unit of home. She was gone, and the family house was going gone, but in my most indwelling place I still had her. What is remembered, home.

Mississippi might be frustrating, at times infuriating, the place and its politics despairingly slow to change and maddeningly contradictory, but it was mine in ways that Mexico, and even New York, never could be. "You'll never be Mexican," my Spanish teacher and friend Enrique had said during year one of my life in his country, when I was trying so hard to learn the language and culture. In my quintessential American way I thought I could be anything. But he was right, I could only be who I was raised to be. Though Mexico would always be part of me, and I would be a part of Mexico.

Not long after the duplex was sold, on an early spring day, we were in the Yazoo cemetery again with Nick, who was half immersed in the fountain, trolling for pennies, his red T-shirt sopping. I saw the lazy blue sky, the brown, lacy branches of the trees against it, and I thought how it was all of a piece, again past and present mixing with an awareness of our future. And I felt the wholeness of my life, alive in this place of the dead, of our history, with my mother nearby. It had always been this place, it had always been of a piece: it was land, sky, trees, earth, birds, and water, it was all this, that was home.

Author's Note

This is a work of nonfiction, meaning the events really happened. It's also a memoir, drawn from my memory, which like all memory is selective, although to write about my mother I've also drawn from my interviews with her and from our letters, along with my emails and diaries. All the conversations and correspondence quoted in the book should be accurate, though some may have been edited or shifted around in time. All the characters are also real people, and none represent composites. To maintain privacy, some names have been changed, while others, especially those of family and public figures, have not. It's my hope that despite any infelicities that may have crept in due to the faultiness of memory, the story told in these pages is above all faithful to the truth, and to the memory of my mother.

Acknowledgments

I would like to express heartfelt thanks to the following people whose encouragement helped me write *The Mama Chronicles*: my sisters, Lisa Maria Nicholas and Deborah Adele Nicholas, and my aunt, Willie Belle Hood, who lived through these times with me; Amy Boorstein and Miriam Schneir, first readers of these pages; and Andy Baltimore, Roger Brudno, Ellen Ann Fentress, Julie Hoffman and the staff at Martha Coker, Martha Kaplan, John Langston, Kate McCorkle, JoAnne Prichard Morris, Sam Olden, Enrique Ramírez, Georgette Thomas, Dr. Will Thompson, and Rickey Flynn Wendling. Thanks also to the dedicated and talented staff at the University Press of Mississippi, especially my editorial team, Craig Gill and Carlton McGrone. Thank you to Evan Young for his sensitive but thorough copyediting and to Mark McCauslin for his careful proofreading. Above all I wish to thank Gerry, Gerard Marion Helferich, friend, editor, husband, and enthusiastic partner in this crazy writing life.

About the Author

Teresa Nicholas has written two previous books, *Buryin' Daddy: Putting My Lebanese, Catholic, Southern Baptist Childhood to Rest* and *Willie: The Life of Willie Morris*. Her articles and essays have been published in *The Bitter Southerner*, NPR's *Opinion Page*, *South Writ Large*, and *Delta* and *Mississippi* magazines, among others. She was born in Yazoo City, Mississippi, and attended Yazoo City High School. After graduating Swarthmore College with a BA in English literature, she worked in book publishing in New York, where she became vice president of production for the Crown Publishing Group, a division of Random House, Inc. She lives with her husband, the writer Gerard Helferich, in Jackson, Mississippi, and San Miguel de Allende, Mexico. For more information, visit her website at teresanicholas.com.